Thomas Gottron

Content Extraction

Thomas Gottron

Content Extraction

Identifying the Main Content in HTML Documents

Südwestdeutscher Verlag für Hochschulschriften

Impressum/Imprint (nur für Deutschland/ only for Germany)
Bibliografische Information der Deutschen Nationalbibliothek: Die Deutsche Nationalbibliothek verzeichnet diese Publikation in der Deutschen Nationalbibliografie; detaillierte bibliografische Daten sind im Internet über http://dnb.d-nb.de abrufbar.
Alle in diesem Buch genannten Marken und Produktnamen unterliegen warenzeichen-, marken- oder patentrechtlichem Schutz bzw. sind Warenzeichen oder eingetragene Warenzeichen der jeweiligen Inhaber. Die Wiedergabe von Marken, Produktnamen, Gebrauchsnamen, Handelsnamen, Warenbezeichnungen u.s.w. in diesem Werk berechtigt auch ohne besondere Kennzeichnung nicht zu der Annahme, dass solche Namen im Sinne der Warenzeichen- und Markenschutzgesetzgebung als frei zu betrachten wären und daher von jedermann benutzt werden dürften.

Verlag: Südwestdeutscher Verlag für Hochschulschriften Aktiengesellschaft & Co. KG
Dudweiler Landstr. 99, 66123 Saarbrücken, Deutschland
Telefon +49 681 37 20 271-1, Telefax +49 681 37 20 271-0, Email: info@svh-verlag.de
Zugl.: Mainz, Universität, 2008

Herstellung in Deutschland:
Schaltungsdienst Lange o.H.G., Berlin
Books on Demand GmbH, Norderstedt
Reha GmbH, Saarbrücken
Amazon Distribution GmbH, Leipzig
ISBN: 978-3-8381-0408-9

Imprint (only for USA, GB)
Bibliographic information published by the Deutsche Nationalbibliothek: The Deutsche Nationalbibliothek lists this publication in the Deutsche Nationalbibliografie; detailed bibliographic data are available in the Internet at http://dnb.d-nb.de.
Any brand names and product names mentioned in this book are subject to trademark, brand or patent protection and are trademarks or registered trademarks of their respective holders. The use of brand names, product names, common names, trade names, product descriptions etc. even without a particular marking in this works is in no way to be construed to mean that such names may be regarded as unrestricted in respect of trademark and brand protection legislation and could thus be used by anyone.

Publisher:
Südwestdeutscher Verlag für Hochschulschriften Aktiengesellschaft & Co. KG
Dudweiler Landstr. 99, 66123 Saarbrücken, Germany
Phone +49 681 37 20 271-1, Fax +49 681 37 20 271-0, Email: info@svh-verlag.de

Copyright © 2009 by the author and Südwestdeutscher Verlag für Hochschulschriften Aktiengesellschaft & Co. KG and licensors
All rights reserved. Saarbrücken 2009

Printed in the U.S.A.
Printed in the U.K. by (see last page)
ISBN: 978-3-8381-0408-9

Preface

Most HTML documents on the World Wide Web comprise far more than the article or text which forms their main content. Navigation menus, functional and design elements or commercial banners are typical examples of additional contents which can be found along with the main text. In the context of web data mining applications or technical solutions to improve accessibility via screen readers or small screen devices it is necessary to draw the distinction between main and additional content automatically.

The solutions for determining the main content in a web document can be divided into the two categories of content extraction and template detection. Content extraction solutions are operating on single documents and are based on heuristics. Template detection algorithms instead analyse a collection of several training documents to determine a common template structure and use this knowledge to find the main content.

This thesis gives an extensive overview of existing techniques and algorithms from both areas. It contributes an objective way to measure and evaluate the performance of content extraction algorithms under different aspects. These evaluation measures allow to draw the first objective comparison of existing extraction solutions. The comparison also reveals typical problems of these solutions. The newly introduced content code blurring extraction filter overcomes at least some of the problems and proves to be the best content extraction algorithm at the moment.

An analysis of methods to cluster web documents according to their underlying templates is the third major contribution of this thesis. In combination with a localised crawling process this clustering analysis can be used to automatically create high quality sets of training documents for template detection algorithms. As the whole process can be automated it basically allows to perform template detection on a single document, thereby combining the advantages of single and multi document algorithms: the independence of a manually created training set of the former with the better theoretic underpinning of the latter approaches.

Acknowledgements

Writing a thesis is a large project. While writing I have been supported and encouraged by several people. Those people I do owe thanks and any list to mention all of them will very likely be incomplete and short of someone who has been forgotten. However, there are few who have to be mentioned in particular.

I would like to thank my supervisor for his support throughout the whole time it took to realise this project. Also the other colleagues and members of the institute of computing science at Mainz have always been available for a discussion or an advice from other fields of expertise. In particular I would like to mention the members of the by now traditional coffee meetings after lunch and the secretaries of the institute. The experience gathered while working in industries about web site management and engineering have been invaluable for the thesis as well. The people there were always understanding when the research at university required more time than foreseen. Also my friends and relatives supported me during this thesis. I would like to thank my old highschool friends in particular for some interesting discussion about the topics of web mining and content extraction. My parents supported my interests and provided me with the possibility to follow my ideas about studies and higher education. To my brother, his fiancée and my grandmothers I owe thank for the good times, when I needed to relax and be distracted. A special thank you goes to my mother-in-law, who is definitely gifted for motivating people by her notion of "having a break" from work.

Finally remain the people dearest to me: my wife and my daughters. They supported me in writing this thesis by sacrificing their time, by cheering me up when necessary and by sharing the moments of success. The children have always been able to swipe away all the tiredness of a full day of hard work at university with their filial love and joyful characters. My wife has kept me grounded and without her love I certainly would not be at the same point in life. She is and always has been the good wind in my life.

Contents

1 Introduction   **7**
    1.1   Contents on the World Wide Web   7
    1.2   Contents of a Web Document   12
    1.3   Content Extraction   16
    1.4   Contributions   19

2 Basic Terms and Concepts   **21**
    2.1   Web Documents   21
         2.1.1   (X)HTML   21
         2.1.2   SAX   23
         2.1.3   DOM   23
         2.1.4   Templates   26
    2.2   Information Retrieval   28
         2.2.1   Concepts, Instances and Attributes   29
         2.2.2   Distance and Similarity Measures   30
         2.2.3   Query, Result Set, Ground Truth and Gold Standard   32
         2.2.4   Evaluation and Visualisation   33
    2.3   Web Documents and Text Mining   36
         2.3.1   Document Representations   36
         2.3.2   Case Folding, Stemming and Stop Words   38
         2.3.3   Methods   39
    2.4   Further Reading   40

3 Related Work   **41**
    3.1   Content Extraction and Related Topics   41
         3.1.1   The Problem of Content Extraction   41
         3.1.2   Wrappers   43
         3.1.3   Recognition of Named Entities   45
         3.1.4   Text Summarisation by Extraction   46
         3.1.5   Applications Using Content Extraction   46
    3.2   Single Document Content Extraction   48
         3.2.1   Crunch   49
         3.2.2   Body Text Extraction   49
         3.2.3   Document Slope Curve   50
         3.2.4   Link Quota Filter   53

Contents

- 3.2.5 (K-)Feature Extractor 57
- 3.2.6 elISA 59
- 3.2.7 Other Applications 60
- 3.3 Multi Document Template Detection 61
  - 3.3.1 Page Partitioning 62
  - 3.3.2 InfoDiscoverer 65
  - 3.3.3 ContentExtractor 67
  - 3.3.4 Site Style Trees 68
  - 3.3.5 RTDM Tree Edit Distance 71
  - 3.3.6 Document Frequency Based Filter 74
  - 3.3.7 LAMIS and WISDOM for Web Structure Mining 74
  - 3.3.8 Methods to Determine the Usage of Web Templates 76
- 3.4 Evaluation of Content Extraction Algorithms 78
  - 3.4.1 Human User Evaluation 78
  - 3.4.2 Application Specific Evaluation 80
  - 3.4.3 Indirect Evaluation 81
  - 3.4.4 Evaluation based on Information Retrieval Measures 82
- 3.5 Structural Similarity of Web Documents 83
  - 3.5.1 Tree-based Similarity 83
  - 3.5.2 Path-based Similarity 84
  - 3.5.3 Sequence-based Similarity 85
  - 3.5.4 Other Approaches 86
- 3.6 Summary 87

4 Content Extraction   89
- 4.1 The Main Content of a Document 89
- 4.2 A Formal Definition of Content Extraction 92
- 4.3 Content Extraction in Practice 94

5 Evaluating Content Extraction   97
- 5.1 Motivation for New Evaluation Measures 97
- 5.2 Measures for Evaluating Content Extraction 101
  - 5.2.1 Creating a Gold Standard 101
  - 5.2.2 Comparing Gold Standard and Extracted Contents 102
- 5.3 Implementation of an Evaluation Framework 107
  - 5.3.1 Design Decisions 107
  - 5.3.2 Implementation Characteristics 109
  - 5.3.3 An Entire Evaluation Run 113
- 5.4 Comparison of Existing Single Document Algorithms 114
  - 5.4.1 Creating Test Data 114
  - 5.4.2 Algorithms 117
  - 5.4.3 Evaluation Process 122

	5.4.4	Results	124
5.5		Summary	133

6 New Single Document Algorithms — 135
- 6.1 Locating the DOM Sub-Tree of the Main Content 135
- 6.2 Largest Size Increase 137
  - 6.2.1 Concept and Idea 137
  - 6.2.2 Adaptation and Implementation 138
- 6.3 Largest Pagelet 139
  - 6.3.1 Concept and Idea 139
  - 6.3.2 Adaptation and Implementation 139
- 6.4 Content Code Blurring 140
  - 6.4.1 Concept and Idea 141
  - 6.4.2 Blurring the Content Code Vector 144
  - 6.4.3 Adaptation and Implementation 146
- 6.5 Evaluation 149
  - 6.5.1 Fixing the Parameters 149
  - 6.5.2 Results 150
- 6.6 Summary 158

7 Template Clustering and Detection — 161
- 7.1 Clustering Template Based Documents 162
  - 7.1.1 Distance Measures for Template Structures 162
  - 7.1.2 Clustering Techniques 166
  - 7.1.3 Experiments 170
  - 7.1.4 Preliminary Results of Template Clustering 178
- 7.2 Automatic Training Set Creation 179
  - 7.2.1 Bootstrapping Template Detection 180
  - 7.2.2 Entropy Based Template Detection 181
  - 7.2.3 Evaluation of Bootstrapped Template Detection 182
  - 7.2.4 Conclusions about Bootstrapping Template Detection 185

8 Conclusions and Future Work — 187
- 8.1 Results and Conclusions 187
- 8.2 Future Work 190
- 8.3 Content Extraction and Web-as-Corpus 191
- 8.4 Content Extraction and HTML 5 191

A Test Data — 193
- A.1 Evaluation Packages for Single Document Algorithms 193
- A.2 Evaluation Packages for Multi Document Algorithms 199

B Evaluation Results — 201

Contents

B.1	Single Document Algorithms	201
B.2	Multi Document Algorithms	211

C Glossary   217

D Abbreviations   223

List of Tables   225

List of Figures   227

List of Algorithms   231

Bibliography   233

Index   249

1 Introduction

A modern HTML document on the World Wide Web (WWW) contains different kinds of content. In particular it usually contains far more than its main content. A document on a news web site, for instance, might contain an article reporting about a recent event but it most likely consists also of some other contents, like navigation menus, commercials or a copyright notice. The latter contents do not contribute to the information the document wants to communicate, they serve other purposes. Hence, a human user who is primarily interested in the news article usually ignores these additional contents and focuses on the main content. Ignoring uninteresting contents is a very common behaviour and humans can actually distinguish quite fast and quite well between the main content and other kinds of content.

A computer program which accesses a web document in order to retrieve some information from it should be able to make the same distinction. The task of automatically identifying the main content in a web document is not easy, though. Where a human user can use all his background knowledge, the semantic context or the visual arrangement and design layout of the web document, a computer program lacks all this additional information. Thus, algorithms which want to detect the main content in an HTML document use different approaches to accomplish their task.

It is these algorithms, the techniques they use and the evaluation and comparison of their performance which lie in the focus of this thesis. In other words: we are interested in how a computer program can find the main content in an HTML web page automatically.

In this introductive chapter we will first take a look at how the presentation of information has evolved in the environment of the WWW. Of particular interest is how web documents have changed under the aspect of their contents, as these changes have had a strong influence on how human users perceive web documents and how the search for information on the web is organised. In this context we will also describe several situations which motivate the need of finding the main content in a web document automatically and we will come to a first general definition of content extraction as the task of finding the main content.

1.1 Contents on the World Wide Web

The WWW has become a huge resource for information. Nowadays the impression might arise, that there actually is no information which cannot be found on the web. Several publications which wrap the size of the web in dry numbers seem to confirm this impression. Benoit, Slauenwhite and Trudel [BST07] have systematically analysed a representative part

1 Introduction

of the Internet's IP address space to look for publicly accessible web servers. Scaling their result up to the entire address space led to an estimate of about 10.7 million public servers on the WWW. Each of those web servers may host several web sites, and each web site in turn contains several web pages. An article [KK07] on Pandia – a web site devoted to topics related to search engines and searching information on the web in general – summarised a few other estimates about the size of the web. Referring to different sources the article comes up with numbers between 15 and 30 billion unique web pages provided by between 109 and 433 million web sites. All those estimates were independently published around the end of the year 2006 and the beginning of 2007, so they were all formed roughly in the same time period. The counterpart to this vast offer of information on the WWW is a large group of consumers: the same article on Pandia mentions a number of above one billion users. Independently of the quality of all those estimates they do give an idea of the magnitude of the WWW – and its growth rate does not seem to decline. Quite the opposite, the recent trends of user or community generated contents which are commonly subsumed under the term "Web 2.0" might cause another leap in the growth of contents on the web.

However, the constantly increasing size of the web gave raise to two problems already much earlier: how to find information as a consumer and how to organise and manage the information as a content provider. *Web directories* and *search engines* have become the main solutions to the first problem, *web content management systems* (WCMS) in all possible variations the solution to the second one. The functionality of the mentioned systems has changed over the time and evolved with the web to adapt to shifts in the presentation and style of web contents. At the same time the changes of the systems have often affected the contents on the web and the style of documents themselves.

Web directories are probably the oldest way to organise the access to the information of the web. Yahoo, for example, started in 1994 as a general web directory. While today the directory service plays a minor role on the Yahoo web portal, lots of other web sites are still organised as web directories. The Open Directory Project – also referred to as DMOZ – certainly is one of the more renown representatives.

Any directory consists of a collection of addresses on the web, usually classified and categorised according to a hierarchic scheme. It can be compared to a very big, well organised and publicly available collection of link bookmarks. The link entries are usually made manually, either by the editors of the web directory, by the authors of a web site themselves or by independent third parties like normal web users who found and reported an interesting page on the web. While typically also the classification into the topical categories and the order in which the entries are listed are determined manually, these processes might nowadays be computer aided.

Managing manually all the information on the web soon started to become more and more difficult – even for professional web directories like Yahoo with employed, full time editors and open projects like DMOZ based on a huge workforce of volunteers. The continuous and fast growth of the web was beyond the capabilities of the human editors of web directories.

Though web directories do still exist, their role as central source for finding information has long since been taken over by search engines.

Search engines basically consist of two main components: crawlers, which are automatic agents browsing and indexing the web along its hyperlink structure, and a retrieval engine, which finds the relevant pages among those crawled and indexed when given a query for some information [Glö03]. An important point in the development of search engines was the capability not only to find web documents containing the significant keywords of a query, but to rank the documents in a way that lists the more relevant and thereby best results first. The advent of the Google search engine was a ground-breaking success in this field, and its good performance at ranking the results has lead to its predominant position among web search engines – a position which Google has managed to defend up till today.

Brin and Page's *PageRank* [BP98] – the algorithm underlying Google – and Kleinberg's *HITS* [Kle99] allow to identify good sources of information in a hyperlinked structure like the web. Both algorithms have been developed independently and more or less at the same time and both use the web's hyperlink structure to deduce the quality of a document. The basic idea of PageRank and HITS is that if a web page is a good resource for information, a lot of other pages will reference it via hyperlinks. And further, if a good source for information is referring to another page, this referenced page very likely is a good source, too. Though the algorithms have been adapted and refined since their first presentation, their basic concept remains unchanged.

While web directories and search engines provide a practical solution to keep the problem of finding information on the web under control, the management of information from a provider's point of view has essentially been solved by WCMS. By now, these systems have become a generally available mainstream technology and cover a wide range of applications for different scenarios. They appear in many different forms and with different ranges of functionality: from complex enterprise content management systems (ECMS) to relatively easy to use blogging systems, from high priced commercial products to free open source software and from general purpose solutions for all kinds of content to specialised programs designed for small market niches or even a single web site only. In any case, when chosen appropriately to the field of application and the needs of a given environment, all approaches improve the administration and handling of a web site. To distinguish this kind of managed sites from manually maintained web sites, Kao, Lin, Ho and Chen introduced the term *systematic web sites* [KLHC04].

The basic features of all WCMS should be roughly the same, as the management of a web site requires at least the separation of structure, content and layout [ABS00][1]. This separation of the content of a web document from the presentational aspects is usually achieved by a system of *document templates* and a presentation independent storage of the contents. The final documents on the web are created dynamically by filling the contents into the template framework. The possibility to further combine a content with different

---

[1]Quite often, the functions for user and workflow management, content syndication options or a sophisticated publishing concept are considered important, too. However, they do not affect the way contents are presented on the web and, hence, are not of importance in our context.

1 Introduction

templates allows to reuse it in different contexts. The most obvious and straight forward example is to offer a printer friendly version of a document, which has a simplified layout and e.g. omits the navigation menu.

The template concept also allows to separate the structure of a web site from its presentation and the contents. The structure of a web site mainly corresponds to the organisational hierarchy of the documents and the hyperlinks connecting them. In a WCMS, this hierarchy information of a document is modelled independently from the template and the content data. Only when a document is compiled into its final form in an HTML format by combining template and contents, the link structures and navigation menus are dynamically created and fitted into the template as well. This allows to easily add, relocate, archive, delete or interlink single documents, as in a systematic web site all hyperlinks affected by such actions are adapted automatically to the new situation.

This automatism tends to stimulate the creation of enriched web documents. As adapting the navigation structure, intra-site hyperlinks or presentation styles does not involve changing manually every single page, a WCMS reduces a web site manager's reservations for doing so. The content providers actually seem to become much more willing to provide several interrelated navigation structures on their web site that improve handling and usability of the site, but which would be impossible to manage without a dedicated information system. Accordingly most systematic web sites nowadays come along with different views on the navigation, several kinds of relations between the documents, references to other articles or special functions like user added comments, the option to send articles by e-mail or even the possibility to personalise the appearance of a web site to the user's needs. All the mentioned examples illustrate functions intended to aid a user when looking for information on a web site. And all of them cause the web documents to become richer in contents and the network of hyperlinks on the web to become much denser – mainly on an intra-site level, but due to content syndication, the effects can be observed on inter-site link structures as well.

It has to be said, that all these additional contents do not provide additional information. They are solely intended to help the users to find what they are looking for. So, where an additional content provides more data than, for instance, a simple link, it has to import information from another document. This causes a lot of information to be kept in a redundant way, when looking at the resulting documents on the web.

The fact that WCMS allow the creation of larger and more complex web sites is increasing this problem additionally. While larger sites certainly contribute to the web's growth rate, they in turn also create most of the redundant contents. Gibson, Punera and Tomkins [GPT05] estimated in 2005 that the redundant content generated by WCMS makes up approximately 40 to 50% of the content on the web.

Redundancy can spread beyond a document or web site level as well. Kao, Lin, Ho and Chen distinguish in [KLHC04] between intra-site redundancy and inter-site redundancy. Yi, Liu and Li [YLL03] described the same phenomenon a bit earlier but less specific as local and global noise disturbing web mining applications. While the first kind of redundancy is mainly a side effect of template usage in systematic web sites and it describes contents occurring repeatedly in several documents, the inter-site redundancy is caused by content syndication, several web sites being managed by the same WCMS software, mirror pages, illegal copies or older versions appearing in web archives. Inter-site syndication and exchange of contents or the multiple publication of the same content on several managed web sites causes a redundancy even of the informative contents in documents at several locations on the web.

Most human users do not have problems to cope with the additional contents on a systematic web site – they simply ignore them. Web designers are nowadays aware, that a user does not really read a web document, but solely *scans* it [Kru06]. By "scanning" the designers mean, that a user is taking a glimpse at a web page and tries to identify the interesting parts of the document. To do so, he or she passes quickly with the eyes over the screen, takes up the layout, the structure and merely reads a few words here and there. This entire scanning process takes only a few seconds – even less time is needed for the user to simply get a first subjective impression whether he likes or dislikes a web page [LFDB05]. If and only if this fast scanning reveals that the document might contain interesting information, the user starts reading. And even in this case the user will usually not read all of the web page but just those parts which promise to be interesting.

While making life easier for the content providers and most consumers looking for information, the additional contents can cause problems at another point. The crawlers of a search engine, for example, have several problems with the additional contents. They cannot scan the documents in the same way a human user does. Hence, they have to handle much more data and a richer hyperlink structure. The latter aspect further influences the performance of PageRank and HITS. The idea underlying those algorithms is based on assumptions which do not reflect any more the changed usage of hyperlinks. A web page that is referenced by many other pages might not necessarily be a good source of information, it might simply be part of the dense network of WCMS generated documents with a high rate of intra-site links. Bar-Yossef and Rajagopalan [BYR02] described several scenarios in which the results of modern ranking algorithms are severely influenced by template generated documents.

But also human users might encounter problems: users which do not use the classical way to access web pages via the visual user interface of a standard browser. A visually impaired user, for instance, does not see the entire web document at once, but has to wait for a screen reader program to read the contents in a more or less linear way. Recalling the observations of Gibson et al. of a rate of 40 to 50% of additional contents, in the most unlucky case the user might have to wait for about half of the page to be read before even noticing, that it is not interesting. Obviously, reading half of the document will take far longer than the few seconds most other users need to scan the page. There are several other scenarios, where it is impossible to quickly flicker with the eyes over a web document to find the possibly interesting parts, e.g. if the screen resolution or size does not permit to display the entire document, or where a low connection bandwidth limits the speed of data transmission.

1 Introduction

In all these situations the users – may they be human or the crawlers of a search engine – cannot scan the documents as a human user normally would do. Hence, they have to cope with more content and invest more time in finding the relevant information in a document. Looking at the perception of web documents from this point of view leads to the conclusion that what the web designers describe as "scanning" can be compared to a filtering process. Experienced web users have learned how to distinguish the interesting from the additional contents simply by looking at a document. Noteworthy about this relatively intuitive description of how documents are perceived is also that it underlines once more the existence of different kinds of content in web documents. We are now going to take a closer look at these contents.

1.2 Contents of a Web Document

The different kinds of content appearing in a web document can be seen best when looking at an example. Figure 1.1 shows a screenshot of a web document as it is rendered and displayed by a modern web browser. It is an article taken from the Spiegel online web site in late 2006, reporting about the failure of the German-French Quaero project, a project intended to produce a European search engine to tackle the dominance of Google[2].

As mentioned above a human user has no problem to get a rough idea of what the article is about by taking a brief look at it. Given the necessary background knowledge, a human probably knows quite well already by reading the headline and the teaser (the introductory paragraph) what the main topic is. Having spotted those two fragments of the document, it comes quite natural to continue reading below. The paragraphs to the right and below the image complete the main content of the document as perceived by the user.

For most users with a certain experience in browsing the WWW the just described behaviour will be the typical way to approach a new document. This behaviour corresponds perfectly to what was described above as scanning a document and then reading the relevant parts. As now we want instead to take a look at all the contents in the documents we will have to deliberately avoid the natural approach we humans take when reading a document – or better: when perceiving it.

Overcoming the temptation to just focus on the main content and paying instead attention to all the present contents, the vast amount of other contents becomes "visible". Looking more closely at the screenshot in figure 1.1, the first thing we notice when reading a document entirely and top down will be the header of the document. The most prominent part of this header is the large red horizontal bar bearing the logo of Spiegel online, depicting additionally that it is the international section which is currently visible. The grey bar positioned above the logo provides short links to pages offering services like an RSS feed or a subscription to a newsletter. Another grey coloured bar below the logo is instead

---

[2]The project actually has not been stopped, but the German-French cooperation broke up. The development of Quaero is now driven mainly by the french partners, while on the German side the work is continued in the Theseus project.

1.2 Contents of a Web Document

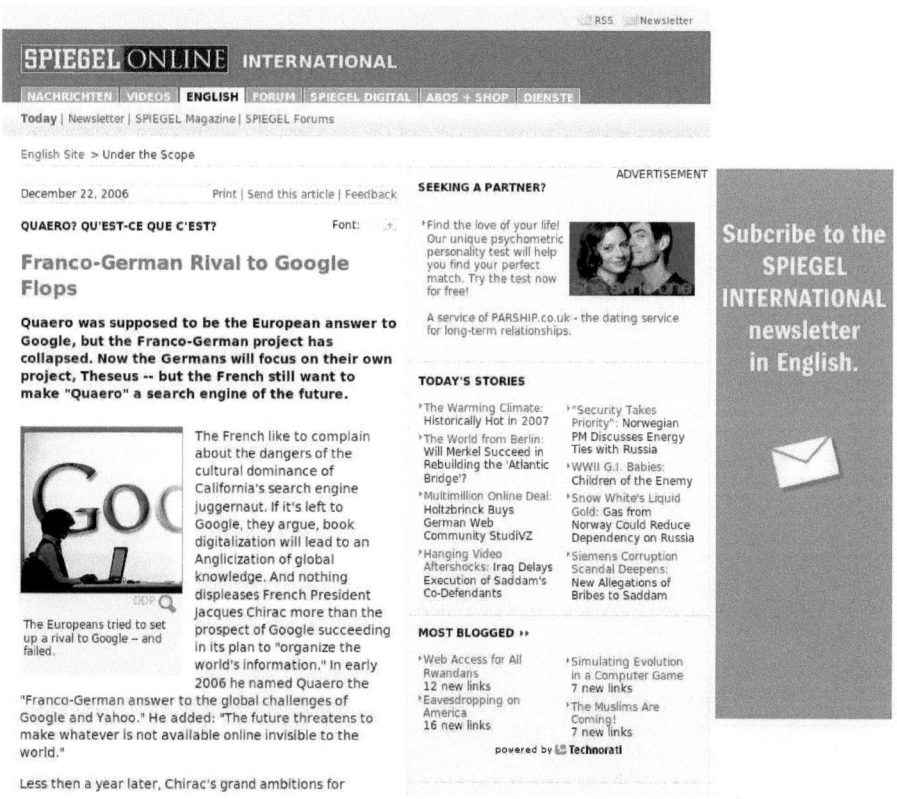

Figure 1.1: An example of a WCMS generated web document as it is presented by a standard browser.

the main navigation element, providing links to all major topic categories, highlighting the currently selected category and showing its sub-categories.

Below the header the document splits into roughly three parts, which form a column each: the article to the left, a collection of references in the middle and a commercial banner to the right. It can be argued, whether the commercial banner is a column at this level or if it lies parallel to the entire document. As it is aligned with the top of the other two columns, the layout of the document suggests the three parallel columns interpretation. Anyway, the description of the three columns is not very precise either, as at least the first two of them can be further subdivided. The article itself is preceded by a link to a printer friendly layout of the document and by the options to send the article by e-mail, to send a feedback message to the authors and to modify the font size of the text.

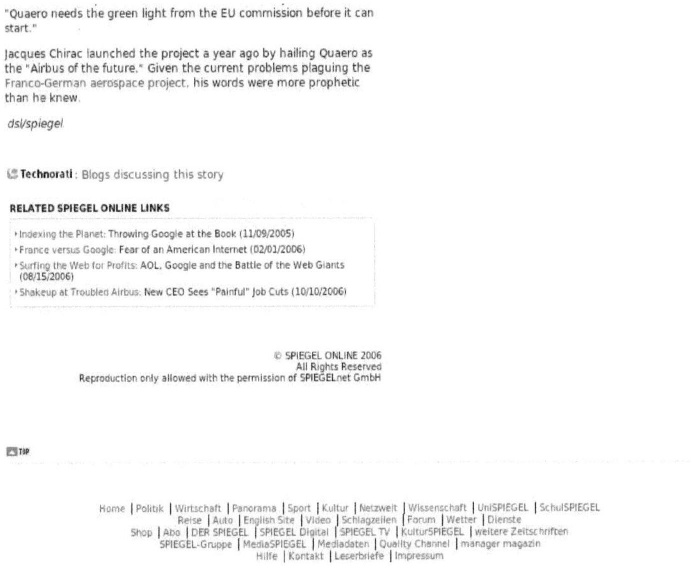

"Quaero needs the green light from the EU commission before it can start."

Jacques Chirac launched the project a year ago by hailing Quaero as the "Airbus of the future." Given the current problems plaguing the Franco-German aerospace project, his words were more prophetic than he knew.

dsl/spiegel

Technorati: Blogs discussing this story

RELATED SPIEGEL ONLINE LINKS

- Indexing the Planet: Throwing Google at the Book (11/09/2005)
- France versus Google: Fear of an American Internet (02/01/2006)
- Surfing the Web for Profits: AOL, Google and the Battle of the Web Giants (08/15/2006)
- Shakeup at Troubled Airbus: New CEO Sees "Painful" Job Cuts (10/10/2006)

© SPIEGEL ONLINE 2006
All Rights Reserved
Reproduction only allowed with the permission of SPIEGELnet GmbH

TOP

Home | Politik | Wirtschaft | Panorama | Sport | Kultur | Netzwelt | Wissenschaft | UniSPIEGEL | SchulSPIEGEL
Reise | Auto | English Site | Video | Schlagzeilen | Forum | Wetter | Dienste
Shop | Abo | DER SPIEGEL | SPIEGEL Digital | SPIEGEL TV | KulturSPIEGEL | weitere Zeitschriften
SPIEGEL-Gruppe | MediaSPIEGEL | Mediadaten | Quality Channel | manager magazin
Hilfe | Kontakt | Leserbriefe | Impressum

Figure 1.2: The lower part of the WCMS generated web document.

The article itself consists of the title, the teaser, the main text body and an image. Some other indirectly related information like the date of publication is interspersed as well. The first element in the second column is an advertisement, followed by a collection of articles published recently on the same web site and some references to articles on other web sites. The elements in this column are clearly separated from each other and, again, could be still subdivided further.

The three parallel columns have different length. In particular the article is much longer in terms of space. The lower end of the document is shown in figure 1.2. Only the left column is reaching that far down; the other two columns are shorter and do not have any contents in the lower section of the document. The column containing the article is concluded by a reference to Technorati[3], a list of related articles on Spiegel online and a copyright note. The footer closing the document is ranging across the first two columns and consists again of a collection of navigation links to provide quick access to central pages of the web site.

So, the document shown here as an example of different contents contains the most common kinds of content, which can be classified as follows:

[3]Technorati is a search engine specialised on blogs and news articles. It aims at keeping its index up to date in real time by allowing web authors to notify the search engine of changes on their web site.

1.2 Contents of a Web Document

Main content: The article of this document is certainly its primary content. It is the payload of the document, the main information which is to be transmitted to the user. Vice versa, it is also the main reason for a user to consider a document for reading.

Navigation: The header and the footer are the main navigation elements in this page. Navigation elements do not contribute to the content but they are necessary for the usability of the document in the context of the hyperlink structure of its web site. Navigation comprises both: elements which allow moving to other documents and elements which allow to deduce the current location in the web site structure.

Link lists: Lists or collections of hyperlinks referring to other documents on the same web site or external resources. Our example provides different kinds of link lists: the most recent stories are documents from the same source grouped according to a time property, i.e. the newest, most recent documents belong to this list. The related links are formed by documents which have a topic similar to the one of the main article. And the links to articles on third party blogs are also related to the main topic, but refer to external documents outside the scope of Spiegel online.

Commercials: Advertisements and commercials are widespread and can be found on most web sites. They represent a common way of providing a source of income, thus partially financing the web site. In this example two different approaches of embedding commercials can be seen: the banner in the right column is a single graphical entity, realised as an animation, using an appropriate technology such as Flash or animated GIF images. The second type is represented by the advertisement in the middle column, which consists of text extended by an image. In fact the layout and the appearance of this second commercial are much closer and more similar to the other parts of the document. As such, it is less prominent than the banner, but vice versa the chance to ignore it altogether as an obvious commercial is reduced as well.

Functional elements: The links which allow to send the article as an e-mail or to alter the font size allow interaction with the document. As the name suggests these elements provide functions related to the document, different from pure navigation.

Template elements: Some parts are common to most or even to all documents found on a web site, such as the copyright notice or the header with the logo of the web site. They provide information common to the entire web site or contribute to the look and feel of a web site.

The above list of content types is not exhaustive and the identification of the kinds of content cannot always be made as clear as in this case.

Staying again with the initial notion of what is interesting for the user and what is not, a much rougher classification used already earlier is to simply subdivide the contents into

1 Introduction

main content and *additional contents*. The main content carries the primary information, the additional contents are simply extensions to it. The names for these two different classes of contents vary in literature. The main content is also labelled as primary, principal or core content. The additional contents instead are sometimes referred to as template generated contents or even as noise, when it comes to the topics of quality and purity of data in the context of text or data mining.

Looking again at the entire document with this simpler subdivision of the contents into two classes, the estimates of Gibson et al. [GPT05] seem quite realistic: nearly half of the contents of the document are template generated, corresponding to the mentioned ratio of about 40 to 50 %.

1.3 Content Extraction

As mentioned above, a human user tends to ignore the contents he or she is not interested in and, thus, will usually focus on the main content. The "scanning" of the document prior to reading it is the process of looking for prominent parts which suggest the location of the main content. Scanning was already compared to a filtering process and – looking at a human user's performance in finding the interesting parts of a document – it is a fast and usually quite reliable filter.

There are several scenarios, where a computer based detection of the main content could be useful or necessary. Supporting web search engines to provide more reliable results or to aid humans with visual disabilities were two of the examples mentioned earlier. When performed by a computer, the filtering process of finding the primary content is called *content extraction* (CE). It was Rahman, Alam and Hartono [RAH01] who used the term CE first in 2001. Since then, it is the expression found most often in publications dealing with this topic, even though also the terms *separation of primary content blocks*, *core content detection* or *extraction of informative blocks* are used to describe the same or very similar concepts.

Obviously, a computer program does not have the ability to access a document in the same way as humans do. First of all it lacks the understanding of the content. While a human user can base the decision about the main content on the semantics of the information in a web page, a computer has no access to the meaning of a document[4]. Further, a program usually must base its operations on the source code of the document or on some derived representation of it. Lacking the visual impression of the document, it has difficulties to find elements with characteristic positions on the screen like the headline, the teaser and the paragraphs which form the main content.

There are few approaches which use rendering information of web browsers to get an idea of how the layout of a web document on a computer screen looks like. But even if a

---

[4]The Semantic Web initiative is working on techniques for describing semantics of contents in a machine readable format. However, the semantic annotation of the a web document will very likely cover only the main content anyway and further is not intended for human speech or writings [BLHL01].

1.3 Content Extraction

rendered version of the document is available it remains difficult to provide general rules on how to locate and recognise the main content. Looking again at the document of figure 1.1 there are some examples of those difficulties. A characteristic of the headline certainly is that it is written by using a larger font size and weight. It is difficult to formalise, though, why the header writings beside the Spiegel Online logo are not part of the headline.

Likewise, a paragraph of the main content can be stated to be a longer text with a normal sized font. It remains the question what is a normal sized font and why the advertisement to the top of the middle column still does not belong to the main content. Even when adding other, additional conditions and restrictions which seem to describe the main content, it soon becomes obvious that they will not fit all documents available on the web. So, even rendering and visually analysing a web document does not provide all the clues necessary to reliably detect the main content. It is likely due to this problem and the computational overhead coming along with it, that rendering information is hardly ever used for analysing web documents.

The search for related work revealed actually only one approach [ZL05] which really incorporated visual rendering information during the phase of document analysis. It used the Internet Explorer's API to deduce the screen position of certain document elements. However, the intention in this case was not to find the main content, but to discover layout structures for wrapper induction – a task which has similarities to CE and which we will look at closer in chapter 3 when dealing with related work.

So, as using rendering information does not seem to be the key to discover the main content, most approaches are solely based on a source code analysis. The thought, that the layout is anyway mainly captured in the HTML structure of a web document certainly corresponds to reality in most cases. There are, however, cases when ignoring everything except the pure HTML information can be misleading to deduce a visual representation. A good example of how much the presentation of the same HTML source code can vary due to the use of additional technologies such as cascading style sheets (CSS) or JavaScript is the web site CSS Zen Garden [She07]. This web site is devoted to the use of CSS as the only technique to influence the layout of a web document. A large collection of examples – some of which are shown in figure 1.3 – shows quite impressively how the same HTML code can have a very different visual presentation simply due to an exchanged CSS style specification.

Given that neither visual information nor the HTML source code can provide definitive clues about the location of the main content in a document, roughly two different kinds of approaches evolved to solve the CE task: heuristic approaches operating on single documents and solutions based on the analysis of template structures in document collections. This division or classification of CE approaches has also been made by Gibson, Punera and Tomkins in [GPT05]. They considered the single document CE approaches as local techniques, while multi document solutions were referred to as global techniques.

The heuristics of the single document approaches are build on assumptions that do usually hold for the main content. The most important and wide spread assumption is that the main content is a continuous text, like in the articles of a news web site. On the

1 Introduction

Figure 1.3: Four screenshots from CSS Zen Garden: the same HTML document has a different appearance due to different CSS definitions.

basis of this assumption, the idea often is to look for a long and rather uninterrupted text. Obviously, on web sites which present main contents other than texts, e.g. collections of photos or mainly tabular data for short product descriptions, these single document methods will usually fail. Certainly, some of those methods could be adapted to look for different kinds of main content, but then they would likely fail on extracting plain text main contents.

The CE approaches based on multiple documents exploit the fact that, in a collection of documents which are all based on the same template, the template portions of the documents occur more frequently or even in every document. By locating these common fragments, the algorithms attempt to deduce the template structure in a reverse engineering approach and use the knowledge about this structure to locate and extract the main content. Therefore, these approaches are often referred to as *template detection* (TD) algorithms. Most TD algorithms are applicable also in other areas than CE, like web site structure analysis or for detecting and differentiating in a more detailed way between the kinds of additional content.

Even though the general problem of deducing a template structure from a set of documents is NP-complete, there are several practical approaches which simplify the task a bit in order to find a solution efficiently. These approaches rely far less on assumptions about the contents and have a much better theoretical underpinning than the single document approaches. Most important, they are usually independent of assumptions about how the main content looks like, and thus can also operate on main contents consisting of images or tabular data. Their drawback, instead, is that they can only be applied to template based documents. If a document is simply not based on a template, there will be no set of documents with common parts. Accordingly the algorithms cannot deduce a template structure – or if they try to, they fail. Under this aspect, TD algorithms do not reflect a human user's approach to find the main content, as humans do not require to see several documents, before they are able to spot the main content. They are able to locate the main content even in documents with a unique layout and structure.

The need of a document collection can be a problem in general, namely as these collections need to be created in the first place. Building clean and reliable document sets is a task which so far has rarely been dealt with. Further, the few attempts to automate the task have hardly brought the desired results.

1.4 Contributions

This thesis deals with several topics in the context of CE. In addition to giving a quite complete overview of methods and techniques developed so far in the field of CE, it makes three contributions which are new to the topic.

Before going into the details of these contributions, we will first provide some basic background knowledge in chapter 2 which is needed to follow the approaches and solutions presented in this thesis. Chapter 3 is dealing extensively with related work in the fields of CE and TD. Some algorithms are described quite in detail, as they are either used later on for comparison, incorporated as a basis to build other solutions on top of them or as they provide an insight into how CE and TD algorithms work in general. This insight is needed to motivate several decisions and developments during the discussions of the evaluation methodology and for the general conversion of multi document TD into single document CE algorithms. For the same purpose, we give a formal definition of CE in chapter 4 and a summary of possibilities on how to realise the extraction process in practice.

The first major contribution is made in the context of evaluation of CE methods. Though there is relatively little research work dealing with CE methods, there is even less dealing with their evaluation. Most publications do contain a section about evaluation, but hardly any develops an objective and application independent way to analyse the performance of a CE algorithm. In the context of developing the evaluation measures, several existing CE algorithms have been implemented, analysed and, for the first time, compared directly with each other under performance aspects.

1 Introduction

In a second step, several new single document based approaches have been developed. Two approaches have been translated from closely related domains to CE by adopting algorithms from applications for wrapper generation and for TD. Content code blurring, a third algorithm, is a completely new approach to CE which is overcoming several drawbacks of existing single document CE methods.

The last contribution of the thesis is dealing with solutions to bridge the gap between single document based CE algorithms and multi document TD solutions. As it was already mentioned before, the first approach lacks the theoretic underpinning while the second has the drawback of being in need of manually created training sets. In this context, we will analyse several approaches to compare document structures and automatically build clean training sets for TD.

Finally, we conclude with a summary of the results and will take an outlook at future work in chapter 8. In particular we will look at the upcoming HTML 5.0 standard, the technical challenges in the Web 2.0 environment and the recently increasing interest of computer linguists to exploit the web as a source for building large scale text corpora. These trends will very likely influence the importance and the role of CE in the near future.

Some of the results presented in this thesis have been published in a condensed form at different conferences. The evaluation framework and a comparison of some existing CE algorithms were presented at the International Conference on Internet Technologies and Applications ITA'07 in Wrexham [Got07]. The results about template clustering were presented at the European Conference on Information Retrieval ECIR'08 in Glasgow [Got08b] and the process of automatic training set creation for TD at the European Conference on Internet and Multimedia Systems and Applications EuroIMSA'08 in Innsbruck [Got08a]. A paper on the content code blurring algorithm has been accepted at the International Workshop on Text Information Retrieval TIR'08 in Turin [Got08c] and will be published in the proceedings in September 2008.

2 Basic Terms and Concepts

CE is a concept which appears in different fields of application. Depending on the focus and the purpose of those applications they involve a wide range of technologies, concepts and methods from different areas of computing science.

This chapter provides a basic introduction to some of these fields and an explanation of the terms, methods and techniques which are necessary to understand the concepts of CE algorithms, motivate certain evaluation decisions or are used frequently throughout this thesis. Three essential fields are addressed here: first, some common data models for web documents and their representation, second, an overview of basic issues from the field of information retrieval (IR) and finally methods and data structures used to represent documents for data and text mining applications. All the topics are dealt with only briefly and in the light of their relevance for CE. This introduction should provide the reader with the knowledge required to follow the algorithms and methods presented in this thesis. At the end of the chapter some further reading is suggested which may – in case of interest – give a deeper insight into the discussed topics.

2.1 Web Documents

CE is operating on web documents, rendering them thereby into the central objects of interest and analysis in this thesis. As mentioned already in the introduction, CE is approaching the documents from a different perspective than a human user. It hardly ever operates on the commonly known visual presentation of the documents in a web browser, but rather accesses them via their source code or some derived structure. Therefore, the technologies and formats behind the documents and in particular the ways to work with them might need to be looked at briefly in the given context.

2.1.1 (X)HTML

The string representation of a web document corresponds to an HTML format. Nowadays the most commonly used formats follow the recommendations of the *World Wide Web Consortium* (W3C) for *HTML* 4.01 [RHJ99] or its XML based successor *XHTML* 1.1 [W3C07][1]. Both are markup languages which structure a plain text by outlining specific structural elements of the document. The elements are marked by parenthesising the

---
[1] The XHTML 2 specification [W3C06b] have so far reached only the working draft status at the W3C. The works on the specifications are still ongoing and the format is not yet adopted in practice.

2 Basic Terms and Concepts

according text fragments in tags – special character sequences that do not belong to the text itself. The string representation of a web document is more commonly referred to as its *source code* and it is the basis for all other higher and more elaborate representations, both visual for presentation in a web browser or structural for computational purposes. The technical information which text encoding is used for transforming the characters of the source code into bytes and vice versa on how to decode the bytes again into characters is contained in the document itself.

The major difference between HTML and XHTML is the stricter syntactic regulation deriving from the underlying XML of the latter, compared to the less rigorous *SGML* basis of the former. Element names, for example, are case sensitive in XHTML and all elements need to be closed, i.e. they have to consist of an opening and a corresponding closing tag or have to be explicitly marked as empty tag. The advantage of the reformulation of HTML using XML as a basis is that it allows to operate on XHTML documents with all applications supporting the XML standard as data format. This becomes especially handy when parsing, analysing or modifying web documents.

Two technologies to be mentioned in this context are *XSLT* [W3C99b] and *XPath* [W3C99a]. XSLT is the transformation component of the *Extensible Stylesheet Language* (XSL) for XML. It allows the transformation of documents from one XML format into another one. XPath is a path language for XML and it finds its use also in XSLT. It allows to address parts of an XML document in a standardised way. Both technologies are frequently used when working with XML documents and they appear in the context of CE as well. The elISA system [VdC04], for example, which is described in 3.2.6, uses XSLT transformations extensively.

Unfortunately, not all documents on the web are written in XHTML format, neither do all of them comply with the HTML 4.01 recommendation or at least a prior version. A large number of documents contain syntactic errors, and accordingly do not fulfil the requirements of the specifications. There are, however, a number of tools and programs available that allow to fix a syntactically broken document – a procedure performed by most web browsers, too[2]. One of the more known and established programs for this purpose is *Tidy* [Rag03]. The Tidy project was originally launched by Dave Raggett at the W3C itself and is now actively developed by a group of volunteers. Tidy is able to turn the source code of virtually any web document into valid HTML or even XHTML code. For easier inclusion in Java based applications, as the ones developed in the course of this thesis, the Java version *JTidy*[3] [GTG+08] represents a comfortable and suitable alternative to the original Tidy.

---

[2]It is a kind of vicious circle – the good will of browser programs to render even syntactically broken documents causes the web document authors to be more lax about adhering to the standards, thus causing the need of browsers to be error-tolerant when handling the documents.

[3]Unfortunately the JTidy project seems not be developed further, even though there is a list of open problems with the program. However, it proved to be functional enough for its intended purpose in the context of this thesis.

2.1.2 SAX

Given the possibility to convert all web documents into XHTML code by applying JTidy, it is always possible to assume XML syntax when working with a document, and thereby providing the option to work with all XML aware tools. One commonly used method to access XML documents is via *SAX*, the *simple API for XML*. Originally designed as a Java programming interface to XML documents it spread to other programming languages and is nowadays considered a de facto standard. SAX parses an XML document and notifies a content handler about the encountered parts in the document, such as tags, parsing instructions, comments or texts. Though a very common way to parse an XML document, it also is a very simple and lightweight approach: it does not provide by itself a data model for storing an entire document. Accordingly SAX does not directly permit to perform more complex operations on a parsed document. For this purpose the DOM representation of an XML document presented in 2.1.3 is a more suitable approach.

As the SAX implementations are meant to be generally applicable to all XML documents and as they require to pass a web document beforehand through JTidy, an additional solution for working with raw HTML files was used for the major part of the applications in this thesis. By implementing a SAX oriented parser, tailored in particular to handle HTML documents, it was possible to be more error tolerant while parsing. This solution allowed an easier, more specific and very robust access to HTML documents if needed. Even though performance issues were not the primary interest, the specialised parser was also faster than a full SAX implementation in combination with JTidy. For parsing 500 HTML documents of different origin and size, JTidy took about 22 seconds to check and correct all documents. Feeding the result afterwards to Apache's Xerces SAX parser resulted in an overall parsing time of 698 seconds. The specialised SAX oriented HTML parser performed the parsing in less than six seconds, therefore even faster than JTidy on its own. Certainly, JTidy is fixing more mistakes in the code, asserts a well formed and valid XHTML document as output and additionally constructs a DOM representation during the process. Xerces, furthermore, comes with all the features of a full fledged XML parser. However, most of those functionalities are not required for the CE algorithms which can be implemented on top of a SAX parsing process.

2.1.3 DOM

The *Document Object Model* (DOM) is described and extended in the W3C specifications [W3C98], [W3C00] and [W3C04]. It is a standard interface to access and modify all XML/SGML based documents, thus, in particular HTML and XHTML documents. The specification does not provide an implementation itself, but actually is a programming language independent model outlining objects and methods for a data structure to represent a document as a tree. The strictly nested structure of the elements induces a natural parent-child relation which is translated by the DOM directly into a tree structure. The texts which appear between the tags of the elements form leaf nodes which are inserted

2 Basic Terms and Concepts

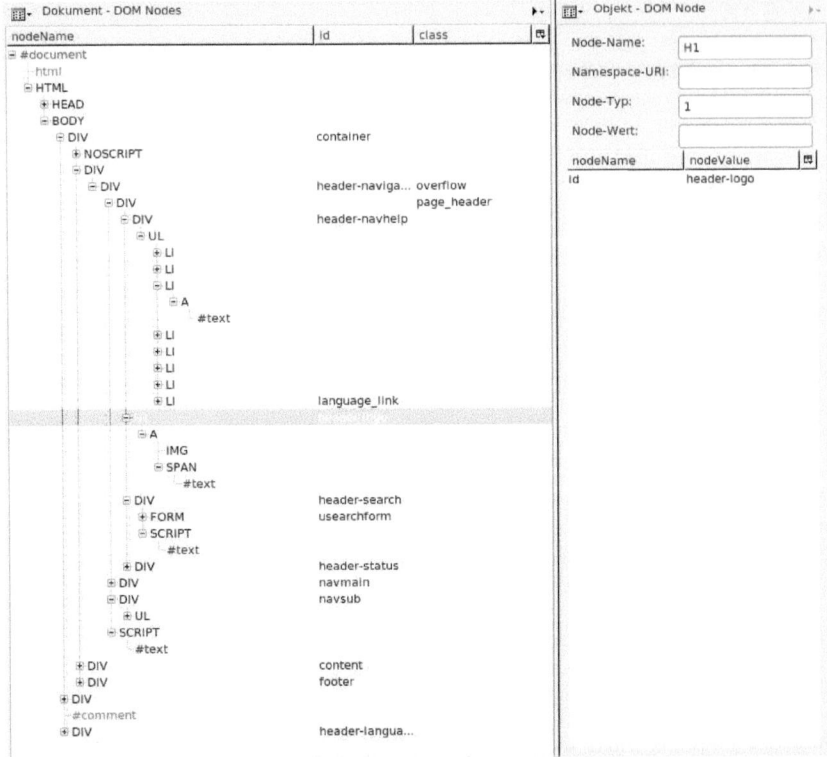

Figure 2.1: The DOM inspector of the Mozilla Firefox browser allows displaying the DOM tree of an HTML document.

into the tree at the according positions. The DOM further specifies standardised methods to access and even modify the information attached to each element.

Several applications make use of the DOM tree representation of HTML documents. The most commonly known is probably the access via scripting languages like JavaScript in web browsers. The script code is embedded in the web documents themselves and uses the DOM to access and modify the client side copy of the document while it is being displayed by the browser – usually to generate client side dynamic and interactive web pages. The Mozilla Firefox browser provides a graphical user interface for viewing, analysing and modifying the DOM model of a web document. Figure 2.1 shows a screenshot of this *DOM inspector*. The application also gives a first idea of how the DOM tree looks like. Given the purpose of the DOM inspector, the tree representation is very technical, though.

2.1 Web Documents

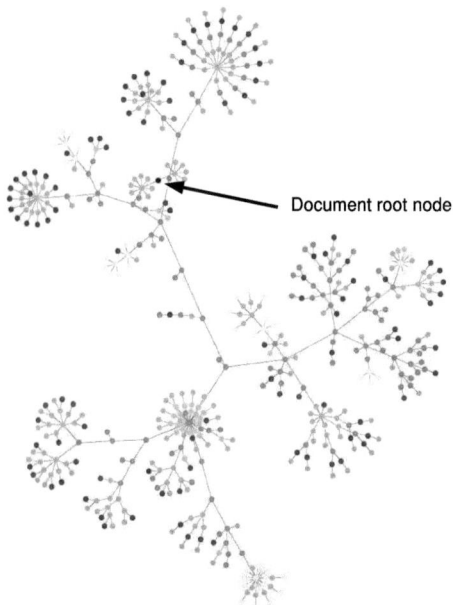

Figure 2.2: A more vivid and artistic representation of the DOM tree of a web document.

Figure 2.2 shows a much more vivid representation of the DOM tree of a web document. It is a more artistic approach [Sal08] making use of DOM parsing, the Processing [FR08] visualisation framework and a physical library for simulating the attraction and repulsion of atomic particles. The nodes are coloured according to their type and the overall image gives a quite nice impression of the tree structure and the complexity of its branches.

The methods provided by the DOM cover counting and accessing the child nodes attached to an element node and determining its parent. Combined with the possibility to locate the root node, i.e. the root element of the document, the DOM allows all basic operations necessary to work with trees. A few other methods allow simpler access to commonly used operations, such as getting the siblings of a node, search operations and the retrieval of lists of nodes. On a node level the DOM specifies access to the element name, to XML namespace information, to the attributes of the element and to their values. While it is not possible to change all of this data directly, it is possible to generate new nodes and insert them at any point as new children or to replace existing nodes. The replacement of a node can be realised either directly or – as some implementations do not support this operation – indirectly via deleting the old and inserting the new node.

While the possibility to modify the structure of a document is coming handy when removing or changing contents or other parts of the document, the tree structure representation is particularly interesting itself: it allows the application of tree based algorithms. The possibility to handle elements as nodes in a tree, having at hand the information about the number and the kind of the child elements, the parent element and the root of the tree is interesting for a number of methods like tree alignment, search or tree cover algorithms. Several applications which will be discussed in more detail in chapter 3 make extensive use of the DOM model for documents because of its tree structure and the easy way to access and modify the information inside a document.

2.1.4 Templates

As already mentioned in the introduction, the increased use of WCMS is one of the main reasons, why web documents nowadays contain more contents – in terms of both volume and diversity – than a few years ago. WCMS increase the maintainability of a managed web site by separating the content from format, layout and structure information. This key functionality is realised via templates.

Templates can be seen as empty framework documents with slots which are filled with different contents to compile the final documents. They allow to reuse contents for different presentation styles or to include the contents only partially, e.g. for the inclusion of title and teaser texts in link lists. Apart from the slots for classical text contents, like news articles written by human authors, the templates commonly also provide slots for automatically generated or derived information, such as a hierarchical structure for the navigation menu, the date of publication or the name of the author of an article. Another kind of slots are those which are filled with external or syndicated contents. Typical external contents are commercials or news feeds from other web sites.

An example of the slot structure of a template is included in figure 2.3, which shows a manually annotated screenshot of a news website. Seven possible slots[4] have been highlighted and numbered to show different kinds of contents which have been fitted in.

1. The *main navigation*: An automatically generated navigation menu which represents a hierarchical structure of the articles. In this case the hierarchical structure is imposed by a pre-defined set of categories and sub-categories in which the articles are classified. This menu is the main and most general mean of navigating between the pages of the web site.

2. A *location display*: Provides the user with an orientation and a secondary mean of navigation. It is dynamically generated from both the navigation structure and the category of the currently displayed document.

3. The *date of publication*: A visually represented meta data information of the document. Though strictly related to the document it is automatically generated and not

---

[4]The true template and slot structure remains hidden, but looking at several documents from the same origin suggested a configuration at least similar to the one outlined in the screenshot.

2.1 Web Documents

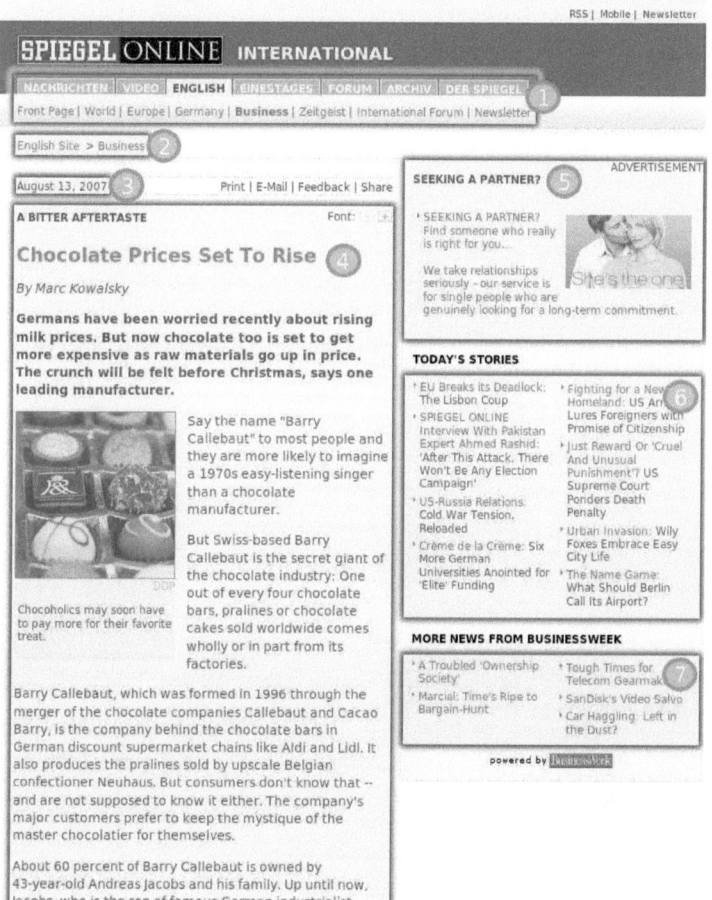

Figure 2.3: Screenshot of a template based web document in which the content slots are highlighted.

part of the article itself. Some more meta data might be hidden in the source code of the document and is not directly visible.

4. The *news article*: The "meat" of the page. The main content and the primary information the document intends to transmit to the user. Though outlined as a single content, the article is very likely not fitted into a single slot, but consists of a collection of slots itself. Title, teaser, author, news body text and images including their captions are typically structured in a presentation independent way. The layout

and arrangement of this information within the main content slot is imposed by the template as well and, thus, the final appearance of the article in the document is created dynamically.

5. *Commercials*: This example of a commercial is perfectly blended into the template structure. It fits both in style and presentation. Other, more frequent forms of commercials are the classical banners which usually harmonise less with the rest of the document.

6. A list of *related links*: In this case the related links comprehend the articles which have been published recently. So, the relation connecting the documents is based on a time criterion. Other criteria could be articles published in a series, written by the same author or texts which deal with similar and related topics.

7. *External links*: While in the previous slot the content was composed of internal links within the same web site, this element offers links to external resources from another news web site. It is an example of content syndication.

This example shows once more how template based documents seem to foster the inclusion of additional contents in a web page: it is mainly the content in slot 4 which makes the document interesting for a reader. While maybe the related and external links are still interesting for further reading, they usually would not attract a user to browse this document in the first place and can be – together with the contents of all other slots – counted among the additional contents.

Apart from providing the managed web sites with an easy to handle uniform look and feel, templates affect the structures of the eventually created web documents as well. Since the framework code of the template is common to all documents, they have a source code which is very similar from a structural point of view. This side effect is particularly interesting for CE applications and underlies several TD algorithms. In a collection of documents which are based on the same template the recurrent source code fragments allow to infer the template structure and hence to deduce the location of the slots.

2.2 Information Retrieval

To a certain extent, CE can be seen as a special task of *information retrieval* (IR), as it corresponds to finding the relevant information in a larger pool of data[5]. The main content represents the relevant information, while the entire document, with all its contents, forms the data pool. Hence, CE can be seen as a kind of IR on a document level.

---

[5]Quite often the term IR is bound to the domain of retrieving relevant documents from a larger collection. However, leaving the document requirement aside, the IR definition of Van Rijsbergen in [VR79] fits the CE task very well.

So, finding the main content can be interpreted as the task of locating the relevant contents in a document. Therefore the process itself might involve technologies and methods taken from the IR domain and the closely related fields of *data mining* and *machine learning*. Especially for the evaluation of CE it is necessary to give a short overview and explanation of the terms and measures used in these fields.

2.2.1 Concepts, Instances and Attributes

In order to gain a deeper understanding of some data, i.e. to conduct data mining (DM) or to apply machine learning, we have to provide three things: a concept – or better a concept description – the instances or examples and the attributes of the data.

The *concept* can be described as the aim of the learning task, the kind of understanding to be derived from the data. A concept can be the assignment of categories to web documents, e.g. the general topic they deal with, or it can be the grouping of documents which belong together, e.g. because they are all based on the same template. As the concept itself might not be obvious and not all concepts hidden in a data set might be known or of interest, the input for the machine learning task is considered a *concept description* This description outlines the intended concept which is to be learned: a classification scheme, the cluster groups of the data, a decision tree, etc. The example of finding the topic category for a web document would correspond to a classification scheme, the example of the document groups based on the same template to a cluster analysis. Providing the concept description for a machine learning task might be the most difficult parameter to set, as it requires to have already a feeling or an idea about what might be hidden in the data. Providing the wrong or an unsuitable concept description might cause the results to be meaningless or wrong in the light of the intended purpose.

Once the concept description has been fixed, any algorithm needs data to learn from in order to provide a result for the concept. This data comes in the form of a set of *instances* or *examples*. To follow again our previous examples the instances would be the web documents for which we want to find the topic category or the groups of common underlying templates. An instance can be seen as a single realisation of the concept which has to be learned and thus provides some experience from which to learn the concept.

The instances are inseparably tied to their *attributes*. Comparing the instances to objects in an object-oriented programming language, the definition of the attributes corresponds perfectly. So, if an instance is said to be the realisation of the underlying concept, it is de facto realised by the values its attributes take. Following the above mentioned examples, the attributes interesting for a topic classification might be the words in a web document. For the template clustering instead the HTML structure might be more important. The attributes in this case would more likely be the tags or the DOM nodes.

In general, the nature of the attributes can be very different. On the lowest level attribute values are divided into numeric or nominal values. Numeric values are continuous and have basically no limits, neither in bounds nor in precision, e.g. there is, at least theoretically, an unlimited number of real values in a fixed interval. Nominal values on the other hand do not have this continuous characteristic. They can be considered as items drawn from a finite set of alternatives. Some attributes are handled as nominal values, even though they correspond to an apparently unlimited set of values. Texts or words are examples for this. The problem with this kind of data is that it is hardly possible to make assumptions on which realisations might occur for these attributes and how to handle previously unseen occurrences. Under this aspect numerical values can usually be dealt with in an easier way due to their continuous character. The range of temperature values, for instance, can be predicted and instances with previously unseen attribute values can be compared with instances with similar values.

Each single instance has at least one attribute but can have an arbitrary number of them; and all instances in a data set have the same attributes. It is, however, possible that some attribute values for some instances are missing. Missing data is – just like faulty or biased data – an issue that has to be faced, but these topics are beyond the scope of this short introduction.

If all attributes of the instances have a numeric character, the instances can be represented as vectors. This translation of the instances into a vector space allows to apply various mathematical functions for operating on the instances. Most important is a nearly self evident concept of comparing two instances by computing the distances in the vector space. However, distance and similarity measures can be defined more generally and valid also for instances which do not map into a vector space.

2.2.2 Distance and Similarity Measures

To compare instances and their attributes it is necessary to provide some kind of function to formalise the comparison. Typically these functions are formulated as *distance* or *similarity functions*.

A distance function $d : I \times I \to \mathbb{R}$ for comparing instances from a set I in a DM or IR context should ideally be a *metric*, thus should satisfy several requirements:

Non-Negativity: the distance between two instances $x, y \in I$ is at least zero:

$$d(x, y) \geq 0.$$

Nonidentical instances have positive distance: the distance function for two instances $x, y \in I$ has a value of zero, if and only if they are identical:

$$d(x, y) = 0 \Leftrightarrow x = y.$$

Symmetry: the distance between two instances $x, y \in I$ is the same, no matter from which perspective:

$$d(x, y) = d(y, x).$$

Triangle inequality: given three instances $x, y, z \in I$, the distance between x and y is less or equal to the sum of the distances between x and z and between z and y:

$$d(x, y) \leq d(x, z) + d(z, y).$$

Not in all cases all these requirements are needed and not always they are met. As usually the instances are compared directly, the triangle inequality might not be necessary. Likewise it might be possible, that two nonidentical objects have a distance of zero, or that even the requirement of symmetry can be violated. Especially in cases where no mathematical or algorithmic way exists to calculate a distance, but human experts are asked to estimate distances between the instances, the properties of a metric distance function are very likely not fulfilled. In these cases the distance function is sometimes referred to as a *dissimilarity function* (e.g. in [Kru64]) to state explicitly that it is not a metric. However, as the term distance function is commonly used throughout domain specific literature for both metric and non-metric distances it is adopted in this thesis for dissimilarity functions as well.

A *similarity measure* $s : I \times I \to \mathbb{R}$ is less restricted. It has to satisfy:

Non-Negativity: similarity values are never below zero:

$$s(x, y) \geq 0.$$

Identical instances have a similarity of 1: the similarity of two instances $x, y \in I$ is 1, if they are identical:

$$x = y \Rightarrow s(x, y) = 1$$

Note that two instances may have a similarity of 1, even if they are not identical.

Symmetry: the similarity between two instances $x, y \in I$ is always the same, no matter from which perspective:

$$d(x, y) = d(y, x)$$

Maximality: a similarity measure has a maximum value of 1:

$$d(x, y) \leq 1.$$

Further, a similarity value of 0 states that two instances are entirely different. The semantic meaning of the statement, that two instances are entirely different depends on the scenario and might not always be easy to define. A similarity lying in the interval $(0, 1)$ states that two objects are similar to a certain degree. The higher the similarity value, the more similar the objects are. As for the distance measures, in some cases the demand for symmetry is omitted.

Any similarity measures can be converted into a (non-metric) distance measure d' by simply subtracting it from the maximum value 1:

$$d'(x, y) = 1 - s(x, y)$$

It can easily be verified that d' satisfies the requirements of non-negativity and symmetry (if s is symmetric). Non-identical instances will have a positive distance if and only if they have a similarity different from 1.

2 Basic Terms and Concepts

Likewise a distance measure d can be used as a basis for a similarity measure. If a maximum distance $d_{\max}$ is known, the distance can be normalised and subtracted from 1 to obtain a similarity s':

$$s'(x,y) = 1 - \frac{d(x,y)}{d_{\max}}$$

If no such maximum is known, there are two other commonly adopted strategies to construct a similarity measure, one based on a fraction and one based on the exponential function (see e.g. [SGM00]):

$$s''(x,y) = \frac{1}{1 + d(x,y)}$$

$$s'''(x,y) = e^{-d(x,y)}$$

All three methods provide a possibility to construct similarity measures which satisfy the requirements of non-negativity, maximality, symmetry (if d is symmetric) and that identical objects have a similarity of 1. The last two approaches though will never result in a similarity of zero. Accordingly they will never state, that two objects are entirely different. This reflects the fact, that as no maximum distance is known, there might always be another object with an even bigger distance, thus being even less similar.

2.2.3 Query, Result Set, Ground Truth and Gold Standard

The tasks of DM and in particular of IR can often be formulated as a query on a set of data. A classification can be seen as a query to retrieve the correct class for an instance or the instances for a given class, and a clustering task as a query for the instances that belong to the same cluster. A decision can be interpreted as a query for the correct decision within given options and a prediction task as a query for the predicted value. The answer provided to a query is the *result set*, consisting of no, one or several items.

When it comes to evaluating the performance of a learned DM scheme, it is often necessary to provide external knowledge about the data. In case of a classification task this would mean to provide the correct classification, for a cluster analysis it would be a desirable cluster configuration. This external knowledge of the correct clustering or classification – usually provided by an expert – is referred to as *ground truth* or *gold standard*. An evaluation of an IR method can then be evaluated by comparing the result sets it provides with the result sets the gold standard suggests, and by how far they conform to each other. Van Rijsbergen [VR79] uses the terms *retrieved items* (instances actually retrieved by an IR method) and *relevant items* (instances which are interesting according to some gold standard).

Providing a gold standard for an evaluation set is difficult and/or time consuming. A typical approach is to subdivide the set of instances which are available for training a machine learning algorithm, and to use only a part of the instances as training set while employing the remaining ones as evaluation set. This is possible as the instances in the training set often provide a gold standard themselves, as they usually have to contain e.g. the correct classification.

In IR, quite often the ranking of the results is very important. The ranking describes the order in which, for example, relevant documents are presented to the user. For CE ranking is a less relevant issue. The results, i.e. the words of the main content, are provided in the same order as they appear in the analysed web document.

2.2.4 Evaluation and Visualisation

For the evaluation of a learned concept, there are various measures and approaches. *Accuracy*, the *confusion matrix*, *recall* and *precision* as well as the deduced *F1-measure* are common quality measures for DM tasks and are predominantly used throughout this thesis. We will now look at their definition and discuss the way they evaluate the quality of a learned concept.

Most simple, the result of a classification task can be correct or incorrect. A correct classification is the desirable result, any incorrect classification is an error to be avoided. The accuracy of a learned classification scheme is the ratio of correctly classified instances among all classified objects. Optimally the accuracy is 1. A problem of the accuracy measure is that neither it goes into the details of the errors nor it specifies where the correct classifications have been made.

In the simple case of a binary classification, i.e. a classification of objects into two disjoint classes or simply deciding for a given object and a given class whether the object belongs to this class, exists a better and more detailed approach to look at the performance.

For each binary classification task there are four possible outcomes when assigning an instance to a class. The most obvious outcome: an instance belongs to a given class and has also been assigned to it. In this case the result is considered a *true positive* (TP) – a positive assignment to the class which corresponds to the truth. Accordingly a *true negative* (TN) is an instance which has been classified correctly as not belonging to a given class. The cases in which the classification is wrong, i.e. does not comply with the ground truth, are called *false positives* (FP) (has been assigned to a class, but does not belong to it) and *false negatives* (FN) (has been declared as not belonging to a class, but in reality does lie in the class). While the first two are the desirable cases, the last two cover the errors made by a classifier. Further, there is usually a trade-off between the FN and FP classifications. Designing a system to be very strict in demanding the attributes of an item to comply with the requirements might avoid FP assignments of instances but increases the risk of FN. Vice versa setting up the system to be very lax it is very likely that FN classifications are reduced at the risk of increasing FP errors. Depending on the scenario, it might be possible to estimate which of the two errors is worse and accordingly should be avoided. However, the consequences and accordingly the preference of FP and FN errors cannot be estimated in general.

2 Basic Terms and Concepts

Table 2.1: The confusion matrix assigns the result of a binary classification of a single item into one of four categories.

		item was assigned to a given class (item has been retrieved)	
		yes	no
item actually belongs to the class (item is relevant)	yes	true positive (TP)	false negative (FN)
	no	false positive (FP)	true negative (TN)

The *confusion matrix* is a common method used to visualise how TP, TN, FP and FN classifications are distributed. Table 2.1 outlines the structure of a confusion matrix, with the results of the classification in the columns versus the actual class according to the ground truth in the rows.

Changing the point of view from classification to the query interpretation of an IR task, the instances that appear in the first column (assigned to class = yes) correspond to the instances in the result set, the instances in the first row (actually in class = yes) to those in the expected result set conforming to a gold standard.

The *recall* and *precision* measures are following more the idea of the query interpretation. The recall is the ratio of retrieved relevant instances to all relevant instances, so the ratio of true positives to the sum of true positives and false negatives. Expressed in a simple way: the recall tells which ratio of the items that would be interesting in the notion of a given query was actually retrieved.

Definition 1 (Recall) *An IR application returns for a given query a result set of retrieved items R. According to a ground truth the set of relevant items is Q. The recall r for this query is calculated by:*

$$r = \frac{|R \cap Q|}{|Q|} \left(= \frac{TP}{TP + FN} \right)$$

Note that for an empty set Q this formula is ill defined as the denominator becomes zero. The recall in this case can generally be set to a value of 1, with the explanation that all the interesting instances (which were none) have been retrieved.

The *precision* measure is looking at the composition of the result set from a different angle. It computes the ratio of relevant instances in the result set to the overall number of retrieved instances, so it is the ratio of true positives to the sum of true positives and false positives. Again expressed in simpler words: the precision shows which ratio of the retrieved items was actually interesting under the given query.

Definition 2 (Precision) *Given the sets of retrieved items R and of relevant items Q for a query as above, the precision p is calculated by:*

$$p = \frac{|R \cap Q|}{|R|} \left(= \frac{TP}{TP + FP} \right)$$

2.2 Information Retrieval

Here the formula becomes ill defined for an empty set R, i.e. if no instances were retrieved. Also in this case the precision is often defined to have a value of 1, as the result set is very precise in the sense that no uninteresting items are contained.

Both, recall and precision, are bound to have values in the interval $[0, 1]$, and for both the performance of an IR application is better if the value is higher. For most IR methods the size of the result set can be controlled more or less directly via parameters. In this way the resulting recall and precision measures can be influenced as well. As explained in the definition, empty result sets score a perfect precision. On the other hand, if the result set contains all items from the data set, the recall is perfect, i.e. has a value of 1, since in this case $R \cap Q = Q$. Obviously, increasing the recall is usually counterproductive to the precision score and vice versa. Out of the two measures the recall value can usually be more directly influenced by increasing the number of items to be included in the result set. An ideal trade-off between recall and precision, though, cannot be decided generally. As one involves the FP and the other the FN errors made, as above, it depends on the scenario whether to prefer a high recall or a high precision.

However, there is a commonly used measure which combines the recall and precision rating into a single score: the *F1-measure*, sometimes also simply referred to as F-measure. This measure – like recall and precision – can have values in the interval $[0, 1]$, where, again, high values correspond to a good performance. To further reward good performance under recall and precision and penalise a bad performance of either of those measures, the F1-measure is designed to have a value of 0 if either recall or precision are zero, and a value of 1 if both recall and precision have a value of 1.

Definition 3 (F1-measure) *For a recall value of r and precision value of p, the F1-measure is defined as:*

$$F1 = \frac{2 \cdot r \cdot p}{r + p} \left(= \frac{2 \cdot TP}{2 \cdot TP + FP + FN} \right)$$

Also F1 may become ill defined: if both recall and precision are zero. It is obvious, that the F1 value in this case is best defined to be zero itself.

The F1-measure was formally introduced by Lewis and Gale in [LG94] but is basically a reformulation of the E-measure with parameter β presented by Van Rijsbergen in [VR79]:

$$E_\beta = 1 - \frac{(\beta^2 + 1) \cdot r \cdot p}{\beta^2 p + r}$$

Lewis and Gale defined $F1 = F_{\beta=1} = 1 - E_{\beta=1}$ to get a measure which gives equal importance to recall and precision, and for which higher values correspond to better effectiveness.

Comparable to the confusion matrix for the different kinds of outcome of a binary classification there are some diagrams that allow a quick overview of the recall and precision performance of a method.

2 Basic Terms and Concepts

Most commonly used are the precision recall charts which plot the precision score of a method for given recall values. This kind of chart allows to see quite easily how precision and recall are developing together. Further visualisation methods are ROC curves, which plot true positives in the result set against the contained false positives, both as percentage of the total numbers of positive and negative hits. This kind of diagram is originating from the field of communications, when it comes to transmission of signals over noisy channels. Hence the name, which stands for *receiver operating characteristics*. In the business world – in particular for marketing analysis – *lift charts* are a widespread visualisation tool. They plot the number of true positives against the result sets percental size relative to the entire size of the data set.

2.3 Web Documents and Text Mining

Classification of web documents often comes down to or is based on classification of text documents, web mining (WM) on a document level is closely related to text mining (TM) and the clustering of web documents often relies on clustering texts.

As one large field of application for CE is to aid WM, it is interesting to see how documents can be represented for WM purposes and how clustering and classification methods operate on these representations. The influence of CE on the representations is different and will be discussed in more detail in chapters 4 and 5.

2.3.1 Document Representations

The simplest representation of documents for mining tasks is to build an *inverted index* of contained words. An inverted index lists the words found in all documents and contains for each entry the references to the documents which the word appears in. A good comparison for such an index is the index of a book, as for example it can be found at the end of this thesis. Whether listing all appearances of all words or just the appearances of interesting words at relevant positions is just a matter of the intended purpose. A book will very likely list only interesting or relevant terms, a database with a full text search option will build a complete index of all words. But even for a full text search usually stop word reduction and stemming are performed in order to reduce the size of the index both in terms of words and references. The concepts of stop words and stemming will be described in more detail in 2.3.2.

An inverted index considers only the presence or absence of a word in a document, thus a document is technically represented by a set of words. As it does not cover any mean to deduce some notion of importance of the words in the document, it is used in WM environments merely as a data structure to quickly retrieve single documents which contain a particular word. A higher analysis of the documents is difficult to base on the index alone. The *bag of words* model for a text is already a more suitable and also very common representation. Opposite to the set approach of the index, the bag of words stores how often each word appears in a document. A common way to implement bag of words is through vectors. Enumerating the words of the document (e.g. in lexicographical order) allows to assign each word to an entry in a vector. Hence, for n different words in the document, the document can be stored in an n-dimensional vector. As for the index, a stop word reduction and an application of stemming algorithms prior to the bag of words construction can reduce the dimension of the vector drastically. This step is necessary especially when converting a whole set of documents into their bag of words representations, as for an increasing number of documents, the dimension of the vector space can become very high. The reason for this lies in the need to measure the similarity or dissimilarity between documents: to be able to compare two documents, they usually have to live in the same vector space, thus requiring the vectors to provide entries for all the words appearing in the document collection – even if a word does not appear in the particular document the vector represents.

Not withstanding this drawback, the bag of words model for documents is one of the most preferred and used as it allows the application of vector based algorithms. Further, the vector representation even opens up all the possibilities that come along with a vector space, for example a variety of distance and similarity measures, the possibility of transforming the whole space into another coordinate systems or applying other geometric constructions.

Other representations and analysis methods are built on top of the bag of words model. Knowing the number of words per document, again with the assumption of having at hand a whole set of documents, allows the calculation of entropy values, e.g. based on Shannon's information theory [Sha48] or the *TF-IDF* (term frequency-inverse document frequency) [SM83] value, or to analyse correlations between document categories and word appearance, e.g. using the χ^2 test [YP97].

The bag of words model does not take into consideration the word order or word context. *Bi-grams* – or more general *n-grams* – try to find a compromise between preservation of context and the benefits of remaining in a vector based environment. An n-gram builds n-tuples of consecutive words in a text. Common values for n are 2 and 3, resulting in the particularly denominated bi- and tri-grams respectively. The n-grams can be retrieved from a text by sliding a window with a length of n words over the text and storing the visible text fragments as entries of the vector.

A commonly adapted alternative to the vector storage are in this case the *proximity matrices*. The *bi-gram proximity matrix* (BPM) is a square matrix in which the value of entry a_{ij} corresponds to how often the i-th word is followed immediately afterwards by the j-th word. Likewise the *tri-gram proximity matrix* (TPM) realises the same concept with a three dimensional matrix of cubic shape for word triples.

An alternative to building the n-grams on the basis of words is to use characters as atomic elements for the tuples. This character based variation is sometimes referred to as *k-mer* and uses a window with a fixed length of k characters to determine the text fragments. The context and the words are preserved to a certain degree by the overlap of the single character tuples and the restricted number of combinations appearing in real language. This approach has the advantage of being relatively tolerant to mistakes in spellings and flexions of words as a subset of the k-mers of a word is very likely not affected by a spelling mistake or the changes due to flexions. In fact, for longer words and a small k the chances are good that most k-mers remain unchanged and thus allow to assert a certain degree of agreement between the original word and a misspelled or flexed version of it.

2.3.2 Case Folding, Stemming and Stop Words

As several techniques and approaches are based on words, there are three concepts which are interesting in this context: case folding, stop word reduction and the process of stemming. All of them are intended to reduce the amount of data to analyse by reducing the number of differently spelled but semantically equivalent words.

Representing a text or a word as a string raises the problem that small and capital letters are considered to be different characters. Accordingly two strings are different if there are differences in capitalisation though they might contain the same character sequence. On the other hand, a word can appear with a small or a capital first letter simply due to its position in a text, e.g. at the beginning of a sentence or in a title. These positions, in general, do not change the meaning of the words though. TM applications therefore often use *case folding* to unify the writing of words by converting them completely in upper or lower case writing. This process is not without drawbacks. In languages different from English a capital letter might change the meaning. For example, in German a capital letter marks nouns and the word "Weg" (path, way) is semantically different from "weg" (away, missing). Differences might occur also in English, for instance, if it comes to names of people or companies: "General Motors" has a different meaning than the words "general" and "motors".

Stop words are words which appear very frequently in texts, but are not meaningful by themselves. Typical examples are adjectives, prepositions or other particles. They are needed to construct syntactically and semantically correct sentences, but they are useless for an index, as they contribute to the meaning only in combination with other words. Therefore they are filtered from an inverted index or similar data structures. Common practice is to use a manually created and language dependant list of stop words for filtering, though this lists vary very much from application to application. E.g. in [Ran07] it is estimated that the English stop word list used by the Google search engine consists of 36 words, the internal stop word list of the MySQL database server used for text indexing consist, according to its manual, of 544 entries [MyS07].

Even though they filter out a lot of words from a single document, stop words do hardly reduce the number of different words. Staying with the example of Google: if the estimate given above is correct, the search engine's inverted index for English words is shortened by 36 entries – a negligible reduction considering the total number of English words. So, stop word reduction mainly reduces the space needed to store the references to documents, not so much the amount of words in the index itself.

Another procedure to reduce the number of different words is *stemming*. Stemming is the process of reducing flexions of words to a stem – either the grammatical ground form of the word (e.g. "to go" for "gone" or "went") or an artificially constructed stem

2.3 Web Documents and Text Mining

which is computationally more convenient (e.g. "berr" for "berry" and "berries"). As creating a complete list of all words, their grammatical ground form and their flexions is difficult and very time consuming, the second approach is probably more commonly used in WM and TM applications. It is realised by applying a so called *stemming algorithm*. Stemming algorithms use a set of rules to deduce the stem of a given word. The rules are set up in a way to work for most words of a language, but they never cover all cases of flexions. One of the most prominent algorithms in this field is the Porter-Stemmer [Por80] for the English language. However, there exist a variety of other stemmers, also for other languages. Opposite to the stop word reduction, stemming does not reduce the number of references in an index. The references are simply attached to the word stem instead of the original version. The list of different words in the index is reduced remarkably though.

Further linguistic operations, like recognition of multi word expressions, resolution of synonyms, disambiguating homonyms or part of speech tagging, are rarely used at this level of document representation. They involve the need for a sophisticated *natural language processing* (NLP) system which often causes too much overhead.

2.3.3 Methods

A category of algorithms frequently used for clustering and classification tasks of web or text documents are instance based methods. These methods refer to a portfolio of documents and decide the class or cluster of new documents by comparing them to the documents in the portfolio. According to a similarity or distance measure, instance based algorithms assign an unseen document to a class or cluster by evaluating its similarity/distance to the known documents. The most common instance based clustering method is the so called *k-means* approach. For classification tasks, instead, the *k nearest neighbour* algorithm is very wide spread.

Another group of algorithms is formed by statistical methods. Based on models for probability they deduce from e.g. correlations of words and categories a classification scheme. The *Naïve Bayes* (NB) classifier is the most prominent representative of this category and works with conditional probabilities and, as the name says, is based on the Bayes theorem.

We will describe some of those methods in more detail later on in chapter 7. As they will merely be needed in the context of clustering web documents with respect to their underlying template, we will describe them directly in the scenario we use them in.

Less used methods for text classification are *rule deduction* systems, *artificial neural networks* and kernel based methods like *support vector machines*.

Another important topic in the context of WM are algorithms to determine a relevance ranking of the retrieved documents. Google's PageRank and Kleinberg's HITS are the most prominent and representative algorithms in this field and have already been mentioned in the introduction. In the environment of CE algorithms, ranking the extracted contents has never been dealt with and so far is of no significance.

2.4 Further Reading

While providing the reader with enough background knowledge to follow the ideas and algorithms discussed and developed in this thesis, the concepts and techniques dealt with in this chapter are much richer both in theory and practice.

The first address for further reading in the field of technologies and formats for web documents are certainly the recommendations and quasi-standards published by the W3C. In addition to the already mentioned technical papers about the formats for HTML [RHJ99] and XHTML [W3C07], the Consortium provides a vast amount of information and tutorials. Best starting points are certainly the web sites of the corresponding working groups at [CSP08] and [Pem08] respectively.

Accessing XML documents via SAX is described in most books on XML. Brownell [Bro02] is one of the few authors dealing with SAX only. However, the homepage of the SAX project [Meg08] provides itself several resources and a brief introduction.

Like SAX also the DOM is dealt with in most XML books in more or less detail. A good introductory description can be found in [Spe99]. The specifications of the Document Object Model are located at the W3C and are spread over several documents [W3C98], [W3C00] and [W3C04]. The consortium's working group provides some additional publications on the DOM at [HWW08].

A good introduction to WCMS is given by Büchner, Traub, Zahradka and Zschau in [BZTZ00]. The technical realisations of templates are differing too much from system to system to offer a single and complete resource for further reading. The articles of the portal ContentManager [Zsc08] offer brief introductions to the topic, usually without being too specific and restricted to a single WCMS. Abiteboul, Buneman and Suciu deal with the general task of publishing data on the web in [ABS00]. Aside from other related topics they also describe the abstract layout of a web site management system, which in its functionality corresponds to a WCMS.

There is a vast amount of books dealing with IR and its evaluation. Classical introductions are the already mentioned book of Van Rijsbergen [VR79] or the one of Salton and McGill [SM83]. More modern and very good introductions are given by Witten, Moffat and Bell in [WMB94], Witten and Frank in [WF00] or Berthold and Hand in [BH03]. Ferber [Fer03] concentrates more on the application of DM in the area of text collections, similar the book of Heyer, Quasthoff and Wittig [HQW06]. When focussing on WM and search engines, the book of Liu [Liu07] is an excellent overview of the current state of research and practice. In [Cha03] Chakrabarti is emphasising more on search engines, discussing the related techniques and algorithms in a more detailed manner. Dealing with very different aspects, some of the chapters on Internet computing and WM in [Sin04] might be interesting as well.

3 Related Work

CE is a topic which is rarely addressed directly and on its own. Often it is merely a tool to support other tasks, therefore the methods to perform CE are frequently developed within other applications. One typical scenario is to extract the main content in order to improve the performance of a text classification system. This inclusion in other systems is probably also the reason why the CE methods themselves are rarely compared with each other.

In this chapter we will follow the development of CE in literature and will position it among other, similar tasks. By outlining the similarities and differences, we will try to create a quite clear profile of what CE is and to provide a rough classification of existing algorithms. A part of this profile analysis is represented by the collection of application scenarios where CE is useful.

The publications on the application of CE often come along with suggestions for CE algorithms. We will take a look at the more important and well developed approaches among those algorithms. After a quite complete survey of CE and TD algorithms follows an overview of approaches and techniques which are useful to evaluate CE or to create the document collections which serve TD as training sets.

3.1 Content Extraction and Related Topics

This chapter starts with a glance at the development of CE and a survey of related topics. We will outline the similarities and differences of CE with the close by field of information extraction (IE) and address the question of applications which benefit from CE.

3.1.1 The Problem of Content Extraction

As mentioned already in the introduction, CE is the task to identify the main content in a document. The main content is defined in opposition to the additional contents such as navigation elements, related links or commercials. In chapter 4 the problem and task of CE will be specified more formally. Until then, this intuitive notion will be sufficient to understand the related work discussed in this chapter – especially because none of those works formulates a precise definition of CE itself.

The spreading use of WCMS was already mentioned earlier as one reason for an increase in the amount of additional and redundant content. Gibson, Punera and Tomkins [GPT05] analysed the phenomenon in 2005 to quantify the amount of template generated content on the web. Based on an analysis of several large web sites, they estimated that the template generated content makes up approximately 40 to 50% of the content on the WWW. Using

3 Related Work

historic data of the same web sites they were even able to determine a growth rate of template contents of approximately 6% per year.

Gibson et al. further provided a rough classification of solutions which address the task of detecting and filtering template generated contents. They differentiated between local techniques, which operate on single documents and are based mainly on heuristics, and global techniques, which are based on multiple documents and exploit the fact that template generated contents appear more frequently.

The local, single document based approach of CE is basically the more universal solution, as it can be applied on virtually every HTML document. In particular also on documents which have not been created by a WCMS and do not have an underlying template structure. The works of Rahman, Alam and Hartono from 2001 [RAH01] probably describe the first solution for single document CE. In addition to formulating for the first time the task of finding and extracting the main content in a document, Rahman, Alam and Hartono coined in this context the term of "content extraction" for the process of building "a faithful reproduction of the original pages with the important content intact". Later on Gupta et al. picked up and established the term CE in several of their publications on the Crunch framework [GKNG03], which will be presented in more detail in 3.2.1.

The techniques Gibson, Punera and Tomkins used to calculate the ratio of template generated contents in a web document, instead, are based on a multi document approach. Multi document solutions are usually more reliable in their extraction performance, but can only operate on documents based on a common template. The algorithms Gibson et al. employed will be described in 3.3.8 and are based on the works of Bar-Yossef and Rajagopalan [BYR02]. It is commonly agreed that Bar-Yossef and Rajagopalan were the first to describe the problems induced by template based web documents in the environment of search engines and that they formulated the task and necessity of template detection within a set of documents.

The actual theoretic problem of using a set of web documents to deduce a template structure was analysed in more detail in 2003 by Yang, Ramakrishnan and Kifer in [YRK03]. They assumed a scenario of a web template which is filled with data from a background database and further considered the possibility that some attributes of the data items can have null values. An attribute with a null value is omitted in a generated web page and thus does not create the local frame embedding the data either. Hence, certain table cells or formatting instructions might be missing for the according web pages. The task to deduce from a set of given web documents a common schema describing the implicit template information is the basic idea underlying wrapper induction and multi document based CE.

Yang et al. show that finding an unambiguous schema for template description is equivalent to finding an unambiguous list of *union-free regular expressions* (UFRE) which is consistent with respect to a set *POS* of positive and a set *NEG* of negative examples. UFRE are defined similar to regular expressions, but do not allow the use of the union operator | or any other mean to define alternatives. The consistency of the list of the expressions with the positive and negative examples demands that they describe all the words in the *POS* and none of the words in *NEG*. The negative examples are created

3.1 Content Extraction and Related Topics

automatically from the positive examples by swapping the slot contents, which in this way intentionally causes the ambiguity the negative examples are meant to prevent. Thus, the demand for unambiguity of the schema states that for each example in *POS* exists exactly one expression in the list of UFRE which describes this word.

By reducing the SAT-problem to the problem of finding a consistent UFRE for a set of positive and negative examples and to the problem of finding an unambiguous consistent UFRE for a set of strings they show that those problems are NP-complete. The idea of the reduction is to formulate the SAT clauses of conjunctive normal form into positive and negative string examples in a way that the entire expression of SAT is satisfiable if and only if exists an UFRE which is consistent for these examples.

3.1.2 Wrappers

IE is the process of extracting structured data from documents on the WWW. To harvest structured data is a typical task in scenarios where web pages always present data of a similar type or kind, such as online catalogues, telephone lists, product descriptions or the results of online search engines. These pages are mainly generated via WCMS and are based on templates which are filled with database stored information about the listed or presented items. *Wrappers* are programs which are extracting again the original information from a compiled web page, thus, they extract a certain target data from the document context.

The web documents suitable to harvest information from are generally subdivided into two categories: *detail pages* and *list pages* [Liu07]. A detail page describes one single item in detail. Using the example of an online catalogue, an according detail page would present a single article from the catalogue with all the data available. A list page instead is usually appearing as part of the navigation structure and lists a briefer description for several items. For example, the catalogue web site would list all products from the same category, providing an overview of information like the name of a product, its price, manufacturer, a small image and a hyperlink to the corresponding detail page. The essential difference between detail and list pages is that a detail page is equivalent to one entry in the database, while a list page contains several data items. However, wrappers can be built for both kinds of web documents.

Liu [Liu07] further subdivides the creation of wrappers programs into three categories: creating wrappers manually, through wrapper induction and by automatic extraction. *Manually created wrappers* are hand made by a human expert after analysing extensively the source code of some web pages containing the target data [GRVB98]. Looking for patterns, the expert tries to find a way to locate the nested data in the web pages. Once the patterns have been established, specific and dedicated wrapper programming languages or development frameworks like Jedi [HFAN98], TSIMMIS [HMGM97], Minerva [CM98] or the Lixto project [GKB+04] with its extraction language ELOG [BFG01] aid the expert in realising the wrapper itself.

Wrapper induction is the first step to automate the creation procedure for wrappers. It corresponds to a supervised learning process. Providing the wrapper learning algorithm

3 Related Work

with documents for which the target data has been previously outlined, it deduces the patterns for extraction itself. A standard approach is to automatically look for the so called *landmarks* in the code: sequences of tags or particular words which delimit the information fragments. Being able to learn and confirm the extraction patterns of a wrapper on a training set larger than a human programmer can handle, wrapper induction leads to more robust results, which might even be able to deal with exceptions and special cases. An intermediary step to full automation is to aid the human user in the process of creating the training data. Algorithms finding and filtering similar documents are used to streamline the search for suitable training documents.

Full *automatic extraction* is reached when the algorithms are able to deduce the data items from the training set without the need to previously outline the target data. The process is usually based on determining the template structure (see also 3.3) and its content slots. In a second step the data found inside the slots of the documents is interpreted by the program as the data items from the database background and is used to build a wrapper. It is still left to a human user to attach a semantic meaning to the extracted data and eventually check the results for correctness. But, leaving aside this interpretation of the data, automatic extraction can be achieved without human contribution. It is therefore suitable to operate on large amounts of data. The computational costs, though, might restrict the size of the training set, as the learning process often involves the alignment of multiple strings or DOM trees.

One approach for automatically building wrappers is particularly interesting in the context of CE: the *XWRAP elite* system of Han, Buttler and Pu [HBP01]. It incorporates an analysis component to find those nodes in the DOM tree of a document which are likely to contain important structured contents. The overall system is aiming at the development of wrappers for finding particular and structured or semi-structured information in web documents and converting them into XML files. XWRAP's mode of operation is described as a three step process, consisting of the phases of document preparation, primary content location and object separation. The second step is of particular interest in the context of CE. Han et al. developed three heuristics to pin-point the primary contents in a document: *largest tag count* (LTC), *highest fanout* (HF) and *largest size increase* (LSI). While LTC and HF are methods to find in particular the structured content for a wrapper induction system, LSI is closer to finding a main content in the sense of CE. We will take a look at this method in more detail in chapter 6.

Another topic to mention is *wrapper verification*. It belongs to the task of maintaining wrappers and is discussed e.g. by Kushmerick in [Kus00]. As the template structure of a web site may change due to a relaunch or a change of style, a wrapper built to fit them will very likely fail with a new layout. Verification that a wrapper is still working, recognition of a failure and eventual provision of an option to fix it are the procedures needed to monitor and maintain wrappers in a production environment. The recognition of a failure incorporates some mean of measuring the performance of wrappers. The evaluation models for wrappers developed in this context unfortunately cannot be translated to the evaluation of CE. For a wrapper program it is legitimate to demand a perfect extraction and thus to use a binary evaluation basis for correctly and wrongly extracted data. The data to be extracted by a CE method is usually not defined as clearly as for wrappers. We will discuss this problem in more detail when dealing with the evaluation framework in chapter 5.

Wrappers and CE programs have a lot in common: the extraction paradigm, operating on web documents and the IE character. The difference is represented by the data in the focus of the two approaches. Wrappers head for structured or at least semi-structured data. Ideally, they can be used to feed their output into a database, by associating the atomic data items of the extracted data to table columns in a relational database scheme. CE, instead, is aiming at the discovery and extraction of unstructured or, at most, weakly structured texts. Even though also the text in a single slot of a template could be described as the single attribute of a data set, wrappers are usually not suitable for this detection task. The irregularity of the structures within the text might confuse the learning algorithm immediately or the deduced rules will not correspond to the main content in new and previously unseen documents.

3.1.3 Recognition of Named Entities

Named entities (NE) are words or sequences of words which denote the name of a location, a person or a company or which contain information about a date, time, phone number, e-mail address or an amount of money in a certain currency. The categories of NE used in a particular application depend on the scenario and the context of the application and do usually classify the words according to some domain specific terminology. In general, NE can be said to be expressions which represent instances belonging to a given set of categories. In some publications, NE are also referred to as *named tokens* or simply as tokens in a text.

Discovering and outlining or extracting the NE in a document is different from the aim of the wrappers in 3.1.2. NE usually do not appear in the semi-structured way necessary for building and utilising a wrapper. It might be difficult or impossible to find the landmarks signalling the beginning and the end of NE. As they can appear even in continuous text, recognition solutions apply other methods to discover the NE.

Witten, Bray, Mahoui and Teahan [WBMT99], for example, used a corpus of marked up documents with different categories of NE to deduce individual compression schemes. New entities are assigned to the category which provides the best performing compression scheme.

While the task of identifying NE can be considered a very specific kind of CE itself, it can aid finding the main content or information in a text. Paradis and Nie [PN05] used a collection of positive and negative examples for NE to determine the informative parts in web documents which in turn helped a classification process. They used a very specific scenario in which it was possible to differentiate between categories of NE which very likely help in classifying a document and those which represent a kind of noise and therefore might mislead the classification algorithm.

3 Related Work

The system of Paradis and Nie is an example where NE recognition can help to accomplish a CE task. However, the problem in general is different from CE as NE are usually short and appear as part of the text. NE recognition is actually even independent from web documents. CE, instead, is a problem specific to the web environment and it usually encompasses the discovery of an entire text. But, CE can aid NE discovery tasks when they are performed on web documents. Being able to focus on specific parts of the text in a web document might improve at least the time performance of NE recognition.

3.1.4 Text Summarisation by Extraction

The aim of computer based text summarisation is to provide a shorter version of a text, which is still providing all or the major part of the information contained in the original text. A reason driving the development of text summarisation software is the problem that human users are often confronted with too much information to handle in the available time – a problem commonly referred to as *information overload*.

Automatic text summarisation is a field of *natural language processing* (NLP) can be subdivided into extracting or abstracting approaches. Abstracting text summarisation is a field of research closely related to text understanding. It corresponds very much to a text summary as made by a human author. Abstracting summarisation algorithms analyse a text and then formulate a new, shorter text with the same or at least the essential part of the information. Accordingly it requires an at least basic understanding of syntax and semantics of a language and in particular of a given text. Extracting approaches, instead, reuse partial or entire sentences of a given text to express the important issues in fewer words. Described in a different way: an extracting text summarisation solution does not formulate a new text, but simply shortens an existing one by omitting certain parts while maintaining the meaning.

This extracting approach shows parallels to CE. Also CE applications, in fact, strip off certain parts of the textual contents of a web document in order to shorten the text. Even though the intention is not to provide a brief summary of the text, but rather to free the text from additional contents, the parallels can be used when it comes to evaluation of CE applications. The evaluation framework introduced in chapter 5 is incorporating evaluation measures which are similar to the ones used for extrinsic evaluation [GS93] of text summarisation by extraction, e.g. as described by Marcu in [Mar99] or by Dorr et al. in [DMO+04].

3.1.5 Applications Using Content Extraction

CE is used in a variety of applications. As mentioned already before, CE algorithms are rarely developed as such but usually in combination with an application based on or benefiting from the CE part. Web mining, improving accessibility, web page restructuring and streamlining, personalisation and web site structure analysis are some of the applications

3.1 Content Extraction and Related Topics

which may incorporate CE algorithms. We will now take a short look at some specific applications to give examples for where CE is used in practice.

Finn, Kushmerick and Smyth [FKS01] classified web documents into opinionated or factual articles. For not getting their classifier confused by additional contents which did not belong to the actual article, they incorporated a CE algorithm.

Pinto et al. [PBC+02] used a CE related technique to filter from a set of documents those pages which are not article pages. They distinguished between article pages and web pages which serve mainly navigational purposes but do not contain much information. Looking for data to feed into a question answering system, they improved the performance of the system by cleaning the input data from unsuitable documents via a CE approach.

Vieira et al. [VdP+06] observed a general improvement in classification and clustering of web documents after passing them through template cleaning filters. Those filters were essentially extracting the main content.

The IsaWiki system of Vitali, Di Iorio and Campori [VdC04] allows a personalisation of virtually any document on the web. To prevent the users from destroying the structure of their personalised copy by editing layout critical regions in a document, the write access is restricted to those regions which actually contain relevant contents. To discover zones which are interesting for editing, Vitali et al. also involved methods to discover the main content.

Several applications like Crunch (see also 3.2.1), the system of Buyukkokten, Garcia-Molina and Paepcke [BGMP01] or the core-content clipping approach of Mantratzis, Orgun and Cassidy [MOC05] aim at optimising web pages for presentation on devices other than the standard computer screens. Freeing pages from unnecessary clutter or restructuring their layout serves in particular the presentation of documents via screen readers for visually impaired users or applications running on small screen devices, such as PDAs and mobile phones.

CE is, to a certain degree, related also to the topic of analysing the HTML markup of web pages to deduce the presentation to the web user. In [HMS02] Henzinger, Motwani and Silverstein listed current challenges for web search engines. Even though the challenges were formulated already some years ago, most of them remain unsolved till the present day. Among those challenges is the problem of divergence between how HTML code is structured in the source code and how it is finally rendered and presented to the user. This divergence corresponds to the possibility to mark up words in a more prominent way than how they are presented on the screen. Vice versa it is possible to display certain texts in key positions on the screen and provide them with a certain layout to attract the user's attention, while the source code hardly reveals this feature. The differences between presentation and source code might mislead search engines and, hence, are often exploited for search engine spamming [GGM05], causing irrelevant web sites to be listed for certain queries.

The structure imposed on the text by the markup – Henzinger et al. refer to most web documents as being *vaguely structured data* – might suggest hints for such attempts. The

3 Related Work

task could also be reformulated as finding the most prominent content. Hence, CE could find application in the field of preventing search engine spamming as well.

3.2 Single Document Content Extraction

CE methods which are based on single documents perform the extraction by analysing only the document at hand. No further information is used except for what the document itself provides. Therefore the algorithms are usually based on heuristics and assumptions of what makes up the main content of a document.

The major advantage of these methods is that they can be used out of the box: no adaptations – optional adjustments of the parameters left aside – or training phases are necessary. As most of these methods are additionally quite fast they are perfectly suitable for on-the-fly extraction. This is an important feature for all scenarios where a CE system is installed as a transparent layer between the user and the WWW. These systems are often realised as local proxy servers or browser extensions and perform the extraction task whenever a web document is received from the web and before passing it on to the requesting client. Hence, in an on-the-fly system the CE operation must not take too long.

The heuristics underlying the single document methods are usually based on user experience and an analysis of a wide range of documents. Accordingly, they work quite well in most cases. However, if a document does not satisfy the underlying assumptions the methods might fail miserably. A common assumption is, for instance, that the main content is a long text with no or few tags. If the main content of a web page consists only of a few words or maybe even of an image, a CE algorithm based on the afore mentioned assumption will locate no or a wrong main content.

The first research work about single document based CE was presented by Rahman, Alam and Hartono [RAH01] in 2001. They described the problem and some fundamental properties a CE system should comply with.

They also presented a CE application which involved an analysis of the HTML structure of documents in order to segment a web page into zones. The overall process is described only vaguely, but comprises an analysis of the proximity of the single zones, the classification of the zones into different content types like summarised content, table of contents or detailed contents and finally an NLP based analysis of the content itself. Incorporating the results of these analyses, Rahman et al. suggested to find semantically similar content fragments of the same kind and to label them as the main content of a web page. Though they presented screenshots of a system demonstrating the described process, the authors provided absolutely no information about the implementation details or the incorporated algorithms.

However, several other applications have been developed since this first approach to the problem and most have been described and presented better and in more detail. We are now going to take a closer look at solutions, which are based on particular approaches or which are representative for an entire category of CE algorithms.

3.2 Single Document Content Extraction

3.2.1 Crunch

The aim of the *Crunch* framework is to rewrite HTML documents for displaying them on small screen devices or to improve accessibility via screen readers. Hence, it addresses specifically the impact that the increased use of additional contents has on these ways of accessing web documents: additional contents cause screen readers to take much longer to read a document and diminish the available space for the main content on the small screens of mobile phones and PDAs.

Gupta, Kaiser, Neistadt and Grimm introduced Crunch in [GKNG03] as a framework bundling a collection of heuristics to find the main content and perform some other transformations of a web document. The framework is set up as a proxy server performing extractions and transformations on-the-fly.

As mentioned above the extraction process is based on a collection of heuristics. Operating on the nodes of the DOM representation of an HTML document, the heuristics are all designed to discover characteristic structures of additional contents. The main filters which come along with Crunch are intended to remove advertisements and discover link lists by determining the link-ratio (see also 3.2.4). Those link lists are then deleted or relocated in the document. All deleted links can, for example, optionally be appended at the end of the document in order to keep the web page navigable within the context of its web site. Other operations aim at simplifying tables, e.g. by removing empty cells, or at unifying the layout of text blocks. Aside from the filters which are incorporated by default, Crunch provides a plug-in mechanism to keep it extensible for new heuristics and filters.

In other publications [GKG+05, GKS05, GBKS06] the Crunch framework has been refined further. One improvement is a genre classifier for web pages. Before processing a web document, it is allocated to a genre category like international news web site, shopping, tech news, etc. Assuming that layout and style of all web sites which belong to the same genre are similar, the parameters for the extraction process in Crunch are set to values which have been discovered to provide the best results for documents belonging to this kind of genre. So, the parameters are fixed according to the genre and, thus, the style of a document.

Crunch is written in Java and publicly available. The latest version 2.0 can be found along with the source code and further information about the project at [KGB05]. Version 3.0 seems to be under development but is not yet available.

3.2.2 Body Text Extraction

A common alternative to using the DOM tree of a document as basis for a CE algorithm is to tokenise its source code into a sequence of atomic elements and operate on these tokens. The first approach making use of this technique was the *Body Text Extraction* algorithm (BTE).

In the context of using the WWW as a repository of information for digital libraries, Finn, Kushmerick and Smyth analysed in [FKS01] whether a news web document presents an opinion or reports facts. As they realised, that additional contents often mislead the

3 Related Work

classification into factual or opinionated articles, they incorporated BTE as a pre-processor for extracting the main content of a web document.

The BTE algorithm is based on the assumption that the main content is a single continuous block of text containing few or no HTML tags. To find this block the first step is to tokenise all the text segments in the document into words using white space characters as delimiters. Then, after having represented all HTML tags as another kind of token, the whole document can be seen as a sequence $B_0, \ldots, B_{N-1}$ of N word and tag tokens. The idea underlying BTE is to find two token indices i and j in the token sequence of a document, for which the number of text tokens between i and j and the number of tag tokens before i and after j is maximal.

By assigning the tag tokens a value of 1 and the word tokens a value of 0, solving the optimisation problem becomes equivalent to maximising the function $T_{i,j}$ defined as:

$$T_{i,j} = \sum_{n=0}^{i-1} B_n + \sum_{n=i}^{j} (1 - B_n) + \sum_{n=j+1}^{N-1} B_n$$

Finn et al. also introduced the interpretation of the cumulative distribution of the tag tokens as a function in which a continuous plateau would represent the main content in a web document. Figure 3.1 shows how a document can be represented as a function following this method. The example demonstrates quite nicely how the main content causes the graphs to show a plateau approximately between the tokens with the indices 600 and 1000.

The BTE algorithm itself has not been tested, but it seemed to perform well in the application it was designed for. However, the main drawback of the algorithm is its limitation to find exactly one continuous block of tokens. If the main content consists of several parts scattered across the whole document and is possibly interrupted by other, additional contents BTE is bound to make a mistake. Either, it will discard fractions of the main content by cutting them off from the main block together with the intermediate additional contents. Or BTE makes the opposite error and includes the additional contents into the extract together with the enveloping parts of the main content.

A simple reference implementation of BTE as a Python module is available at [Fin05] together with a short explanation of the algorithm. Algorithm 3.1 outlines the formal algorithm as it has been implemented in this module. The Python module further uses a more compact representation for the token vector to combine sequences of consecutive tag or word tokens and thereby speeds up the process a bit.

3.2.3 Document Slope Curve

The largest drawback of BTE certainly is the restriction of extracting one continuous block from the document only. Pinto, Branstein, Coleman, Croft, King, Li and Wei [PBC+02] extended the BTE idea for usage in their QuASM system to look for several plateaus in the cumulative tag distribution function and thereby basically overcame this weakness.

3.2 Single Document Content Extraction

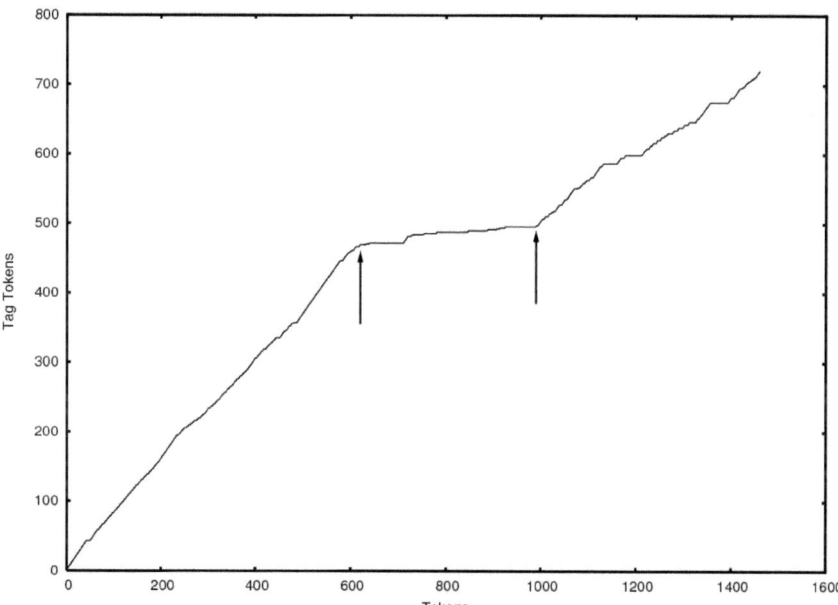

Figure 3.1: The cumulative tag token distribution in a web document represented as a function. The arrows mark the plateau which corresponds to the main content.

QuASM is a question answering system based on web documents. Instead of providing documents containing the information fitting to a search query of a user, QuASM tries directly to give an answer to a user formulated question. When crawling web pages, QuASM does not take into consideration every document as a possible source to extract information for answering questions. Instead, it first determines whether the document contains an article and consequently any useful information at all.

For this purpose Pinto et al. tokenised the document in the same way as Finn et al. were doing for BTE. But, instead of maximising the function $T_{i,j}$, they took a closer look at the function describing the cumulative tag token distribution. They referred to this function as *document slope curve* (DSC) d and formally defined it as:

$$d(i) = \sum_{n=0}^{i} B_n, \text{ for } 0 \leq i \leq N-1$$

In the curve representation they interpreted long regions with a low slope as content, on the basis of the same assumption of the main content being mainly text with few interspersed tags. Having transformed the original problem into an analytical task it is sufficient to look at the curve alone and discover the above mentioned regions of low slope.

51

3 Related Work

Algorithm 3.1: Finn's BTE algorithm.
Data: B: Token vector of an HTML document of length N, where B_i corresponds to the i-th token and has a value of 1 for tag tokens and 0 for word tokens.
Result: Index tuple $t_{index} = (i, j)$ with $i \leq j$ denoting the token range with the main content

begin
    $t_{index} \leftarrow (0, N-1)$;
    $T_{max} \leftarrow 0$;
    // count tag tokens till index i
    lookup0N[0] $\leftarrow B_0$;
    for $i = 1 \ldots N-1$ **do**
        lookup0N[i] $\leftarrow$ lookup0N[i-1] $+ B_i$;
    // count tag tokens after index i
    lookupN0[N-1] $\leftarrow B_{N-1}$;
    for $i = N-2 \ldots 0$ **do**
        lookupN0[i] $\leftarrow$ lookupN0[i+1] $+ B_i$;
    // Search optimum
    for $i = 0 \ldots N-1$ **do**
        for $j = i \ldots N-1$ **do**
            $T_{i,j} \leftarrow$ lookup0N[i] + lookupN0[j];
            for $k = i \ldots j$ **do**
                // Add word tokens
                $T_{i,j} \leftarrow T_{i,j} + (1 - B_k)$;
            if $T_{i,j} > T_{max}$ **then**
                $t_{index} \leftarrow (i, j)$;
                $T_{max} \leftarrow T_{i,j}$;
    return t_{index}
end

This goal is achieved by applying a windowing technique. The window size depends on the document length in terms of tokens. For documents of up to 200 tokens the window is set to a size of 8 tokens. For longer documents a larger window is applied, up to a maximum size of 50 tokens for documents containing 5000 or more tokens[1].

The window is passed over the slope curve of the document with an overlap of half of the window length l. If the average slope of the document section within the current window is less than 50% of the average slope of the entire document, the section is declared to be a low slope section. For a window starting at index i this condition formally corresponds to checking if:

---

[1]The paper does not mention how to increase the window size for documents with a length between 200 and 5000 tokens, but a linear increase seems an obvious approach.

3.2 Single Document Content Extraction

$$\frac{d(i+l-1)-d(i)}{l} < \frac{1}{2} \cdot \frac{d(N-1)-d(0)}{N}$$

If three consecutive sections have been declared to have a low slope, they are considered to be the beginning of a low slope region, which continues until three consecutive sections have an average slope of more than 50% of the average slope of entire document.

Having outlined low slope regions in this way, QuASM uses them for two tests before considering a document to be suitable for further processing and for harvesting information for question answering.

In the first test, the length of the low slope regions in terms of tokens is summed up. If the amount of tokens in low slope regions makes up less than 10% of the tokens in the entire document, the document is classified as not containing an article and hence is discarded from the list of possible sources of information for QuASM.

In a second step the average slope of the sections in the low slope regions is calculated again and once more compared to the average slope of the entire document. If the average slope of the selected sections is less than 50% of the average document slope the document is finally accepted as containing an article and passed on for further processing. This second test is not motivated any further. Rechecking the slope properties of previously checked regions is probably intended to cover such cases in which the end rule of three consecutive windows with a high slope does not occur or is met too late in the document.

As the low slope areas in the documents are not used further in the processes of the QuASM system, it becomes obvious that this adaptation of BTE was never intended to perform CE, but simply for the binary classification of documents into those containing articles and those which do not. Given this intention, Pinto et al. observed a recall of 0.862 and a precision of 0.688 for their classification task on a collection of 188 documents of which 87 were really containing articles, while the others did not.

However, it is fairly straight forward to construct a CE algorithm out of this DSC approach, by simply considering the low slope regions as main content. The algorithm in 3.2 determines for each token in the document whether it lies in a low slope region, hence it is general enough to realise both, the original purpose and extraction of the main content.

3.2.4 Link Quota Filter

Link Quota Filters (LQF) are implementations of an intuitive heuristic for identifying and removing link lists and navigational elements. Those elements typically consist mainly of hyperlinks and little or no other text. Vice versa, normal text as found in the main body of an article might contain hyperlinks but usually with an overall low ratio compared to the entire text. Accordingly, if a part of a document consists mainly of hyperlinks it is very likely to be a navigational element or a link list.

The determination whether a document fragment consists mainly of hyperlinks is done by calculating the ratio of hyperlink content to the overall content – as demonstrated in

3 Related Work

Algorithm 3.2: DSC algorithm.

Data: B: Token vector of an HTML document of length N, where B_i corresponds to the i-th token and has a value of 1 for tag tokens and 0 for word tokens.

Result: L: Vector of length N denoting whether token i is in a low slope region. L_i is 1 for token in low slope regions, 0 otherwise

begin

    // Create document slope curve
$d[0] \leftarrow B_0$;
for $i = 1 \ldots N - 1$ do
    $d[i] \leftarrow d[i-1] + B_i$;
// Determine window size
$w \leftarrow= 8$;
if $N > 5000$ then
    $w \leftarrow= 50$;
else if $N \geq 200$ then
    $w \leftarrow= \lceil 0.00875 \cdot N + 6.25 \rceil$;
// Determine low slope regions
$s_{total} \leftarrow d[N-1]/N$;
// History for last two windows
$h \leftarrow [0, 0]$;
// Flag if currently in low slope region
$lr \leftarrow 0$;
for $i = 0 \ldots N - 1 - w$, **stepwidth** $w/2$ do
    $s_i \leftarrow (d[i+w-1] - d[i])/w$;
    // Determine if low slope section
    $ls \leftarrow 0$;
    if $s_i < 0.5 \cdot s_{tot}$ then
        $ls \leftarrow 1$;
    // Check history and update low slope region status
    if $lr = 0$ then
        if $(ls = 1) \wedge (h[0] = 1) \wedge (h[1] = 1)$ then
            $lr \leftarrow 1$;
    else
        if $(ls = 0) \wedge (h[0] = 0) \wedge (h[1] = 0)$ then
            $lr \leftarrow 0$;
    for $j = i \ldots i + w - 1$ do
        $L[j] \leftarrow lr$;
    // Update history
    $h \leftarrow [ls, h[0]]$;
return L

end

3.2 Single Document Content Extraction

algorithm 3.3 – or alternatively to the none-hyperlink contents. The resulting ratio is sometimes also referred to as the link/text removal ratio [Gup06].

Algorithm 3.3: Linkquota function.

Input: n: DOM node
Output: q: quota of links to overall text
begin
    $C \leftarrow \text{descendants}(n)$;
    $t_{tot} \leftarrow 0$;
    $t_{link} \leftarrow 0$;
    foreach $m \in C$ **do**
        if $\neg\text{isBlockNode}(m)$ **then**
            if $\text{isTextNode}(m)$ **then**
                $t_{tot} \leftarrow t_{tot} + \text{length}(\text{getText}(m))$;
            else if $\text{isLinkNode}(m)$ **then**
                $t_{tot} \leftarrow t_{tot} + \text{length}(\text{getText}(m))$;
                $t_{link} \leftarrow t_{link} + \text{length}(\text{getText}(m))$;
            else
                $t_{tot} \leftarrow t_{tot} + \text{length}(\text{getText}(m))$;
                $t_{link} \leftarrow t_{link} + \text{Linkquota}(m) \cdot \text{length}(\text{getText}(m))$;
        else
            $C \leftarrow C \setminus \text{descendants}(m)$;
    $q \leftarrow t_{link}/t_{tot}$;
    return q
end

Implementations of LQF are relatively wide spread and can be found in several variations. These depend on the three ingredients referred to above: the document fragments observed by the filter, how the contents in these fragments are incorporated to calculate the link/text removal ratio and the threshold value for this ratio. While the threshold ratio usually is a parameter, the document segmentation and the way to calculate the link ratio afflict the algorithms in some details. A very simple LQF is outlined in algorithm 3.4 and it can easily be adapted to different ways of calculating the link quota or to consider nested blocks as well.

Gupta incorporated a Link Quota Filter in Crunch [GKNG03], which calculates the link/text removal ratio, by counting the words in- and outside the hyperlinks within the scope of particular DOM structures, mainly table cells. The approach does not count the words themselves, but estimates the number by dividing the number of characters in the respective parts of the DOM structure by a constant number of characters per word. This number is preset to be five, but may be changed via parameters of the algorithm. Under this aspect Gupta's approach can be reduced to counting and comparing the number of

3 Related Work

Algorithm 3.4: A simple LQF algorithm
Input: D: Document, t threshold
Output: D': modified document without link list blocks
begin
    $N \leftarrow$ descendants(D) ;
    foreach $n \in N$ **do**
        if isBlockNode(n) **then**
            if Linkquota$(n) > t$ **then**
                $C \leftarrow$ descendants(n) ;
                foreach $m \in C$ **do**
                      if $\neg$isBlockNode(m) **then**
                          if isTextNode(m) **then**
                              deleteNode(m);
    return D
end

---

characters inside and outside hyperlink anchor texts. The default threshold in Crunch is preset to a value of 0.35 but this setting may be altered by the user as well.

The most obvious drawback of this implementation is its restriction on table cells as only notion of document fragments. As nested table structures used to be a major design approach for laying out web pages, the solution is certainly historically motivated but will have difficulties with modern layouts. The recent tendency to realise the layout of web documents solely by div-layers in combination with CSS formatting instructions renders this approach unsuitable for a large number of today's web sites.

Possibly this is one of the reasons, why Mantratzis, Orgun and Cassidy [MOC05] extended the list of DOM objects which form document fragments. They added other block level elements such as the above mentioned div as well as table and tr. Mantratzis et al. referred to those elements as *structurally significant elements*, as they highly influence the layout of a web document. Another major change in their LQF implementation is to take into account the effect of structurally significant nested elements. This means that the link/text removal ratio calculated for one DOM element influences the ratio of all parent block structures to a certain degree. In this way the algorithm is supposed to be able to handle link lists which are built in a more complex manner, e.g. consisting of several nested tables. For one of the structurally significant elements to be classified as the root element of a link list it has to satisfy two conditions: the ratio of the contained non-empty anchor elements over all contained elements has to be higher than 0.5, the ratio of the characters in link elements over the characters in the entire text has to be above 0.4. The ratios of nested blocks are taken into account but reduced by a factor which represents the distance of the according child element to the potential link list root node in the DOM tree.

3.2 Single Document Content Extraction

Considering the nested elements might have drawbacks, though: a short text can get polluted by nested link lists with a high link/text removal ratio. Hence, choosing a suitable influence factor of the nested blocks becomes a crucial parameter. Mantratzis et al. unfortunately did not mention their choice for this factor.

A general problem with all kinds of Link Quota Filters is that they are specifically designed to locate link lists but are not capable of detecting any other kind of additional content. Accordingly, contents like headers, footers, functional and layout elements are very likely not recognised as additional contents, as they do not fall in the category of link lists. Therefore, a LQF can only be part of a larger system – as in the case of Crunch – and should not be the only way to approach the problem – as suggested by Mantratzis et al.

3.2.5 (K-)Feature Extractor

The link quota filters in 3.2.4 were based on analysing DOM block structures. Two other approaches also using blocks as objects of analysis are the *FeatureExtractor* algorithm and its extended version *K-FeatureExtractor* of Debnath, Mitra and Giles discussed in [DMG05a] and [DMG05b] respectively. Both algorithms segment a document into blocks and select for extraction those blocks which are particularly rich in a certain kind of content, e.g. in text for classical CE applications.

Quiet obvious, the definition of blocks and the way how to split a document into these blocks is a central element of the algorithms. A block corresponds to a sub-tree in the DOM and the criteria for building blocks are based on particular elements in the document which define the root node of a block. The elements Debnath et al. list as the ones denoting blocks are `table`, `tr`, `p`, `hr`[2] and `ul`. After recursively splitting a document into blocks as shown in algorithm 3.5, they assign certain features to the blocks. The features correspond to the kinds of content included in a block. As typical features the authors list the presence of smaller, nested blocks, text, images, applets or contained JavaScript code. The features are detected and recognised via the type and element name of their according DOM nodes.

FeatureExtractor and K-FeatureExtractor are designed to find those blocks which are rich in a certain feature. Obviously, for classical CE tasks the desired feature is text, so, the algorithms extract those blocks which contain mainly text. As the desired feature can be incorporated as a parameter, the algorithms are very flexible and can be used not only for finding the primary text content, but also to locate and extract blocks of another kind of main content, like images, tables or even JavaScript code.

Referring to the ratio of the desired content to all content in a block as the probability for this content, the FeatureExtractor algorithm first filters and discards blocks with a probability of less than 0.5. In a second step the remaining blocks are then ranked according

---

[2]Their works do in fact list the horizontal ruler element as a block structure, even though it is by definition an empty element in HTML and does not contain any content. As such it is unsuitable as root node for a block of content in documents adhering to the W3C specifications for HTML.

3 Related Work

Algorithm 3.5: Decomposing a document into blocks according to Debnath et al.

Input: d: DOM node (first called with root node of a document), T: Set of block defining HTML elements.
Output: B: Set of blocks.
begin
$\quad B \leftarrow D$;
$\quad$ foreach $t \in T$ do
$\quad\quad$ foreach $b \in B$ do
$\quad\quad\quad$ if b hasChildNode(t) then
$\quad\quad\quad\quad B^N \leftarrow$ getBlocks(b,t);
$\quad\quad\quad\quad B \leftarrow (B \setminus b) \cup B^N$;
$\quad$ return B
end
function $getBlocks$(b,t);
begin
$\quad B \leftarrow \emptyset$;
$\quad C \leftarrow$ descendants(b);
$\quad$ foreach $m \in C$ do
$\quad\quad$ if elementType(m) $= t$ then
$\quad\quad\quad B \leftarrow B \cup \{m\}$;
$\quad$ return B
end

---

to their probability and the highest ranked block is chosen to be the *winner block*, i.e. the block presumed to contain the main content.

Let us for example assume a web document which consists of three blocks. The first of which contains two hyperlinks, an image and three words, the second block consists of a hyperlink and four words and the last block of a hyperlink, an image and no words. As we are interested in text, the desired feature is the presence of words. According to Debnath et al., the probability for words in the first block is $\frac{3}{2+1+3} = 0.5$, for the second block $\frac{4}{1+4} = 0.8$ and for the last block $\frac{0}{1+1} = 0$. In the first step, FeatureExtractor discards block number three, as it has a probability for words of less than 0.5. From the remaining two blocks, the algorithms selects the second as winning block. It is extracted as main content because it is the purest block for the desired feature.

As not all main contents of all web documents consist of a single block, the FeatureExtractor algorithm has been extended to the K-FeatureExtractor. Instead of simply choosing one single winning block, the blocks with a probability high enough to pass the first filter are clustered using a k-means cluster analysis[3]. Afterwards the cluster with the highest

---
[3] The paper omits the detailed settings for the cluster analysis. After inquiring the topic with the authors, Mr. Debnath stated that setting the parameter $k = 3$ had empirically been found out to work well.

probability for the desired feature is chosen as the *winner set*, so again all blocks from this set are considered to be part of the main content.

3.2.6 elISA

The *elISA* system is a rule based approach for analysing the structure of web pages. It uses an XML based format to capture an expert's knowledge for detecting the main content. Thanks to an elaborated mechanism for turning the rules into an applicable extraction system based on XSLT, new heuristics can easily be adopted by formulating them as an additional rule in XML syntax.

Vitali, Di Iorio and Campori introduced elISA in [VdC04] as a part of the IsaWiki system. The aim of IsaWiki is to allow users to annotate and even change virtually every public HTML document on the web independently from write permissions on the hosting web server. It is implemented as a client side browser extension, which is backed by a central server. Whenever a user accesses a web document via the browser, IsaWiki checks if a modified version has been stored on the central server. If this is the case, the system incorporates the changes of the modified version into the currently viewed web page. For editing a currently viewed document, IsaWiki provides the user with in-place editing capabilities for certain regions of the document.

The role of elISA in this context is to find those regions in a document, which the user will be offered to edit. Based on the thought that modern web pages have a quite complicated and sometimes even fragile layout structure, the IsaWiki user is supposed to be able to edit the contents of a document only, not the structures supporting the layout. This requirement implies the need that IsaWiki is capable of identifying different kinds of content – among which the main content is the most prominent.

The indications on how to find the different contents in a document are specified as heuristic rules. While the above mentioned Crunch framework uses differently formulated and hard-coded heuristics to identify the main content, the rules of elISA are formulated in a uniform way. They are expressed in an XML based format and do all have a very similar and simple syntax structure. By applying an XSLT stylesheet the rules are transformed into an XSLT stylesheet themselves, which in turn can be applied to an XHTML document. The advantage of the meta-stylesheet of elISA is the simplicity, extensibility and adaptability of the file containing the rules. The editors do not need to have a deep insight into XSLT syntax and XPath functionality, but can maintain the original XML rules easily. To render changes or new rules operational it is enough to issue a recompilation of the XML source code using the meta-stylesheet.

The rules used in [VdC04] to describe content and non-content regions were derived from best practice recommendations described in web design literature and experiences gained from an analysis of the structures of representative HTML pages. The rules were not intended to cover all possible cases, but to provide a starting point for the IsaWiki system. The rule set is certainly meant to evolve and to be extended.

3 Related Work

...

```
<RULE context="IMG">
  <CALL name="AttrSrc" select="./@src"/>
  <CHECK>
    <WHENEVER test="contains(lc($AttrSrc),'logo') or
            contains(lc($AttrSrc),'main') or
            contains(lc($AttrSrc),'home')">
      <SET attr="border">3</SET>
      <SET attr="alt">"logo"</SET>
      <SET attr="elISAtype">"logo"</SET>
    </WHENEVER>
  </CHECK>
</RULE>
```
...

Figure 3.2: Example of an extraction rule formulated in the XML syntax of elISA.

For evaluation purposes Vitali et al. manually annotated 100 documents from different backgrounds to outline content, layout, navigation, form, footer and logo regions in the source code. Using elISA with a set of 19 rules the system managed to correctly identify most of the first four region categories. The poorer performance for recognition of logos and footers was explained to be due to the various possibilities to realise these regions and to achieve similar visual results with different HTML code.

In [Di 07] Di Iorio described another application for elISA. Segmenting web documents and sorting the segments into one of the five groups of content, structure, presentation, dynamics and meta data, he introduced the *Pentaformat* concept to capture the characteristics of a document in a dedicated structure.

3.2.7 Other Applications

The *Opera Mini* Browser is a Java ME (Mobile Edition) based browser for mobile phones and hand held devices. Instead of contacting HTTP servers directly to request a web document, Opera Mini uses a specialised proxy server hosted by the Opera company as a relay. The purpose of the proxy is not only to have a single point for connecting to the WWW, but to enhance the performance of phones and PDAs when accessing web documents. It compresses the data to speed up data transfer and restructures the web pages for screens with a low resolution. The latter modification allows to display also those pages which were designed for resolutions much higher than the ones of the small screens the devices usually provide.

The whitepaper [WJ05] about the Extensible Rendering Architecture (ERA) underlying the Opera Mini browser describes the general processes of preparing and rendering standard web pages for mobile phones and contains hints to the incorporation of CE techniques, even though on a very small scale. The technical details behind the extraction process, however, are not explained at all. In practice, the system causes at most minor and very conservative changes to the contents of a document, a behaviour hinting to the careful use of simple heuristics.

The approach of centrally filtering and restructuring web documents before displaying them on mobile phones has recently become more popular and some other applications like the TeaShark browser [Tea07] are based on similar concepts. However, more and more web sites provide dedicated web documents for mobile devices, a development fostered also by the W3C Mobile Web Initiative [W3C06a]. In many cases, web sites exploit the possibility of an anyway utilised WCMS to publish the same content with different layouts via the template mechanism. So, the overhead of content analysis and extraction is actually becoming less necessary in this context.

To a certain degree, some browser extensions can be considered CE applications as well. In particular, those applications which block commercial banners or codes loaded from external advertisement servers fall in this category. They do not perfectly match the concept of CE, but are more filters removing particular kinds of additional content. However, some approaches are capable of learning and adapting the filter rules, e.g. the solution developed by Kushmerick in [Kus99].

3.3 Multi Document Template Detection

The CE methods discussed up to this point operate on single and isolated documents. They involve implicit or explicit assumptions on how the main content of a web page usually looks like or how a document is commonly structured. In fact, the notion of main content in these cases is usually restricted to textual main content. If the main content is an image or even if it consists of a table structure containing several small texts, the single document methods might fail very likely.

A field of research closely related to the local CE approach is the one of TD and *template recognition*. The problem can be described briefly as the task of analysing a collection of web documents in order to deduce the structure of a common underlying template. Knowing the template structure, in turn, allows to locate the main content. So, TD can be a basis for multi document CE.

A first step in this direction was already taken by the genre detection mechanism in Crunch [GBKS06]. In this case, a global approach was used to deduce a more specific but still heuristic assumption on the presumable structure of the documents, and thereby choose better parameter settings. Other algorithms are looking more specifically at the documents at hand to gain a deeper insight and, hence, base their extraction process in particular on the documents in the collection.

3 Related Work

3.3.1 Page Partitioning

In 2002 Bar-Yossef and Rajagopalan [BYR02] first described the problem of template discovery as a task of web IR and web DM. They gave a formal definition for templates, described the impact of template based documents on typical WM tools and introduced an algorithm to clean template data from web documents, thereby improving the precision of WM tools operating on those documents. The central concept in their template definition and detection mechanism is that of *pagelets*. Pagelets are self-contained regions in a document like the navigation menu, a search function, an advertisement or the main content.

The authors started by defining the three so-called *Hypertext IR Principles*, which are important assumptions underlying most hypertext or reference based IR methods. The principles are the *Relevant Linkage Principle* (a hyperlink references a relevant resource), the *Topical Unity Principle* (co-cite documents or documents with large common bibliography are related to each other) and the *Lexical Affinity Principle* (similar text and links indicate a mutual relevance of documents). These three principles, so Bar-Yossef and Rajagopalan argued, are often violated on the web, especially by template based documents. Detecting the template structures and accordingly ignoring their contents in a WM process might rectify the situation.

To achieve this aim, Bar-Yossef and Rajagopalan described, additional to the above mentioned pagelets, also templates as a structural characteristics of web documents. A template is a collection of HTML documents which have the same look and feel and which are controlled by a single authority[4]. Given these definitions in the paper, the use and appearance of pagelets and templates are clearly correlated. Templates favour the use of pagelets as they can easily combine different sources of content and provide functionality across an entire web site. Vice versa the organisation and management of pagelets without an underlying management system is difficult, on a large scale even impossible. The requirement of an underlying management system in turn favours the use of templates. Altogether, Bar-Yossef and Rajagopalan's definition of pagelets and templates is one of the few attempts to give a formal definition of templates. Most other works adopt an intuitive approach to templates and their characteristics.

In addition to the general, semantic definitions of what pagelets and templates are, Bar-Yossef and Rajagopalan propose a syntactic definition for pagelets. A pagelet is defined to be a DOM node which does not have a pagelet as an ancestor node and does not contain any child node with at least k links. In the course of their works the authors report that in their experiments they chose to set k to a value of 3. According to the syntactic definition they defined a simple *page partitioning* algorithm to locate the pagelets in a web document.

The formal definition of a template is built on top of the definition of pagelets: a template consists of a set of identical pagelets, whose original pages form an undirected connected

---

[4]The single authority as controller of a template is required to consider also special cases like web site mirrors or accidental similarities on one hand and the case of several web sites managed by the same WCMS on the other hand.

3.3 Multi Document Template Detection

component. In other words, a template is a collection of pagelets with the same structure and which occur throughout a set of documents. Further, the documents in this collection are required to be connected at least indirectly by hyperlinks, so for each two documents in the set it has to be possible to find a sequence of links connecting them.

The pagelets of a template correspond to the structure of the template and denote the recurrent fragments causing the common look and feel. The requirement, that the pages in which the pagelets occur form an undirected connected component, is an attempt to formalise the demand for a template to be under the control of a single authority. Note that this definition of templates does not necessarily correspond to the intuitive approach of a framework document. The templates of Bar-Yossef and Rajagopalan correspond more to a code fragment or a frequently used slot content in a framework document. Consequently, the intuitive template concept could be represented as a collection of templates in the notion of Bar-Yossef and Rajagopalan all covering the same pages.

In practice, Bar-Yossef and Rajagopalan relax the strict requirement of identical pagelets in a template and define a template as a group of pagelets which are at least approximately identical. To model this approximate identity they use *shingles* as described by Broder, Glassman, Manasse and Zweig in [BGMZ97]. A shingle corresponds to the idea of n-grams for document representation as described in 2.3.1. Shingles are basically all tuples of n consecutive words. Opposite to the approach for document representation, the frequency of a shingle/n-gram is not of importance in the context of pagelet similarity. Accordingly the shingles for a pagelet are stored in a set structure rather than a vector, and two pagelets are approximately identical if their shingle sets are equal. The intention of this approach is to avoid that a small perturbation in the text of a pagelet causes it to be treated as entirely different.

Given these definitions, the task of TD on a graph of hyperlinked documents $G = (V_G, E_G)$ corresponds to finding all the templates T and their pagelets $p_1, \ldots, p_k$ which are part of the documents in V_G.

The example in figure 3.3 shows five documents d_1 to d_5 which all contain pagelets. Identical pagelets are denominated with the same index, so all pagelets labelled p_1 are identical in the above mentioned notion. Given that p_1 occurs in the documents d_1, d_2 and d_3 which form a connected component satisfies the template requirements for the p_1 pagelets. Likewise p_3 qualifies as a template. Instead neither p_2 nor p_4 appear in a set of documents which are connected. Hence, they are not templates.

As the definition of templates is sensitive to recurrent contents, duplicate pages in a collection have to be removed prior to the application of any TD algorithm. Otherwise, all the pagelets in the duplicates appear more frequently and might lead to a detection of non existent templates. The authors refer once again to the works of Broder et al. [BGMZ97], which provide a suitable algorithm for the purpose of duplicate document detection.

Once the documents have been filtered from duplicates, Bar-Yossef and Rajagopalan present two TD algorithms: one to be applied on a local level, another one for application on a global scale. The local TD algorithm is intended for usage on small data sets with

3 Related Work

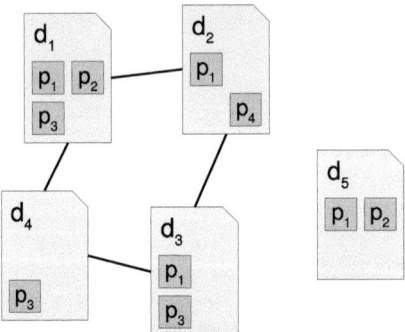

Figure 3.3: Bar-Yossef and Rajagopalan's template criterion: documents d_1, d_2 and d_3 form a connected component for pagelet p_1, hence, qualifying p_1 as template.

few documents. The locality of this algorithm is not to be confused with the locality of CE algorithms that operate on a single document only.

After the documents in G have been decomposed into their pagelets and their shingles, the local algorithm uses the shingles to sort and group the pagelets. At this point, each group already resembles a template. As mentioned above, the algorithm is designed for application on small sets of documents. In this kind of set the requirement that the web pages containing the pagelets of a template are linked to each other might easily be violated as there are few links to tie the pages together. Following this thought the local algorithm does not check this constraint of the definition.

The global scale algorithm, instead, is meant to operate on larger sets and accordingly requires the templates to comply fully with the definition. Its first step is to collect all the pagelet shingles which occur at least twice in the document set. The pagelets of those shingles are considered to be template candidates. In a second step, the documents containing these template candidate shingles are checked for being linked to each other using a breadth first search algorithm. By finding the undirected connected components among the pages, the pagelet groups of the template candidate are partitioned into the final templates. The templates found in this way fully satisfy the formal definition.

For evaluation purposes Bar-Yossef and Rajagopalan compared the performance of the *Clever search system* [KRRT06] when applied on data sets of entire pages versus data sets of pagelets. The core of the Clever system is mainly based on Kleinberg's *HITS* algorithm [Kle98, Kle99][5]. HITS uses the references in hyperlinked systems or similar structures to deduce network nodes which are good sources for information (so-called *authorities*) and those nodes which reference several good authorities (so-called *hubs*). The results of Bar

---

[5]There are actually several publications which refer to the Clever system, when basically they mean the HITS algorithm.

3.3 Multi Document Template Detection

Yossef and Rajagopalan's experiments showed much more precise results when searching authority pages related to a set of given topics.

Bar-Yossef and Rajagopalan explain further, that their notion of template detection in the sense of finding groups of pagelets can be seen as an application of the *frequent item set* problem. The latter is a classical DM problem appearing often in connection with *market basket analysis*, as discussed e.g. by Agrawal, Imielinksi and Swami in [AIS93] and Agrawal and Srikant in [AS94].

3.3.2 InfoDiscoverer

Lin and Ho developed *InfoDiscoverer* [LH02] which is based on the idea, that – opposite to the main content – template generated contents appear more frequently. To find this redundant content, they disassemble the web pages of a training set into blocks of text and calculate an entropy value for each of those blocks. The entropy value is based on the frequency of the words in the text blocks. A too high block entropy value indicates redundant contents, which according to the underlying assumption are deduced to be template content.

While the idea of partitioning a web page into blocks is similar to the page partitioning of Bar-Yossef and Rajagopalan, InfoDiscoverer is based on another understanding of templates and uses a different algorithm for the block building. The blocks in the notion of Lin and Ho correspond to visual components of a web document, rather than to the content and functional oriented pagelets. Instead of defining the blocks over the number of hyperlinks in the child nodes, they use the approach outlined in 3.6 which is based mainly on HTML tables[6].

For the purpose of generality, they assume all documents of a web site to be based on the same template. Once a crawler has grabbed all the documents of a site and stored them in a training set, they begin to break down the documents into so-called *content blocks*. All table cells and some similar structures in a document are considered to be a content block and are represented by the texts contained in them. Nested tables form content blocks on their own and are excluded from their parent's structure. The content blocks are stored in a simple tree structure, where an internal node corresponds to a content block – for example a table cell – and leafs correspond to the text nodes appearing in the DOM sub-tree of this table, without being contained in nested tables. Lin and Ho report a downstream refinement of the granularity of the tree until the classification of content block is unambiguous, but do not illustrate the technical details of this process.

Once the blocks have been found, InfoDiscoverer calculates the block features, i.e. the words in the contained texts after cleaning them from stop words and applying the Porter

---

[6]While nowadays certainly a bit outdated, the major part of web documents did make use of tables structures to realise the layout of a web document when the article was written. Lin and Ho have actually conducted an analysis of the prevalence of table based layouts at the time of publication and claim that this kind of layout structure was used for about 70% of the web documents. However, the concept could certainly be generalised from table cells to other HTML block elements, such as `div`.

3 Related Work

Algorithm 3.6: Building block tree structures in InfoDiscoverer
---
Input: n: DOM node
Output: n': converted node for InfoDiscoverer's tree structure of blocks
begin
    $C \leftarrow$ descendants(n) ;
    foreach $m \in C$ **do**
        if isTableNode(m) **then**
            $C \leftarrow C \setminus$ descendants(m) ;
            n'.addChildNode(BlockBuilding(m)) ;
        else if isTextNode(m) **then**
            n'.addChildNode(getText(m)) ;
    return n'
end

---

stemming algorithm [Por80]. Lin and Ho describe the remaining features roughly as "meaningful English keywords"[7].

The entropy calculation is a two step process. First the entropy values of the features are estimated by analysing the term frequency of the words in the documents of the training set. For this purpose the authors grouped together the features of the content blocks of each document and thereby built a *feature-document matrix* (F-D matrix). For further calculations or reuse in other IR system, they suggested to use term frequencies or term weight values (e.g. TF-IDF) for the entries in this feature-document matrix. The entropy of a feature then corresponds to the probability of a term and can be estimated by the term weights across the documents, if they are normalised to a range between 0 and 1. Using Shannon's entropy formula [Sha48] Lin and Ho arrived at defining the entropy of a feature F_i as:

$$H(F_i) = -\sum_{j=1}^{n} w_{ij} \log_2 w_{ij}$$

where w_{ij} is the entry in the i-th row and the j-th column of the F-D matrix, i.e. the term weight for feature i in document j of the training set[8]. A normalisation of the entropy values to the interval $[0,1]$ is achieved by using the number $n = |D|$ of documents in the training set D as base for the logarithm, so:

$$H(F_i) = -\sum_{j=1}^{n} w_{ij} \log_n w_{ij}$$

The content block entropy is accordingly estimated to be the sum of the feature entropies and is normalised by dividing by the number k of different features in the content block:

---
[7]The paper also covers briefly the aspect of extending the approach to oriental languages such as Chinese – a detail of no importance to the InfoDiscoverer algorithm.
[8]Note that $\lim_{x \to 0} x \log x = 0$, so terms with a zero entry in the matrix do not cause problems.

$$H\left(CB_{l}\right) = \frac{1}{k} \cdot \sum_{j=1}^{k} H\left(F_{i}\right)$$

where the sum covers all the features which are present in the content block CB_l.

On the basis of this definition, a content block is classified as being redundant and part of a template if it has an entropy value above a certain threshold, as high values correspond to a block appearing on many web pages. Vice versa, a content block with a low entropy value is found only on few pages and thus cannot be template generated. The choice of the threshold value t is stated to be crucial to the algorithm.

To solve the problem of an appropriate value for t Lin and Ho propose a greedy algorithm to find a good threshold – the authors considered it even an optimal threshold. The threshold value is increased from 0.0 to 1.0 in steps of 0.1. As long as the increase of the threshold adds new features, the process is continued. If no new features are added, Lin and Ho assume the critical boundary between informative and redundant blocks to be reached.

InfoDiscoverer is evaluated on different data sets of web documents. The content blocks of these documents were manually labelled to be either informative or redundant. Using the above described way to find an optimal threshold setting, InfoDiscoverer performed very well in identifying the informative content blocks. For most tested scenarios, it actually achieved perfect values of 1.0 for both, recall and precision. The value of the optimal threshold setting ranged from 0.1 to 0.7.

3.3.3 ContentExtractor

The idea to find redundant blocks in a collection of web documents is also used by Debnath, Mitra and Giles in [DMG05a]. The differences of their *ContentExtractor* algorithm lie in the way to build the blocks and how to measure redundancy.

Instead of Lin and Ho's content blocks Debnath et al. use a block structure, which is similar to the one used in their works on the (K-)FeatureExtractor and has already been described above in 3.2.5[9]. The blocks are built as shown before in algorithm 3.5 and, equally, also the block features are identified in the same manner as described above. The features cover aspects as the number of contained elements like JavaScript or image elements and the number of words in contained text blocks. A difference to the approach of (K-)FeatureExtractor lies in the handling of the text blocks. To differentiate the texts beyond the number of words, they consider an additional binary vector noting which of the words of the whole document corpus are present in a given text. So, for the purpose of finding the main content, text would be the desired feature again and a block would be represented by a binary vector v of the words appearing in the block.

---

[9] As a matter of fact, the works on ContentExtractor were actually published first and contain suggestions for an early version of the FeatureExtractor algorithm. A more detailed description and the clustering extension of winning candidate blocks was then added later in [DMG05b].

3 Related Work

To be able to account also for similar content blocks, Debnath et al. define a block similarity measure $sim(B_i, B_j)$ using the classical approach of calculating the cosine between the block feature vectors v_i and v_j as described e.g. in [SGM00]:

$$sim(B_i, B_j) = \cos(v_i, v_j) = \frac{\langle v_i, v_j \rangle}{|v_i| \cdot |v_j|}$$

Two blocks are considered identical if their similarity is above a certain threshold ϵ. In their practical realisation Debnath et al. chose the value of ϵ equal to 0.9.

Being able to measure the similarity of blocks and to treat similar blocks as identical, they calculated the *inverse block-document frequency* (IBDF) for each content block B_i in order to discover redundancy:

$$IBDF^i = f\left(\frac{1}{|S^i| + 1}\right)$$

where S^i is the set of all documents containing the block B_i or a similar block B_j with $sim(B_i, B_j) > \epsilon$ as above and f is said to be a linear or logarithmic function. A content block is classified as primary content if it appears in few documents, so if its IBDF value is below a threshold θ[10].

ContentExtractor is evaluated in the same way as Lin and Ho's InfoDiscoverer on a set of web documents for which the primary content blocks have been manually outlined. On all the data sets involved in the comparison ContentExtractor achieves a higher F1 score for retrieving the relevant content blocks, usually resulting from a much higher precision value. Another aspect evaluated is the cumulative execution time of the algorithms for large sets of up to 500 documents. Again, ContentExtractor performs much better than InfoDiscoverer. The reason for the time improvement is not stated clearly, but might result from ContentExtractors ability to work reliably even with a small training set to calculate the IBDF values. InfoDiscoverer instead needs to analyse the whole document set in order to calculate its entropy values. However, the proposal for the FeatureExtractor algorithm is stated to be still faster. The reason for the faster performance in this case certainly is that no training set is needed as it is a single document algorithm.

3.3.4 Site Style Trees

The Site Style Tree (SST) approach of Yi, Liu and Li [YLL03] combines the tree structures of the DOM with layout and formatting attributes of the nodes to find redundant parts of the analysed documents. Accordingly it focuses much more on the visual aspects of web documents than the other TD solutions.

Given the task of classifying web pages with product descriptions and reviews into predefined categories about the product type, the intention of the SST was to purify the data

---

[10] The function finally used for f and the specific value chosen for θ in the experiments is missing in the paper. Neither is made clear the purpose for involving the function f.

3.3 Multi Document Template Detection

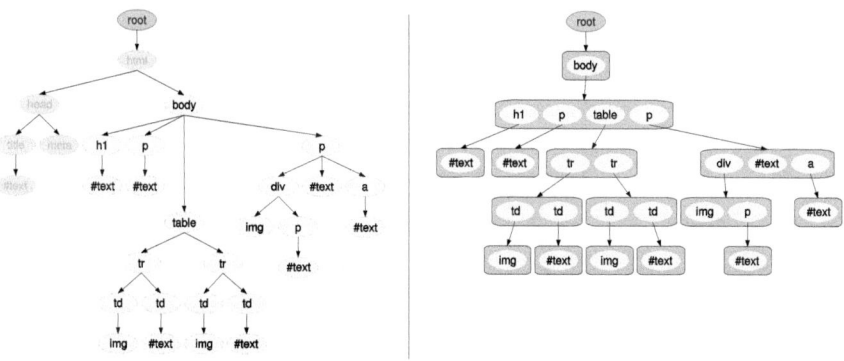

Figure 3.4: The DOM tree of a simple document and the according PST. The rectangular structures in the PST correspond to style nodes, the oval structures to element nodes.

from local noise, i.e. the additional contents. Aim of this purification was to improve the classification results, as the additional contents might mislead the classifier.

For this purpose, Yi et al. developed the SST to analyse the structure of a sample of web pages from the same origin, i.e. the same web site. Ignoring the header part of the HTML documents – as it does not contribute any visual content – they build an SST starting from the body element. An SST is different from the DOM tree, as it contains two different kinds of nodes: style nodes and element nodes.

The *style nodes* basically capture the entire sequence of sibling element nodes occurring at a given level of a sub-tree in the DOM. The contained *element nodes* are similar to the element nodes of the DOM as they contain the name of the element and its representation related attributes. But, instead of directly referring to child element nodes, their children are style nodes, which capture the entire sequence of child elements in a single structure.

Building an SST for a single document is a straight forward process based on the DOM representation of the document. Yi et al. refer to such a single document SST as a *Page Style Tree* (PST). Figure 3.4 shows a very simple document in its DOM and its PST representation. To combine several PSTs into an SST, all possible child style nodes for an element node are collected and attached to the node together with the number of their occurrences. As two style nodes are considered to be equal if and only if they contain the same sequence of element nodes with the same attributes, there is no need to perform complex tree alignments; therefore the computational complexity of building the SST is kept low. The result of this process is a tree structure uniting all the PSTs of a web site in a single SST.

The next step in the process is to identify the nodes of the SST which correspond to noise and those which are meaningful. To achieve this, the first step is to calculate a value reflecting the *importance* of an element node. Similarly to InfoDiscoverer, Yi et al. chose the entropy of the nodes to deduce importance. Given an element node E which appears

3 Related Work

in m documents, if E has l child style nodes and p_i is the probability for the i-th of these nodes to appear with E, the importance of E is:

$$NodeImp(E) = \begin{cases} -\sum_{i=1}^{l} p_i \log_m p_i & m > 1 \\ 1 & m = 1 \end{cases}$$

As this importance value does not incorporate the importance of the child nodes yet, the second step is to build a *composite importance* for the nodes. This composite importance is necessarily defined differently for internal nodes and leaf nodes in the SST, as leaf nodes do not have child nodes. For an internal element node E, again with l child style nodes and their probability p_i of occurrence with E, the composite importance is:

$$CompImp(E) = (1 - \gamma^l) NodeImp(E) + \gamma^l \sum_{i=1}^{l} (p_i CompImp(S_i))$$

γ is stated to be an attenuating factor and Yi et al. set it to a value of 0.9 during their experiments. Further, this equation involves a composite importance of style nodes, which is defined as the average composite importance of the contained element nodes, e.g. for a style node S with k element nodes E_j:

$$CompImp(S) = \frac{1}{k} \sum_{j=1}^{k} CompImp(E_j)$$

As already said, leaf element nodes do not have further attached style nodes, so the composite importance is defined in this case via the actual contents. Actual contents would be words, links, image files etc. and are referred to as the features of the node. Given an element node E which appears in m different documents and has altogether l different features a_i each of which with a probability of p_{ij} to appear in the context of E in page j, E is assigned the composite importance of:

$$CompImp(E) = \begin{cases} 1 - \frac{1}{l} \sum_{i=1}^{l} H(a_i) & m > 1 \\ 1 & m = 1 \end{cases}$$

where $H(a_i)$ is once again the entropy of a_i in the context of E, so:

$$H(a_i) = -\sum_{j=1}^{m} p_{ij} \log_m p_{ij}$$

Once the composite importance of the nodes is found, each element node in the SST is marked as being either *noisy* or *meaningful*. A node is defined to be noisy, if the composite importance of itself and of all its descendants is below a given threshold t. Vice versa a node is meaningful if it is not noisy and does not contain any noisy descendants. Note, that it is possible and even normal to find nodes in an SST which are neither noisy nor meaningful. All the nodes which contain children from both sets fall into this third category. To further reduce the size of the SST, the so-called maximal meaningful and noisy nodes are determined, which correspond to root nodes of completely noisy or meaningful sub-trees. In the SST it is enough to keep these maximal nodes as it is known that they contain only noise or meaning.

For the final task of eliminating the noise in a given web document, this particular document is turned into a PST. Then its element nodes are matched to those in the SST and the nodes falling on noisy nodes are deleted, while the meaningful nodes are kept. If a PST node matches an SST node which has been declared neither noisy nor meaningful, the decision for extraction is relayed to the next level in the tree, i.e. the matching of the child nodes. Nodes finding no counterpart in the SST are considered to be presumably meaningful and are kept as well.

The authors mention a few implemented options for fine-tuning the SST algorithm. Visually similar style nodes, for example, are merged under certain conditions. The leaf nodes in the DOM tree are not used as leaf nodes in the SST but rather their parents in order to avoid a too excessive fragmentation of the tree, and small and rare element nodes with an entropy value below a threshold of 0.1 are ignored when determining the noisy and meaningful nodes.

The SST approach was tested on a collection of web documents describing consumer electronic products from five similar categories across five different web sites. Starting from a random sample of 20 pages from the web sites to empirically set a value for the threshold t to separate noisy from meaningful nodes, the final training set for building the SSTs consisted of 500 randomly chosen pages. Yi et al. then applied a k-means clustering and a Naïve Bayes classifier(NB) on the page collection. They compared the results of the clustering and classification scheme when applied on the original documents, when applied on the documents after having cleaned the template data by using SST and finally when applied on the documents after they were cleaned by the page partitioning approach of Bar-Yossef and Rajagopalan as described in 3.3.1. Yi, Liu and Li observed an improvement of F1 for k-means clustering and of F1 and accuracy in classification with NB, when employing SST data cleaning. Also in comparison with the page partitioning approach, SST yields a significant improvement in classification and clustering performance.

3.3.5 RTDM Tree Edit Distance

Reis, Golgher, da Silva and Laender introduced in [RGdL04] a similar but more flexible tree based solution, which does not look for exactly equal sub-trees only but considers similar sub-trees as well. Their research work is composed of three contributions. First, a fast algorithm for computing a tree matching for HTML based DOM trees. Second, the definition of a pattern concept for trees which is similar to regular expressions. And third, a heuristic based solution to deduce from a matching of a tree pattern to a DOM tree, which nodes of the document contain the title and the main text of a contained article.

The algorithm introduced to find a tree mapping is called *RTDM* (an acronym for *restricted top-down mapping*). The original form of the algorithm is presented in 3.7 and is based on the works of Yang on discovering syntactical similarities in programs via the parse

3 Related Work

trees [Yan91] and the efficient bottom-up tree distance algorithm of Valiente [Val01]. It is a restriction of the top down tree mapping problem as the algorithm looks for identical sub-trees only on the same level and within the scope of the same parent node. This, in combination with the introduction of a threshold for pruning too expensive mapping options, leads to a quite good performance of the algorithm in practice. The computational cost in the worst case is, however, still of quadratic order.

When working with a set of documents which has been downloaded from a web site automatically, Reis et al. suggested a pre-processing step in order to detect groups of documents which are based on different templates. If a TD algorithm is applied to documents which are based on different templates, it will not be able to detect typical common structures in the document. Hence, building groups of documents which are all based on the same template allows to apply the TD algorithm individually for each group and thereby to detect the different template structures.

To discover those document groups with different underlying templates, the authors proposed to build a similarity matrix based on RTDM for all documents in the collection. By applying a hierarchical clustering method with a similarity threshold of 80% the documents in the training set are grouped together and the formed groups are assumed to reflect eventual differences in the underlying templates.

The concept the authors introduced to employ as a tree matching pattern is the *node extraction pattern* (ne-pattern). Those patterns can be seen as a kind of regular expressions for ordered and labelled trees. They offer the possibility to use particular wildcard nodes which can be mapped onto arbitrary nodes or even entire sub-trees. The kinds of allowed wildcard nodes cover the cases of nodes for optional sub-trees (? -node), for arbitrary label nodes (. -node), for an iteration of nodes (+ -node) and for an optional iteration (*- node). The question whether an ne-pattern matches (or accepts) a given tree is answered by computing a mapping with the RTDM algorithm and a particular cost-model. The cost model considers the wildcard nodes in a pattern and might assign an infinite cost for certain mappings. If the overall mapping has less than infinite cost, the pattern matches the tree.

An ne-pattern for a given DOM tree corresponds to the DOM tree itself. To find an ne-pattern, which actually matches an entire set of trees, Reis et al. used an iterative process. On the basis of tree mappings, they define a way to combine two ne-patterns into a new ne-pattern which accepts all trees accepted by the original two patterns. Applying this iterative process to all documents in the initially created clusters of the training set, Reis et al. created ne-patterns corresponding to the according templates of the documents in the clusters.

To finally decide which parts of a new and previously unseen document belong to the template framework, once again a mapping is computed between this document and the ne-pattern. The text nodes which are mapped onto wildcard nodes are deduced to correspond to contents. A heuristic is then used to find those text nodes which are most likely the title and the body of a news text. The body is defined to be the longest text containing more than a 100 words, the title to be a text with a length between one and 20 words, which

3.3 Multi Document Template Detection

Algorithm 3.7: RTDM
Input: Two DOM (sub-)trees T_1 and T_2 with direct child nodes $t_1[i]$ and $t_2[j]$, threshold ε
Output: Tree edit distance for (T_1, T_2)
begin
    $m = $ length (t_1);
    $n = $ length (t_2);
    $M[0, 0] = 0$;
    for $i = 1 \ldots m$ **do**
        $C_{(1,i)} \leftarrow$ descendents $(t_1[i])$;
        $M[i, 0] \leftarrow M[i-1, 0] + \sum_{k \in C_{(1,i)} \cup \{i\}}$ delete $(t_1[k])$;
    for $j = 1 \ldots n$ **do**
        $C_{(2,j)} \leftarrow$ descendents $(t_2[j])$;
        $M[0, j] \leftarrow M[0, j-1] + \sum_{k \in C_{(2,j)} \cup \{j\}}$ insert $(t_2[k])$;
    for $i = 1 \ldots m$ **do**
        for $j = 1 \ldots n$ **do**
            $del \leftarrow M[i-1, j] + \sum_{k \in C_{(1,i)} \cup \{i\}}$ delete $(t_1[k])$;
            $ins \leftarrow M[i, j-1] + \sum_{k \in C_{(2,j)} \cup \{j\}}$ insert $(t_2[k])$;
            $sub \leftarrow M[i-1, j-1]$;
            if $sub > \varepsilon$ **then**
                $sub \leftarrow \infty$;
            else if identicalSubTrees $(t_1[i], t_2[j])$ **then**
                $sub \leftarrow sub + 0$;
            else
                if isLeaf $(t_1[i])$ **then**
                    $sub \leftarrow sub +$ replace $(t_1[i], t_2[j])$;
                    $sub \leftarrow sub + \sum_{k \in C_{(2,j)}}$ insert $(t_2[k])$;
                else if $t_2[j]$ *is leaf* **then**
                    $sub \leftarrow sub +$ replace $(t_1[i], t_2[j])$;
                    $sub \leftarrow sub + \sum_{k \in C_{(1,i)}}$ delete $(t_1[k])$;
                else
                    $sub \leftarrow sub + RTDM(t_1[i], t_2[j], \varepsilon)$;
            $M[i, j] \leftarrow \min(del, ins, sub)$;
    return $M[m, n]$
end

has the largest intersection with the body. The idea underlying the latter requirement is that the words in the title most likely appear again in the main text.

3 Related Work

The overall algorithm was evaluated by its capability to extract news from 35 different online news magazines. On average about 88% of the news were extracted correctly, 9% were extracted erroneously and 3% were not extracted.

3.3.6 Document Frequency Based Filter

A very simple approach based on the document frequency of text fragments was used by Ma, Goharian, Chowdhury and Chung in [MGCC03]. Considering the text fragments in web documents only, they developed an alternative and less complicated approach for detecting redundancy.

The authors segmented web pages according to a quite small predefined set of tags, namely the table tags `tr` and `td`. The texts contained in each of the resulting document segments are considered to be an information unit. Ma et al. then calculated for each unit the document frequency and stored it with the according text fragment in a suitable data structure. The filtering process itself is pretty simple. All text fragments which have a document frequency above a certain threshold are considered redundant, therefore template generated and are hence deleted from the document set.

The intended purpose of this task was to improve accuracy of search operations on a collection of web pages. For evaluation Ma et al. compared the number of relevant pages in the top ten ranked results for given queries[11], based once on the unfiltered and once on the filtered documents. They observed an improvement in precision in most cases. A further evaluation covered how well the segmentation corresponded to the underlying template table. Except for one web site, the so-called *template table detection ratio* reached a value of 1, i.e. a perfect detection ratio.

While the algorithm itself is quite simple, the works are interesting also under another aspect. It is one of the few papers addressing the topic of data cleaning. Especially entropy based TD algorithms are susceptible to artificial redundancy. Duplicates of web pages cause different documents frequencies and skewed entropy values. To remove duplicates, Ma et al. pre-processed their data with *I-Match*, a hash based algorithm for duplicate document detection [CFGM02]. To further detect the occurrence of different templates in the training set, they tried to cluster the documents according to their underlying templates. However, the attempt turned out to be too unreliable and they finally decided against adopting it.

3.3.7 LAMIS and WISDOM for Web Structure Mining

In [KCLH02] and [KLHC04] Kao, Lin, Ho and Chen picked up the ideas of InfoDiscoverer's feature entropy [LH02] described in 3.3.2 and combined it with Kleinberg's HITS algorithm [Kle98, Kle99] to analyse the structure of an entire web site.

The primary intention of *LAMIS* is to harvest the informative structure from the hyperlink network between the pages of a web site. The informative structure is defined to

---

[11]Looking at the precision among the first ten results is a common evaluation measure for IR system which provide a ranking. In literature it is often denominated as precision@10.

be a set of index pages and a set of article pages which are referenced by the index pages. The informative structure can be interpreted as the main hyperlink structure of an entire web site. For this reason, the index pages are considered to be *table of content* (TOC) pages which provide links to the articles. Given this division the article pages correspond to Kleinberg's notion of authorities, i.e. sources of good information, and the TOC pages correspond to hubs, i.e. places which refer to good authorities.

The problem with finding the TOC and article pages via HITS is that intra-site redundancy appearing among pages of a web site can influence the process of determining hubs and authorities. Kao et al. gave an example where an advertisement page gets a very high authority value, simply because it is referred to by many other pages due to common template generated content. This topic drift[12], they said, is a common problem of the HITS algorithm which was observed by Bar-Yossef and Rajagopalan as well. To overcome this drawback, Kao et al. proposed to incorporate weights in the link structure of the web pages. A link is supposed to get a higher weight if it is "more informative".

To analyse how informative a link is, they used the same principles as in the InfoDiscoverer system. The contents of the links are split into features, which correspond again to the concept of meaningful words. For each feature they calculate a normalised entropy value which is based on a normalised F-D matrix. A feature F_i which appears in the j-th out of n documents with a frequency of w_{ij} accordingly is assigned an entropy value of:

$$H(F_i) = -\sum_{j=1}^{n} w_{ij} \log_n w_{ij}$$

The entropy of a link anchor is the average of the entropy value of its features. Using the entropy $H(A)$ of a link anchor, Kao et al. attach a weight of $(1 - H(A))$ to the according link before using the HITS algorithm. They show that this process remarkably improves the accuracy of HITS on a web site level for detecting hubs and authorities.

Once the hubs have been found, the authors used once again the classical InfoDiscoverer to extract the informative blocks and incorporated the same greedy algorithm for finding an optimal entropy threshold. After the informative blocks have been determined, all pages referenced by the hyperlinks in these blocks are considered article pages.

The authors named the process described above LAMIS for "Link Analysis of Mining Informative Structure" and it was tested on snapshots taken from several web sites. The system performed quite well in recognising TOC and article pages when compared with a manually labelled classification. Also the informative structures extracted in this way were quite similar to the manually created ones and did simplify the link graph of the web pages significantly while maintaining the general structure.

In the *WISDOM* system [KHC05], instead, Kao, Ho and Chen adapted the idea of informative structures to the scope of single web documents. This so called *intrapage in-*

---

[12]Topic drift is a term used for a web page which is drifting into another category due to the link structure. An example could be a web page about poetry appearing in the result set of a search for the Java programming language. This can happen simply because a famous Java programmer's homepage features not only Java-related information but also a link to his favourite poetry web site.

3 Related Work

formative structure is defined to be a DOM sub-tree composed by the informative blocks in the document and by the structure carrying them. WISDOM (for Web Intrapage Informative Structure Mining based on the Document Object Model) is designed to automatically recognise and extract the informative structure of a page.

Though developing several new concepts, the basic idea of WISDOM is to find informative blocks in a document, collect them in an *information coverage tree* and perform some filtering, merging and expansion operations to retrieve the intrapage informative structure. All of those steps are again heavily based on the entropy calculation of features (meaningful words) as it was used in InfoDiscoverer. The main achievement of WISDOM is to improve accuracy when searching for dedicated article and TOC blocks in documents.

3.3.8 Methods to Determine the Usage of Web Templates

Though the primary objective of their work was not to detect template structures, Gibson, Punera and Tomkins [GPT05] needed to develop algorithms capable of doing so in order to estimate the ratio of template generated contents on the web. The aim of their analysis was to measure the amount of template material and its evolution on the web in the last years. Template material, in the authors' notion, is content which is present across several web pages. The purpose of this common content, they say, lies mainly in the domain of formatting, navigation and branding of web sites.

Gibson et al. proposed two algorithms for determining a ratio of template generated content. The first algorithm is based on a DOM analysis, while the second uses the mere text contents of a web document. Both approaches take ideas from the works of Bar-Yossef and Rajagopalan and the SST algorithm of Yi, Liu and Li mentioned in 3.3.1 and 3.3.4, respectively.

The first TD algorithm analyses the nodes in the DOM tree of a document and assigns to each node a so called *template-hash*. The template-hash represents the node element, its attributes, its content and all nested elements. Counting the occurrences of the template hashes, it is possible to easily count how often a node and its sub-tree appear in identical shape across all web pages of a web site. In a second step, the algorithm declares a node in a document to be a template node, if its frequency in the web document collection is between a lower and an upper threshold. The lower threshold prevents rarely found document fragments to be declared template content. This reflects the common hypothesis that template structures appear more frequently. Hence, the nodes with a low document frequency simply appear too seldom to be part of a template structure. In the experiments of Gibson et al. this lower threshold was set to a frequency of 0.1. The upper threshold is intended to avoid considering small DOM tree structures as template data, which occur often by themselves. An example given in this context is the br element, which is found often and always has the same template hash, but does not necessarily belong to a template. However, in practice the authors used an upper threshold frequency of 1. In this way they ignored the implications of the previous thought again with the reason that these items will

3.3 Multi Document Template Detection

not influence the overall result remarkably[13]. Aside from a certain frequency, a template node has to follow the maximal noise rule used in the site style trees, that it is not child of a template node itself. The basic algorithm was fine-tuned and made more flexible by adopting a technique to combine several template nodes, if they are separated only by small and rarely changing contents.

The text based approach does not use the document structure but only the text contents of a document. By first removing all HTML tags, comments and contents of `script`-elements[14], this TD algorithm creates what is referred to as *detagged content*. After this pre-processing, the algorithm conducts two passes on the training data.

In a first step only a random sample of P pages from the overall training set is considered. Passing a window of length W characters over the texts in the sample, Gibson et al. calculated a hash value for the currently visible content. To identify redundant text, as in the DOM-based approach, again the occurrences of each hash value are counted. As an option for downsizing the amount of collected data, they introduced another parameter D and used a particular selection mechanism to store only 1 out of D hash values[15]. After all documents from the random sample have been processed, only those hashes which occur at least F times are kept. In their experiments, the four parameters were set to $W = 32$, $F = 10$, $D = 0$ and $P = 200$, which correspond to using 200 documents for this first pass, creating hashes for each 32 characters window, not to use the option of downsizing the collected data and considering only those hashes which occur at least ten times.

Afterwards, in a second step all documents in the training set are scanned for fragments with the same hash values as found in the first pass. By combining overlapping or continuous fragments, once more, a concept of redundant template content is defined and its volume can be compared with the remaining contents of the document.

Using these two algorithms to detect the rate of template generated content in collections of web documents, Gibson et al. analysed a sample of 200 web sites which were required to contain at least 200 web pages each. The type of web sites was manually determined and labelled according to seven different categories like news, catalogue, private or portal web sites. The documents in total and in the single categories were analysed each for the rate of contained template generated content, leading to the results already mentioned in the introduction: approximately 40 to 50% of the content bytes on the web are template generated. However, the results in the single categories vary very much. Comparing further the obtained ratio to the ratios found in older versions of the same web sites taken from a web archive [Arc08], the development showed that the ratio of template content on the web is increasing annually by 6 to 8%. The paper further discussed the results in more detail and introduced a visual representation of template rich web site structures. These topics are omitted here as they fall outside the main scope of this thesis.

---

[13]In fact, in the case of the `br` element no actual content is added, as it is by definition an empty element.
[14]The authors do not mention the removing of the content of `style` elements. However, their deletion can be assumed in analogy with the `script` elements.
[15]To make sure to keep the same hashes across all documents, they demand the hash of a text fragment to be zero modulo D.

3.4 Evaluation of Content Extraction Algorithms

The research work presented in 3.2 and 3.3 is a quite complete list of CE and TD algorithms. If an algorithm is listed in the bibliography but has not been mentioned here it is solely because it represents merely a variation of one of the other approaches.

Most of the publications on CE and TD also address the evaluation of the developed algorithms. The research carried out on evaluating CE solutions can be considered very small, though. A general and objective measure which allows to compare the entire range of different CE solutions does not exist. Accordingly the algorithms presented in the different publications are hardly ever compared with other solutions.

A further problem for comparing the evaluation results is the lack of a collection of benchmark documents. Each approach is evaluated on a different set of documents. A standard collection of documents for evaluation like the TREC data sets for IR tasks provided by the Text Retrieval Conference[16] has not been developed.

Going back to the first problem, the measures applied to evaluate a CE system are quite different, but can be generally divided into four categories: *human user*, *application specific*, *indirect* and *IR based* evaluation. We will look at the different approaches and describe some scenarios in which they are applied. Of particular interest for an evaluation measure is how generally applicable and objective the approach is, if and how it can be automated and how suitable it is for large scale testing.

Before going into the details, the works of Rahman, Alam and Hartono [RAH01] need to be mentioned again. They listed general requirements a CE system for HTML documents should comply with. Being generic enough to work with any website, a fast extraction algorithm and a non intrusive design are the most important aspects for the extraction part of such a system[17]. By non intrusive design Rahman et al. meant, that the system neither requires to be installed on the web server, nor that changes to the web documents need to be made in order for the system to operate on them successfully. The first step in evaluating a CE system should accordingly be to check its compliance with these requirements.

3.4.1 Human User Evaluation

The easiest and most direct way to evaluate a CE system is to have human users judge its performance. As human users have a very intuitive approach to finding the main content in a document, they can easily rate the performance of a CE system when being provided with both the original document and the created extract.

All publications which employed human user evaluation were settled in the context of software systems which were in fact intended to aid a human user when interacting with documents on the WWW via small screen devices like handhelds, PDAs or mobile

---

[16]The TREC conference series [oST08] provides several data collections for different text retrieval scenarios.
[17]Other criteria involve rapid deployment, economical use of network resources and easy configurability, which are more general features applying not only to CE systems.

3.4 Evaluation of Content Extraction Algorithms

phones. Given the aim of these systems, the user based evaluation approach is a self-evident solution.

Already Rahman et al. chose such a way to evaluate a CE system they described in [RAH01]. Giving an example of a web document, they show how their system decomposes the document into single content fragments and how those fragments are classified into the categories of detailed content, table of contents and other navigation elements, like the top bar of the web page. In the presented paper they give only one example of a single document and its analysis. No massive testing has been done and neither has any objective measure been employed in judging the performance. The evaluation was not intended for comparing the system with other approaches, but rather for demonstration purposes. Accordingly it is impossible to base a comparison on such an approach or to use it for a large scale evaluation. However, it might be possible to get a first impression of the performance of a CE system and to spot obvious flaws during the development phase of a CE algorithm.

In order to bring the results of a human user evaluation in a more comparable form, Chen, Ma and Zhang [CMZ03] requested the users to classify the performance of a CE system into the categories perfect, good and error. Using a corpus of 200 web documents selected from 50 popular web sites, they computed a segmentation and classification of the web pages and presented the results to the user. If the user found the segmentation to be without any error, the extraction was considered perfect. If the page analysis contained few smaller mistakes the result was considered to be still good and an extraction which led to a loss of information or an unusable web page was declared to be an error. Providing this rough scale for judging the performance, allows to compare systems to a certain extent. Nevertheless, as the users might still have their own subjective idea of how a web document should be segmented, at which point a web page is considered "unusable" and which segments are important, also the predefined categories bear a certain degree of subjectivity.

One way to overcome this flaw is to not ask the user for their judgement directly, but rather measure some secondary indications for the success of the extraction process. Buyukkokten, Garcia-Molina and Paepcke [BGMP01] gave the users ten tasks to fulfil and measured the time they needed to accomplish their assignments. All the ten tasks were about finding some particular information within the pages of a web site. The tasks were assigned to different users and divided for some to be done with and for some without the help of the CE systems. It turned out that CE reduced the amount of additional and distracting content significantly and allowed the users to focus and complete the tasks much faster. In some cases Buyukkokten et al. observed a speed up of 83% for finding the relevant information.

If the experiments are designed carefully this or similar approaches really do allow to obtain quite objective results based on human users' experience with a CE system. However, the general flaw of human user evaluation remains: it is very time consuming and thus expensive. Especially the obvious lack of automation renders these approaches unsuitable for large scale evaluations.

3 Related Work

3.4.2 Application Specific Evaluation

As the major part of CE algorithms has been developed in conjunction with larger applications, the evaluation is sometimes specifically tailored to the needs of these applications.

The above mentioned work [BGMP01] of Buyukkokten et al. contained another evaluation measure, which – though still user based – falls more into this category of application specific evaluation. The intention of their system was to streamline web documents for presenting them on PDAs. In addition to finding information faster, they also wanted to help finding information more directly. For this purpose they collected data about how many I/O interactions were necessary to arrive at a given information. As an I/O interaction they considered any operation with the stylus pen used for interacting with the PDA. Buyukkokten et al. observed a reduction of up to 97% of the user interactions when applying their CE system.

Gupta [Gup06] developed four measures for evaluating the performance of the Crunch framework. Two of those measures reflected the intended application of Crunch to improve displaying web pages on small screen devices (such as PDAs or mobile phones) or to enhance the accessibility of web pages to screen readers. For the so-called screen reader test two screen reader software packages were used to read a document. Under both screen readers Gupta compared the time needed to read the document once in its original version and once after it had been filtered by Crunch. The test is supposed to measure the time benefit for a visually impaired user when using Crunch to access a web document. The constrained device test instead aimed at the improvements for users with small screen devices. In this test the amount of relevant content visible on screens with resolutions of 320x240 and 640x480 pixels was compared again between documents in the original and in the filtered version. The experiment setup was restricted to considering the number of words of the main content visible on the screen without scrolling.

The last two tests reveal a problem of this kind of evaluation measures: it might be difficult to define what a good performance is. Gupta assumed a better performance of Crunch if the used screen reader software was presenting the document faster or more words fitted on a small screen. As long as the CE filter is working fine, this is correct. But as soon the filter removes also some of the relevant content the actual performance becomes worse. The measures will not reflect this, though. There might still fit a lot of words on a small screen and the screen reading time is certainly improving when the text is becoming shorter.

The third test reflected Crunch's technical layout as a proxy server. Its intention was to test performance and scalability of the implementation. For this purpose a setup of different clients was used, which requested different numbers of web pages simultaneously. Measuring the time needed to load the documents with or without Crunch filtering the data allowed to get an insight into how fast the system can handle a document and how it performs under stress.

In general, application specific tests are very interesting, as they allow the evaluation of CE systems under the very aspect they are intended to be used for. The results provide

3.4 Evaluation of Content Extraction Algorithms

a very specific method for comparing the performance of different systems. A drawback is that the results can hardly be considered for other applications or even to deduce a general performance. Automation might still be an issue as well, as the results of a CE process might need to be interpreted and adapted to the target measure, e.g. Gupta's constrained device test requires a user to count the words visible on the screen.

3.4.3 Indirect Evaluation

If CE is used to pre-process data for other algorithms and if for those algorithms exist standard evaluation measures, the CE performance can be measured indirectly by measuring the improvements in the performance of the downstream algorithm.

The fourth measure used to evaluate Crunch is falling into this category. In the Newsblaster test, Crunch is used as a filter for the Newsblaster [MBE+01, MBC+03] system. Newsblaster is an IR and information analysis system, capable of tracking news web sites and creating multi document summaries of news published by different sources and in different languages. The system crawls news web sites and linked documents, and is able to decide whether a document contains an article and consequently a suitable content for creating a news summary. Passing the crawled pages through Crunch improved the performance of Newsblaster in the sense that its crawler was much more focused on web documents actually containing articles. The rate of web pages crawled but then discarded as unsuitable was reduced drastically thanks to the prior appliance of CE.

Yi, Liu and Li [YLL03] evaluated their SST approach by looking at the improvements in clustering and classification of web documents. Following the idea that CE supports these tasks by cleaning the data from disturbing noise, they expected the cluster analysis and classification to obtain better results. The advantage of this approach is that the evaluation takes place in the world of IR and DM, where objective evaluation measures are well developed, field tested and commonly accepted. The documents were clustered using a k-means algorithm once in the original, unfiltered version, once using Bar-Yossef and Rajagopalan's PagePartitioning and once using SST. The same data was used for a classification task based on a Naïve Bayes classifier. The performance in both cases was measured using the F1 measure, to see the improvements in recall and precision.

Provided the downstream algorithm allows the usage of appropriate performance measures, the indirect evaluation process can be automated very well and the results allow a very objective measure for comparing different CE solutions. A problem with this approach is that it does not directly look at the performance of the CE algorithm. In certain scenarios even a bad CE performance can boost the performance of other algorithms based on the output data. An extreme example could be a CE approach which eliminates all contents except some navigation structure, which, due to some sub menu entries, is perfectly correlated to the classification of the documents. The classifier approach as used by Yi et al. would yield perfect results, while the extraction of the main content in its true sense is an entire failure.

3.4.4 Evaluation based on Information Retrieval Measures

Directly using IR measures to evaluate CE is the aim of the last category of approaches for judging an extraction system. The basic idea underlying all the evaluation methods – even though never stated clearly – is that the main content is the relevant information in a document. So, CE can be seen as the IR task of retrieving this relevant information and filtering out all additional and irrelevant contents.

This approach is similar to measuring the performance of wrappers. Kushmerick, Weld and Doorenbos provided in [KWD97] and [Kus00] manually extracted information as a gold standard. As for a wrapper it is comprehensible to perfectly extract the desired data, it is possible to calculate a success rate based on the results of each single extraction process. If the encapsulated data was outlined perfectly the wrapper was successful, otherwise unsuccessful. This interpretation allowed to determine an accuracy value for the wrapper. For CE this approach is not suitable, as already slight changes in the extracted content would lead to a failure under the evaluation aspect. But in reality it hardly changes the overall success if a few words too much or too little are extracted. Even for a human expert it might actually be difficult to outline precisely which contents belong to the main content and which do not.

Lin and Ho's InfoDiscoverer [LH02] was evaluated using an IR approach which addresses this problem. As described in 3.3.2, InfoDiscoverer segments a web document into blocks and decides for each block whether it is informative or redundant. So, the items extracted by the algorithm are always entire document blocks. To compare those extracted blocks with the actual main content, Lin and Ho manually labelled the blocks in a set of documents to contain either informative or redundant information. The extraction process was then interpreted as a binary classification task in which the blocks were assigned to one of those two classes. To do so across all the manually analysed documents, the classification was not evaluated on each single document, but on the set of all blocks occurring across all documents. In this way it was possible to calculate a global recall and precision rating for finding the relevant main content blocks in the documents.

Debnath, Mitra and Giles [DMG05a, DMG05b] picked up this idea of document block based evaluation for their ContentExtractor and (K-)FeatureExtractor algorithms, which have been described in 3.3.3 and 3.2.5, respectively. As those algorithms operate on block structures as well, it fitted their approach. The document segmentation is calculated in a different way, but the concept remains unchanged. They manually decided for the blocks of a document whether or not they were main content. Afterwards this classification was used to evaluate the results of ContentExtractor and (K-)FeatureExtractor. Different from Lin and Ho they integrated the resulting recall and precision ratings into the F1-measure to characterise the performance with a single value. Additionally they considered the time performance of the algorithms to demonstrate that their approaches performed significantly faster than InfoDiscoverer.

While the IR approach is objective and can be automated – with respect to the initial creation of a gold standard – it still has a few drawbacks if it is performed in the way of

InfoDiscoverer, ContentExtractor and (K-)FeatureExtractor. First of all, not always the main content can be perfectly aligned with predefined block structures; especially Lin and Ho use table cells as main block structure, which contradicts current trends in web design and, hence, might not appear in a modern HTML document at all. Additionally none of the block based evaluation measures seems to take into account the "amount" of content in a block for the evaluation. Under this measure a block with no content is considered as important as a block containing long texts. When developing the evaluation measures in chapter 5 these problems are discussed in more detail together with proposals for their solutions.

3.5 Structural Similarity of Web Documents

Comparing web documents and finding similarities is an essential part of most TD algorithms. Knowing the similarities of the documents corresponds to recognising the template generated parts of the documents and allows conversely to deduce the location of the template slots and their contents. Cruz, Borisov, Marks and Webb distinguished in [CBMW98] three different kinds of similarity measures for web documents: tag frequency based measures, parametric functions and measures based on edit distances. Especially the latter measures have been developed very well and can be generally subdivided in tree edit distances and deduced approaches operating on paths and sequences. As mentioned already in chapter 2 any distance measure can be turned into a similarity measure. Therefore we will look not only at dedicated similarity measures, but also at distance measures for web documents.

3.5.1 Tree-based Similarity

The DOM tree is generally considered to represent best the structure of a web document. It covers all contents, the contained tags, their according elements and brings out the hierarchy of these elements as well. Additionally, trees are well studied structures and a wide range of algorithms for comparing trees has been developed. Furthermore, DOM trees have particular features which are useful in this context: the nodes have labels and are ordered on the basis of their correspondence to elements or texts appearing in a sequence given by the document. Further, the tree is rooted as the document root element is fixed by the W3C specification and there are certain restrictions on which elements can have what kind of child nodes due to the HTML document type definition (DTD). The knowledge of these features and restrictions allows to specialise general tree algorithms in order to improve performance and reduce computational complexity.

Before going into tree matching algorithms for HTML documents, it has to be mentioned that already XML documents have most of the above listed features. Therefore, it is possible to apply any XML document matching algorithm to HTML documents. One representative to be mentioned here is *diffX* of Al-Ekram, Adma and Baysal [AEAB05].

3 Related Work

The authors basically converted Valiente's bottom up algorithm [Val01] for detecting identical sub-trees to suit tree matching for XML DOM trees. However, as HTML is a special case and ideally a particular XML format, further specialisations can be made.

The RTDM algorithm of Reis, Golgher, da Silva and Laender [RGdL04], which has already been described in 3.3.5, is one of those specialisations. The major restrictions used in RTDM to calculate a tree matching are twofold: it is a top down approach and identical sub-trees are found only if they have the same parent. In combination those two restrictions eliminate the possibility to match identical parts of two trees if they are spread in different sub-trees or have a different distance to the root of the tree. A further introduction of a threshold parameter, used to prune off sub-tree matchings which are too expensive, allows to speed up the algorithm in practice. The theoretical worst case complexity remains quadratic though.

A different approach to speed up tree matching is proposed by Shi, Niu, Zhou and Gao in [SNZG06] and comprises a reduction of the tree size. Their aim is to identify parallel versions of web documents in different languages. For this purpose they need to align multiple DOM trees in order to find which documents correspond to each other. Working with an adaptation of a tree matching algorithm used for natural language processing they reduce the size of the trees prior to the alignment. By stripping off all unnecessary DOM nodes like comments or processing instructions, merging text nodes with their parents and unifying image nodes with the texts contained in the `alt` attribute, the DOM tree is reduced both in depth and number of nodes.

Zhai and Liu [ZL05] base their works on the same restricted tree matching algorithm of Yang [Yan91] as Reis et al. did for RTDM. But instead of aligning the whole document, they make a pre-selection of certain sub-trees in the document. Using rendering information obtained from the API of the Internet Explorer web browser, they enriched a simplified version of the DOM tree with screen locations for each element. As wrapper development is the main target of their application, they used this additional information to identify what they called *data regions*. These are regions which have a central position in a document and are considered to be suitable for IE. The relatively small DOM sub-trees of the data regions were aligned to extract patterns for generating a wrapper on this data.

3.5.2 Path-based Similarity

In [But04] Buttler discusses several ways to measure the similarity between XML documents. Tree edit distances are stated to be probably the best but also very expensive approaches to measure the similarity between documents. After having looked briefly at other solutions to calculate a similarity he proposes a new approach based on DOM paths.

DOM paths as an approach to tackle the problem of the high computational costs for aligning DOM trees was already dealt with earlier by Joshi, Agrawal, Krishnapuram and Negi in [JAKN03]. Their approach tries to capture the tree structure by looking at the tree paths which appear in a document. As a tree path they consider only those paths in the DOM tree which lead from the root node to a leaf node. An entire document is then disassembled into the bag of paths[18] (BOP) occurring in its DOM tree. A bag of paths contains each path and how often it appears, but no information about the order in which the paths have appeared in the document. For a whole collection of documents, Joshi et al. further removed those paths, which are too rare or occur in nearly all documents. This feature selection was based on too high or too low document frequencies of the according paths. The document frequency of the paths also serves for calculating the similarity of documents. The similarity of two documents is based on the frequencies $f_j(p_i)$ of path p_i in document d_j and on the maximum of the occurring frequencies $f_{\max} = \max_{i,j} f_j(p_i)$. Each document d_j is represented as an N-dimensional vector $(d_{j1}, d_{j2}, \ldots, d_{jN})$, where the $d_{ij} = \frac{f_j(p_i)}{f_{\max}}$. A similarity for two documents d_j and d_l is finally computed by:

$$Sim_{BOP}(d_j, d_l) = \frac{\sum_{k=1}^{N} \min(d_{jk}, d_{lk})}{\sum_{k=1}^{N} \max(d_{jk}, d_{lk})}$$

Even though Buttler did not refer to this approach of Joshi et al., he suggested himself a variation to the bag of paths technique. Starting from a general representation of a document by the paths occurring in its DOM tree, he developed a way to also handle a partial matching of paths, while keeping the computational cost low. To achieve this he makes use of the shingling technique suggested by Broder, Glassman, Manasse and Zweig in [BGMZ97] already mentioned in the description of Bar-Yossef and Rajagopalan's TD algorithm in 3.3.1. The idea is not to compare complete paths but rather breaking them up into smaller pieces of equal length – the path shingles. The advantage of this approach is that two paths which are differing only for a small part, but are quite similar for the rest, will have a large "agreement" on the shingles. So, if $ps(D)$ provides the path shingles for a document D, the path shingle similarity can be computed by:

$$Sim_{PS}(D_1, D_2) = \frac{|ps(D_1) \cap ps(D_2)|}{\max(|ps(D_1)|, |ps(D_2)|)}$$

3.5.3 Sequence-based Similarity

Path based similarity measures can be considered a vertical approach to simplify the tree structure, as they consider all parent-child relations, but ignore, to a certain extent, information about the sibling relation between nodes. Sequence based similarities, instead, can be interpreted as a horizontal view of the trees. As obviously the sequence in which the tags appear in the source code reflects the hierarchical structure, this sequence can be used for alignment. Parent-child relations, however, are more difficult to track in a sequence – in particular across several hierarchy levels.

Representing the web documents as sequences allows to map the tree alignment problem into a string or sequence alignment problem. But if the problem is simply reduced to computing the longest common subsequence (LCS) of the sequences the complexity remains high. The commonly adopted algorithm of Hirschberg [Hir75] for determining the LCS still

---
[18]The term is derived from the bag of words model used for text mining.

3 Related Work

has quadratic time complexity. For cases where there are few matches between the two sequences Hunt and Szymanski reduced the problem in [HS77] to $O((n+r) \cdot \log(n))$, where r is the number of matches and n the length of the longer sequence. It is probably due to the computational complexity that there are no approaches using LCS to compare document structures.

Also Lindholm, Kangasharju and Tarkoma take a different approach in [LKT06]. They represent an XML document as a sequence of XAS events as described in [KL05]. Those events are similar to the notifications of a SAX parser and correspond to e.g. a start tag, a close tag, an attribute and its value or a text fragment. Instead of looking for an optimal matching, they use a heuristic for sequence matching based on the algorithms xdelta [Mac00] and rsynch [Tri99] which allows to compute good alignments of sequences at linear time cost. The matched sequence is transformed back into an XML document which provides the common part of both original documents.

Another approach was recently proposed by Chakrabarti, Kumar and Punera in [CKP07]. They combine the site-level TD algorithm [GPT05] of Gibson et al. to produce training sets for a classifier, which in turn is supposed to learn typical template characteristics. After being trained, the classifier is said to be able to assign a templateness score to each single node in the DOM tree of a document. Chakrabarti et al. report that the classifier is even capable of generalise the results from the templates of few analysed web sites to all templates on the web.

3.5.4 Other Approaches

In the class of document similarity measures based on tag frequency distribution analysis (TFDA) Cruz, Borisov, Marks and Webb [CBMW98] describe a weighted sum of differences between tag frequencies in two documents. To compute the distance, the documents are first passed through a filter to eliminate everything except the HTML tags. In a second step the frequency for each kind of tag in the document is computed; not occurring tags naturally have a frequency of zero. Provided there exist N different kind of tags and $F_{k,i}$ being the frequency of the k-th tag in document i, the distance function for two documents can be computed by:

$$d_{TFDA} = \sum_{k=1}^{N} (F_{k,1} - F_{k,2})^2 \cdot w_k$$

The parameters w_k are weights for tags and the sum of the weights is restricted to be 1. The weights allow to give different importance to different kinds of tags, e.g. to promote tags which provide the general structure, like `div` and `td`, over presentation oriented tags, like `b` or `i`.

As Cruz et al. further represented the frequencies in percentages, and thus the values of $F_{k,i}$ in a document add up to be 100, the distance d_{TFDA} cannot exceed the value of 10.000. This allows normalisation and an easy conversion into a similarity measure.

When referring to the process of finding parametric functions to calculate similarities of web documents, Cruz et al. distinguish three steps. The first one is to find a suitable data structure for representing the structural aspects of web documents. The second is, to define the parametric functions themselves, which operate on those data structures and whose values, in the third and last step, are aggregated into the final distance or similarity measure.

As an example of a data structure they give a simple string format which represents the hierarchies of the unordered ul lists in an HTML document represented by braces and using numbers to show the number of contained li entries. For the parametric functions the examples are then to count the length of the entire string, the number of opening braces or the sum and average of the numbers of the li elements. The values of these functions are compared for two documents, the differences are weighted and incorporated into a rather lengthy formula for a distance.

The authors state that building a parametric function distance involves a lot of knowledge about the structures and a good portion of heuristics. Indeed, the results can vary very much but allow at the same time to tailor a very scenario specific distance measure.

An entirely different approach is taken by Flesca, Manco, Masciara, Pontieri and Pugliese in [FMM+05]. Though based on the sequence of tags appearing in a document, it is different from other sequence alignment approaches as described in 3.5.3. Starting from the sequence of tags, they use a tag encoding function to assign a unique value to each kind of tag. In a second step a document encoding function uses the tag values and the tag sequence as basis to generate a sequence of numeric values representing the document. Having converted a document in this way into a time series, they adopt the discrete Fourier transformation to analyse characteristic frequencies in the documents and to compute a distance function.

3.6 Summary

Having looked at related research work, we can say that CE – though its exact task is rarely formally defined – has similarities to wrapper engineering, discovery of named entities and text summarisation by extraction. The high level division into single and multi document based TD approaches we adopted is made by other authors as well. Several CE solutions have been developed to an extent that they are ready to be employed and some even provide reference implementations. Also most TD algorithms are presented in sufficient detail.

However, evaluation is an open topic. No publication provides an objective and generally applicable evaluation measure for CE. This gap is devastating to the development of new CE algorithms and the assessment of existing ones. Accordingly, our first task, after formalising the process of CE, will be to develop suitable evaluation measures and to compare the algorithms described in this chapter. Only once the performance of these algorithms is known and their weak points are detected, it is possible to systematically develop new approaches which can overcome the drawbacks of existing solutions.

3 Related Work

For the purpose of comparing web documents from a structural point of view, several distance and similarity measures can be found. Their performance in the context of comparing documents according to their underlying templates has hardly been addressed, though. Further, the few attempts of applying document distance or similarity measures for creating and cleaning sets of training data for TD algorithms have not been evaluated at all. Buttler's statement that tree edit distances are the best measure to compare web documents has never been analysed under the aspect of detecting underlying templates. Hence, in chapter 7 we will compare several approaches for clustering web documents according to their templates under different distance measures.

4 Content Extraction

The topic of CE was already the central part of the last chapters. We used it so far without a precise definition and adopted a very intuitive approach to explain what CE actually is. In this chapter we will go into the details of the general problem of defining the main content of a document, take a more diversified look at the different kinds of content and formalise the concept of CE.

4.1 The Main Content of a Document

CE has been defined in the preceding chapters as the process of finding the main content in a web document. Finding the main content also corresponds to identifying the other, additional contents. Examples for additional contents were already given in the introduction and said to comprise navigation elements, layout structures, link lists, commercials and template generated contents.

The characteristics of the main content of a web document – though intuitively clear – are difficult to describe formally. A general definition of what makes up the main content cannot be given. Even if in other publications the terms principal, primary or core content are used, the described concept is always the same and with it remain the difficulties to capture it formally.

Intuitively, the main content is the central information of a document. It is, so to say, what the document is supposed to communicate and a document might well contain the main content only. Conversely it can be stated that a document without a main content does not make any sense.

In general, the main content may have different forms. In most cases it will be text, as text still is the predominant method to transmit information on the WWW. Hence, the research in this thesis focuses mainly on the extraction of text contents. There are, however, web sites or parts of web sites which provide different kinds of main content. A photo community will have pictures as main content for most documents, video portals deal with movies or animated images. Software collections will provide binary programs or source code, while digital online libraries will feature electronic documents, more likely in a PDF format than in a pure HTML format.

In particular the last two examples of a software collection web site and a digital library are interesting, because very likely the main content will not be visible in a rendered version of the document. Instead, the pages will provide some additional information about the program or the document the user is about to download. While certainly this additional information makes little sense by itself, it is closely related to the main content and, in this

4 Content Extraction

case, it is the only directly visible part of it. Depending on the point of view, this closely related meta data might even be considered to be a part of the main content.

There are other cases, where the separation of main and additional contents is not clear. Good examples are all the web sites, where a central content is extended and enriched – either by the authors or even by the users. After all, user generated content is a scenario which is found more and more often in the course of the booming Web 2.0. But there are other, more classical examples for this phenomenon.

One representative is the Slashdot [MB08] web site, which collects news, rumours and stories from the IT world. While the actual news are usually quite short, the web site allows the users to discuss and comment the news. Opposite to most other sites, the discussions and comments are directly included in the document of the news article. Figure 4.1 shows an example of such an article and the following discussion. The comments are organised in a style similar to newsgroup messages and it is more the rule than the exception that the contributions of the users are much longer than the original message. Again, while the discussion without the reported news is making little sense, it can be debated, whether the discussion is actually becoming a part of the main content. Some users will certainly appreciate the discussions very much and might consider them more entertaining, more interesting or even more informative than the initial news.

A second example is taken from a classical news web site and demonstrates another quite common situation: an article which is enriched with further but optional information. Figure 4.2 shows such an article which was published on the BBC news web site. It reports about a new step in reducing the size of the structures on computer chips. While the main article covers the technological background and consequences of this development, an additional content is blended into the article. A small box provides an explanation of how micro processors work. This extension to the article is general background information. Depending on who reads the article, it can be considered part of the main content or an additional content. A user with a good knowledge of computing technologies and technical aspects of computing science will see it as an additional content, which is not particularly interesting to him and the document could perfectly persist without this information. If the reader instead has no clue about how a computer works, and which purpose there could be in reducing some to him unknown structures on a computer chip, this extension could be extremely useful. For this user the article without the explanation of how a computer processor works would provide far less information, accordingly the extension could be considered as a part of the main content.

These examples demonstrate quite nicely, that even with the intuitive approach it is not always easy to differentiate between main and additional content: the user's interest and background knowledge influence the differentiation. The difference between main and additional content might even be simply a matter of taste. Some users like the offer of related links, others may be annoyed by such extras.

Summarising the observations we can state that it might be difficult to outline the main content in a document. The decision which parts of the document to include also depends on the user and is therefore to a certain extent subjective. Considering this observation as

4.1 The Main Content of a Document

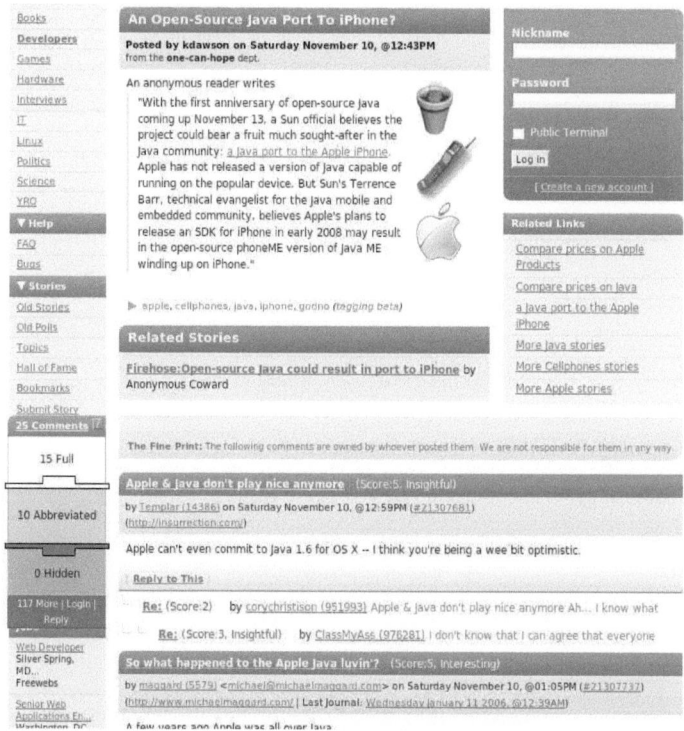

Figure 4.1: Slashdot news article with user discussion.

an intrinsic feature of the main content, we will, from now on, refer to the main content as those parts of the documents which are central due to an expert's notion. On one hand, this ideal expert comes along with the necessary background knowledge to distinguish between contents essential for the document, extended contents which are still related to the main content and unrelated additional content. On the other hand, we rely on the expert to be able to put himself in someone's place who has less expertise and to evaluate the contributions of the closely related optional contents under this aspect. In the course of this thesis we will always try to strike a balance between keeping only the necessary parts of a document for the main content while not excluding too much of the closely related contents by taking a too specialised point of view. The aim of this attempt is to find a definition for the main content of a document, which most people from different backgrounds could agree upon.

4 Content Extraction

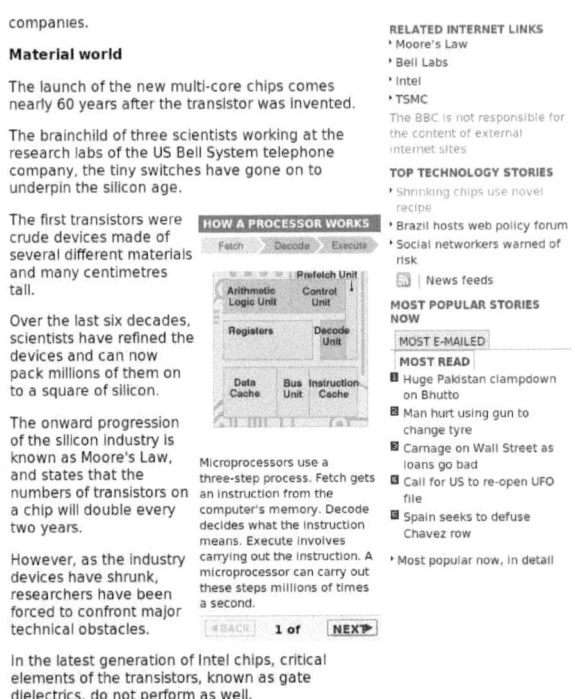

companies.

Material world

The launch of the new multi-core chips comes nearly 60 years after the transistor was invented.

The brainchild of three scientists working at the research labs of the US Bell System telephone company, the tiny switches have gone on to underpin the silicon age.

The first transistors were crude devices made of several different materials and many centimetres tall.

Over the last six decades, scientists have refined the devices and can now pack millions of them on to a square of silicon.

The onward progression of the silicon industry is known as Moore's Law, and states that the numbers of transistors on a chip will double every two years.

However, as the industry devices have shrunk, researchers have been forced to confront major technical obstacles.

In the latest generation of Intel chips, critical elements of the transistors, known as gate dielectrics, do not perform as well.

Microprocessors use a three-step process. Fetch gets an instruction from the computer's memory. Decode decides what the instruction means. Execute involves carrying out the instruction. A microprocessor can carry out these steps millions of times a second.

RELATED INTERNET LINKS
- Moore's Law
- Bell Labs
- Intel
- TSMC

The BBC is not responsible for the content of external internet sites

TOP TECHNOLOGY STORIES
- Shrinking chips use novel recipe
- Brazil hosts web policy forum
- Social networkers warned of risk
- News feeds

MOST POPULAR STORIES NOW

MOST E-MAILED
MOST READ
- Huge Pakistan clampdown on Bhutto
- Man hurt using gun to change tyre
- Carnage on Wall Street as loans go bad
- Call for US to re-open UFO file
- Spain seeks to defuse Chavez row
- Most popular now, in detail

Figure 4.2: Additional information embedded in a BBC news article.

4.2 A Formal Definition of Content Extraction

Following the analysis of what is – or better could be – the main content, comes the question of how to define exactly the CE process. Leaving aside the difficulties to precisely fix the main content of a document, we assume that the main content is known. When talking about CE methods so far, we described the process as outlining the main content, as extracting the core content or as removing the additional contents from the document. These descriptions corresponded to the practical approaches taken in the discussed systems to achieve a certain aim by utilising a CE algorithm. The practical realisations and their intended purpose will be described and discussed in more detail in 4.3.

However, in the context of the practical approaches a formal definition of CE is never really given – probably because the task is intuitively clear and does not need to be formalised in the environment of a specific application. In the light of describing characteristics of CE algorithms and of developing objective ways for evaluating the extraction of a known main content (always with respect to the unclear shape of this main content), a formal definition of CE is needed.

4.2 A Formal Definition of Content Extraction

To remain as general as possible, we base the definition on the string representation of a web document, i.e. the source code. After all, each document content is somehow represented in the source code. As mentioned above we focus on texts and these in particular are clearly visible in the HTML code[1]. Looking at a document in this way the main content is nothing else but a subsequence of this code string. Note, that this subsequence does not necessarily need to be continuous. So, CE is after all a way to mark the according fragments of the source code. These markings which delimit the main content can be most simply realised by denoting the positions in the string.

Hence, CE can be seen as a function from the source code of an HTML document to a set of pairwise indices determining at which position in the string representation of the document the fragments of the main content start and end. We accordingly define CE formally as a function f_{CE} with:

$$f_{CE} : D \to \{(s_i, e_i) : 1 \leq s_i \leq e_i \leq |D|, i \in I\}$$

where D is the source code of a document represented by $|D|$ characters, s_i and e_i are the start and end position respectively of the first and last character of a part of the main content, with $1 \leq s_i \leq e_i \leq |D|$. The index i is from a finite indexing set I allowing to enumerate the main content parts of a document, as there might be several of them.

Though mainly focussing on textual main contents, this definition also suits other kinds of main content to a certain extent. Every content represented in a web document has an according representation in the source code. Images, for example, can be located in the source code via the according img element, links to PDF files via the anchor tag a which defines the hyperlink to the document. For external resources it might even be enough to solely outline the URL representing the location of the according file.

Apart from the practical implication of this definition to suit all those different kinds of CE tasks, there is yet another reason supporting this approach. When dealing with template based documents, the index tuples correspond to the location of the template slot for the main content. Thus, the definition can – for the scenario of template based documents – be motivated as reflecting the correspondence of CE to a reverse engineering of template structures.

There is, however, one kind of content which is difficult to capture in this way: content which is dynamically created via JavaScript on the client side. While the script code itself might still be possible to locate in the HTML source code, it is difficult to capture its dynamic aspect and to decide whether it creates main or additional content. The AJAX technology used in the Web 2.0 environment allows even to contact the web server and obtain further data after the document is displayed in a web browser. Dynamically created contents are big challenge for CE algorithms in the future. So far, no approach is capable of handling this problem. Hence, we will neglect this special case also in the formal definition.

---

[1] A special case might be particular characters encoded in HTML entities. They can, however, be considered to be converted into a decoded form.

4.3 Content Extraction in Practice

According to the formal definition, an algorithm for CE will have to determine the index tuples and use them to outline the main content. Though the above definition basically allows to describe the operational characteristics of all CE solutions, an outline of the main content in the form of the index tuples will rarely occur. Considering the different environments of applications that involve CE, the indices are hardly ever computed explicitly and basically never form the final results of the algorithms. Instead, the observed locations of the main content are used immediately for a further processing of the document. We will now give a short overview of several approaches how applications realise the CE process.

Extraction: The main content found in a document is properly extracted and taken out of the context of the surrounding document structure. The extract is usually filtered to remove the remaining embedded tags, comments or other HTML structures, converting the main content thereby basically into a plain text format. This filter corresponds to the creation of the detagged content as mentioned by Gibson et al. in [GPT05]. CE implementations based on this principle might be adopted by applications that operate on text only and do not need or are even unable to handle HTML formats. Very basic screen readers and text mining applications are examples in this environment.

This particular approach corresponds best to the interpretation of CE as a task of IR within a single document, as in this case the CE solution definitely tries to find the relevant parts of the document for the query "What is the main content?". We will keep this interpretation in mind in the course of developing the evaluation measures.

CE by Marking: The closest to the formal definition of finding index tuples is certainly the option to simply mark the main content by wrapping it into special markup tags. These tags can have a proprietary and application specific form or can be XML/SGML tags, living in their own namespace for not interfering with the HTML code. In the latter case a critical issue might be to pay attention that the document remains well formed and that the main content markup does not spread across several hierarchy layers of the HTML document. This problem can be circumvented by simply adding more tags and splitting the main content fragments into several smaller ones that comply with the hierarchy or by using specific HTML comments to outline the main content, as for comments the hierarchy restriction does not apply.

When analysing documents on the web it can be observed, that some WCMS generated documents do seem to mark the main content exactly in this way. They outline the contents in the slots of a template with comments or dedicated tag structures. It can be assumed that these marks are left either by web designers to indicate the intended locations of the template slots where a programmer then incorporated the design with the WCMS, or the programmers themselves left the marks for purposes of testing, debugging and analysis. As these marks are very individual, not system specific and do not appear in all cases, they are not useful for CE. It is an option, though, to use them for implementing specialised and tailor-made CE systems operating on documents which are all based on the same template with a known marking.

A general disadvantage of this marking approach is that it remains impossible to outline sub element structures like attribute values of HTML elements. Marking e.g. only the URL referring to the image-file in the according img element cannot be done without violating the HTML or the URL syntax.

CE by Deletion: Instead of outlining the main content in a dedicated way to mark its position in the document, it is possible to operate on the additional contents. The main content can, after all, be outlined by simply removing all other contents. The advantage of this approach is, that the HTML structure of the document can be left untouched. Only the text fragments are altered or – when working with a DOM representation – the text nodes in the DOM tree are deleted. An application scenario for this approach are pre-processors for more sophisticated screen readers, which are able to handle HTML data, or WM applications, which benefit from being able to focus their analysis on the main content without sacrificing the knowledge of the HTML structure.

CE by Hiding: Though very similar to CE by deletion at the first sight, there is a significant difference when solely hiding the additional contents, instead of deleting them. Namely that they are still present and can be accessed by downstream applications if necessary. Hiding additional contents is technically realised either by wrapping them into comments, or by modifying the presentation style to render them invisible. The CSS specifications actually provide an according formatting instruction, so that no difficult intervention in the source code is necessary.

CE by Replacing: A third way to handle the additional contents in order to promote the main content is to replace them. Substituting the text with white space characters is very similar to deleting it. Some browsers, however, do distinguish between empty HTML elements and elements which contain white space when rendering a document. Hence, removing the contents entirely might result in a different rendering and altered layout of the documents. This risk is reduced by replacing the contents with white space. Another scenario is to replace the contents with predefined alternative contents or dedicated characters, e.g. the three point ellipsis. This allows a visual impression of how much additional content has been removed.

CE by Restructuring: An option rarely used is to restructure the entire document, once the locations of the main content fragments are known. Mainly those applications pre-processing HTML documents for screen readers or small screen devices make use of such techniques. Instead of removing or hiding the additional contents, they simply move them to less prominent locations. Moving the navigation menu and lists of related links to the end of the document allows the user to get to the main content first, but maintains all possibilities of navigating the web site and accessing

4 Content Extraction

all contents. However, the restructuring might also comprehend the removal of some parts of a document if they are considered entirely uninformative, like elements which purely serve layout purposes.

All these different ways to realise CE comply with the definition given in 4.2, even if the observed effects might be different. The CE solutions described in chapter 3 are all based on one or the other of those approaches. Thus, the formal definition we gave – though it appears to be very simple – describes all practical CE applications well enough to reflect reality. Further, it provides a theoretical model which allows the development of more objective evaluation measures.

5 Evaluating Content Extraction

As CE algorithms often represent only a part of larger applications, they are rarely evaluated on their own. Moreover, as we have seen in the chapter on related work, the methods used to extract the main content have hardly ever been compared with each other directly. This chapter describes a framework for measuring, evaluating and comparing the performance of CE methods based on objective criteria. The framework is designed to be platform independent and extensible for both the evaluation data and the measures to be employed.

We will further use it to evaluate the performance of existing single document CE algorithms. Thereby we will also provide a first and direct comparison of the approaches presented in 3.2 for locating the main content in web documents.

5.1 Motivation for New Evaluation Measures

In chapter 3, talking about related work, we have seen several approaches of how CE methods have been evaluated and on few occasions even have been compared with each other. Already there, we mentioned a few drawbacks of the solutions involving the different ways of evaluation. To motivate the development of a new evaluation approach, we will now look at these drawbacks in more detail. We will in particular pay attention to how they can hinder a large scale evaluation or may even cause distorted or wrong results.

The main drawbacks of the approach of employing *human user evaluation* are twofold: subjective results and lack of automation. As we observed that the perception of what belongs to the main content is subjective, any CE evaluation measure will have a subjective note. While this is an intrinsic problem, human user evaluation contains further subjective aspects. Even if the user is provided with a gold standard for the main content, which the CE algorithm is supposed to extract from the document, there remains a certain space for interpretation. How many mistakes may a CE algorithm make before the extraction is considered a failure? Which deviations in the extraction are exactly to be considered a mistake? Are all mistakes of equal gravity? These are just some of the questions for which it is difficult to give detailed and specific instructions to the user in order to eliminate subjectivity entirely. Accordingly, a comparison between CE methods under human evaluation is difficult, even more so if different people are involved in the evaluation process.

The second drawback – the lack of automation – causes other difficulties. To get a general impression of the performance of a CE system, a large sample of different documents should be considered. This is practically impossible when asking human users to do the evaluation. The time needed to compare in detail a document in its original version, a gold standard

5 Evaluating Content Extraction

for the main content and the extract created by the CE system is quite long. Accordingly, it would take a huge workforce and still a remarkable amount of time to evaluate the performance of even a single system. Thus, human evaluation is first of all simply too time consuming and too expensive to run it on a large scale.

Human evaluation is, however, a useful approach to analyse in detail the specific drawbacks or advantages of single systems. During the development process of a CE application or after an automated evaluation of an existing system, a human expert might be able to spot specifically where a system fails or where it performs well. During the development phase, this analysis can focus on a couple of test documents. After a large scale automated evaluation process, instead, the user can take a look at those documents where the results are particularly good or bad. Insights like "The system tends to fail in recognising the headline of the document" or "Commercials embedded into the main content are not removed from the document" might be easy to obtain for a user. Knowing these details can help improving the performance of a system or in selecting the right kind of system for a given application background.

Another approach for evaluation are the *application specific tests*. While this kind of tests can be tailored to reflect exactly the requirements of an intended application environment for CE, they most of all lack generality. Even if a CE algorithm works well for one application does not necessarily mean that it will also work well for another application. Furthermore, the individual development of a measure and an automatic way to apply it can be quite difficult and time consuming as well. Beyond this problem, it is especially necessary to pay attention on how to define a good performance.

Gupta's screen reader testing[Gup06] is an example where the test is specifically designed for the intended application, but also for a specific extraction approach. Evaluating the Crunch framework by how much faster a document can be read by a screen reader after it has been filtered perfectly reflects the scenario Crunch was designed for. If the documents can be read in less time, Crunch had performed well. When trying to generalise the approach to other CE systems, the results might be questionable. An extreme example is a filter which simply removes all contents from a document. Such an output is obviously not in the intention of a CE system. The screen reader test instead will attest the system to have done a phenomenal job as the document can be read in no time at all. For Crunch the screen reading evaluation made sense, as the system was designed to be quite careful in removing contents. It rather extracts too much than too little content. Other approaches do not behave in this way.

The *indirect evaluation* partially suffers from the same problems. If a particular system is performing better due to the employment of CE methods, it does not necessarily mean that the extraction was done in a good way. A good example of distorted indirect evaluation results can easily be given in the context of WM. A standard approach for classifying web documents is to use a Naïve Bayes (NB) classifier. Employing the Bayes theorem, this classifier deduces from a set of training documents the conditional probabilities of finding each single feature – in this case a feature corresponds to a word – in a document, given that the document belongs to a certain category. For a new document NB analyses

5.1 Motivation for New Evaluation Measures

the probability of this document to belong to a category, given the words contained in it. Using a CE algorithm to filter the web documents prior to using them for training or before classifying a new document should improve the performance of this classifier. In fact, this approach was successfully taken by Yi, Liu and Li in [YLL03]. They observed an NB classifier to perform better when pre-processing the documents with the Site Style Tree algorithm. If the set of documents used for evaluation is instead chosen unluckily, the results can easily turn out the other way. Selecting a large number of documents from few web sites, and using the web sites categories as gold standard for classification is a common approach to obtain large sets of training and evaluation data for classifiers. The chances are quite high, that the documents contain some reference to the categories themselves, e.g. via the navigation menu, small modifications in the template structure or by containing category specific additional contents which are common to all documents in this category. These hints for the categories are discovered by an NB classifier and are strong indicators if they appear in a previously unseen document to put it in the according category. Hence, an NB classifier trained on such data will base its judgement mainly on those additional contents.

When incorporating a good CE system as a pre-processor, these hints will be removed, as they definitely do not belong to the main content. Accordingly the category indicating hints are missing and the NB classifier will quite certainly tend to perform poorer – though the CE algorithm is doing a good job. It can be argued that in this case the original input data is biased and the NB classifier using the unfiltered documents will be overfitted on the training set. However, the point is that the combination of CE and a downstream application might become complex and interwoven in a way that it is not clear how the changes in the performance are caused. A separate and individual evaluation of both systems does not give rise to this problem.

The category of *IR-based evaluation measures* was already mentioned in 3.4.4 to be the approach which allows best to measure the performance of a system in an automated, objective and CE-specific way. The publications mainly using this evaluation approach are the ones of Lin and Ho on InfoDiscoverer [LH02] and Debnath, Mitra and Giles on ContentExtractor and (K-)FeatureExtractor [DMG05a, DMG05b]. All these systems operate on the DOM tree representation of web documents. They incorporate a segmentation of the documents into blocks which correspond to nodes and their sub-trees in the DOM. Each individual block is then decided to be either main or additional content. As this is equivalent to a binary classification of blocks, the authors in all cases provided a gold standard for the block classification and employed measures like recall, precision and F1.

While it seems that this evaluation approach takes very well into consideration the very task a CE system has to fulfil, the results in some cases might not correspond at all with the actual performance of CE algorithms. The problem can again be described best with an example. A web document is segmented into ten blocks, of which five belong to the main content and five to the additional contents. We assume, that a CE algorithm classifies all the blocks correctly except for one mistake: one of the main content blocks is wrongly classified as an additional content. The confusion matrix for such an outcome looks like

99

5 Evaluating Content Extraction

Table 5.1: The confusion matrix for block based evaluation of a CE algorithm which has made one mistake.

		block classified by CE as	
		main content	additional content
block actually is	main content	4 (TP)	1 (FN)
	additional content	0 (FP)	5 (TN)

the one in table 5.1. The relative good performance of the system is also reflected by a precision rating of 1, a recall rating of 0.8 and a F1 score of 0.89. Hence, the overall performance of the system seems to be quite satisfying.

If the blocks and their content are specified in more detail, the picture might change. In our example the five main content blocks shall represent the title, the subtitle, a teaser text, an image with its according text label and the body of a news article. The five additional content blocks can be said to contain the main navigation, a related links list, a commercial banner, the header and some copyright notations. Anyway, as the additional contents were identified correctly their form does not matter any further. For the main content blocks instead it matters, which one has been wrongly classified. If it is the block with the subtitle or the image, the document can still be considered to be dealt with quite well and the evaluation ratings reflect this fact.

If instead it is the block with the article text, which is wrongly classified as additional content, the evaluation ratings are entirely distorted. This block will very likely contain most of the content and can be considered the central part of the main content. Without the article text the other blocks are very likely not making much sense any more. In this case, an F1 rating of 0.89 does not reflect the performance of the system at all.

The reason behind this distorted result is that the block length is never considered during the evaluation. A block containing hardly any content is having the same importance and accordingly the same weight in the evaluation scheme as a block which contains a lot of content. Hence, classifying correctly virtually empty blocks which do not change the perception of the document very much can easily balance misclassification of blocks which heavily affect the content of the document.

A further problem with the block based approach is, that it is not compatible with all extraction methods. Those methods which do not build blocks or are able to extract text nodes from the DOM tree only partially cannot be evaluated straight away by the classification result for blocks. The most important question to answer in this case would be how to evaluate a block which was extracted only partially. The evaluation approaches found in the according publications of Lin and Ho and Debnath et al. did not go into this detail as their block based CE methods do not cause this problem.

Summarising, we can say that none of the evaluation methods proposed so far is really adequate to measure the performance of a CE system. The IR based approach is the most promising but needs to be based on more appropriate data structures.

5.2 Measures for Evaluating Content Extraction

As most other performance measure we will base our evaluation approach on a comparison with a gold standard. The latter is created by experts and will serve as reference for what a CE algorithm is supposed to extract. On the basis of this reference data we will develop evaluation measures which compare the gold standard with the extracted contents. As already mentioned we will focus on textual main contents. It should, however, not be too difficult to adapt the described techniques to contents of different formats.

5.2.1 Creating a Gold Standard

In order to be able to measure the performance of a CE algorithm on a particular document, we need first of all independent experts to define what exactly is the main content of this document and thereby to create a gold standard. It remains the question of which experts to employ in this task. Two practical approaches can be taken: human experts or dedicated and specialised CE programs which are suitable to extract the main content from a particular document format of a single web site.

Employing human experts to outline the main content in a document allows to create gold standards for very different kinds of documents. The term "experts" in general is actually a bit exaggerated. As we mentioned already in the introduction, every halfway experienced web user is capable of finding the main content in a web document. However, there remains the tricky decision of which closely related contents might still be considered part of the main content. To overcome this problem we will adopt the approach suggested in chapter 4 about the definition of CE, i.e. the expert will strike a balance between keeping only the necessary parts of a document which contain the main content and not stripping off closely related contents. Hence, we can rely on the expert user to provide a good gold standard. In this way, the human user approach can provide diverse evaluation documents covering a wide range of document types. As the main problem of involving human users remains, namely that it is a very time consuming task, this approach will not provide large amounts of data.

The specialised content extractors instead aim exactly at the creation of evaluation data for massive tests. A specialised content extractor is a program which is particularly designed to work on one type of document only – or better on documents which are all based on the same template. The implementation of such an extractor is again to be based on the knowledge or a document analysis of a human user. Just that in this case the user formulates the way of recognising the main content in a way that allows to create a pattern for extracting the main content automatically. This pattern is then applied to a large collection of web documents. The development of specialised CE solutions can make use of tools similar to the ones for wrapper generation. Using landmarks like particular words or tag combinations in the source code to identify the slot of the main content is a common and well performing method.

5 Evaluating Content Extraction

As the specialised content extractors are based on a human's opinion of what makes up the main content as well, they also suffer from the same kind of subjectivity as the first approach of humans outlining the main content manually for each individual document. Hence, we will have to keep in mind that all gold standards are after all nothing more but a very good guess on which parts of the document make up the main content. It is important to keep this problem in mind when evaluating CE algorithms. After all, the algorithms are developed following some notion of what defines the main content and how to locate it. So, if an algorithm tends, for example, to always extract too much, it might simply be due to a difference in the underlying notions of main content of the algorithm designer and the expert providing the gold standard. Hence, we usually cannot expect a perfect match.

5.2.2 Comparing Gold Standard and Extracted Contents

Once a gold standard for the main content of a document has been established, the next task is to find a way to compare it with an extract created by a CE algorithm. To distinguish between the two notions of the main content in the further course of this thesis we will refer to the gold standard provided by an expert simply as the *main content* and the text extracted by a CE system as the *extracted content*.

A primary objective in an evaluation process must be to measure how similar the extracted content is to the expert's main content. Clearly, it should reward large accordance, while both possible deviations – extracting too much or extracting too little – should be penalised.

The interpretation of CE as a document level IR task of retrieving the relevant content suggests to handle CE like a binary classification of contents into main content and additional content. The clear advantage of bringing CE into the IR world is – as already mentioned for the block based IR evaluation – the wide range of evaluation measures that has been developed for IR methods. Accordingly, we will base the evaluation on the well known and accepted recall, precision and F1 measures.

The blocks created during a web document segmentation process have already turned out not to be fine-grained enough for a reasonable evaluation process. As it is not clear which level of granularity is needed we take four different approaches to define the atomic items, i.e. the smallest unit of content, which can be retrieved in the extraction process. The approaches reflect four different models for representing web documents, which have a different resolution of the document contents themselves.

Character Sequence: Each character is a fragment of the document and as such can be part of the relevant main content or of an irrelevant additional content. The evaluation accordingly compares the agreement between the actual main content and the extracted content on a character level. The addition of representing the contents not only by the characters contained in it, but as a sequence of characters reflects that not only the right amount of characters has to be extracted, but that the characters have to be in the correct order as well.

This approach is certainly the most fine-grained one and is closest to our formal definition of CE in 4.2. It is capable of detecting whether a word was extracted only partially and takes the correctly extracted part of it into account for the overall extraction performance. Though it is theoretically possible that a CE system extracts words only partially, it will usually not occur in practice. There is simply no sense in extracting only a part of a word. Words can probably be considered the smallest unit of information in a text which cannot be divided further without altering or destroying its information. The advantage of such a fine resolution for evaluation is instead that longer words influence the performance more and that even punctuation marks or other particular symbols are taken into account.

To apply recall, precision and the F1 measure we have to find a way to determine the overlap of relevant and retrieved items, hence of extracted and main content. Given the character sequence representation of the contents and the fact that the extracted and the main content do not necessarily need to be a continuous sequence in the document, the best way to calculate the overlap is to determine the longest common subsequence (LCS). The LCS is a sequence of characters which can be found in both texts, possibly interrupted by other interspersed characters, and there is no longer sequence with this property. Considering this longest subsequence to be the intersection of relevant and retrieved items, the calculation of recall and precision can then be based on the length of the character sequences m of the main content, the extracted content e and their common subsequence c by:

$$r = \frac{|c|}{|m|} \quad , \quad p = \frac{|c|}{|e|}$$

The special cases of an empty main content or extracted content can be handled as described in 2.2.4 for empty result sets and empty sets of relevant items.

Word Sequence: We just mentioned words to be the probably smallest unit of information in a text. A way to model a text on a slightly higher level is accordingly to consider single words as the items retrieved by CE systems when answering the question "What is the relevant content?". The string representation of the text in a web document is tokenised into words and, given the gold standard for the main content, it is again possible to classify each single word as being either main or additional content. While all the following evaluation measures are based on words as the smallest unit of the content, there are still differences in how they are considered in order to model a document.

The first approach is to maintain the order of the words as they appear in the text, thereby constructing a sequence of words. The biggest differences between the word sequence and the character sequence model is, that punctuation marks and word length are not taken any more into consideration. This model corresponds best to all document representations which are based on words and which maintain the word context at least to a certain degree. A common representative for this document model are the n-grams which group n words together to form a fragment of the document.

The agreement between the actual main content according to the gold standard and the extracted content provided by a CE algorithm can be computed, similarly to the character based measure, via the LCS approach. The only difference is, that the LCS is defined on word sequences instead of character sequences. The recall and precision are again defined in the same way as above via the sequence lengths.

Bag of words: The next step to a more coarse-grained evaluation measure is not to take into consideration the word order. This corresponds to the bag of words model for a document, which simply counts how often each word occurs in a document.

There are two reasons for developing a measure based on this model. First, this document model is among the most wide spread in the domain of text mining. And second, while ignoring the word order will not change performance very much for most CE algorithms in comparison to the word sequence approach, it allows to consider systems which restructure the web document. If some content is moved to another place in the document, the sequence based measure will result in a lower score, as the longest common subsequence of the agreement is not capable of handling moved contents. If, instead, the word order is ignored, a restructured document can be handled as well.

In chapter 2 we said that a bag of words can be represented as a vector by enumerating all possible words. Hence, if the main content is represented by a vector $m = (m_1, m_2, \ldots, m_n)$ and the extracted content by a vector $e = (e_1, e_2, \ldots, e_n)$, where m_i and e_i count how often the i-th word appears in the respective contents, the intersection of the two contents can be given by a vector $c = (c_1, c_2, \ldots, c_n)$, where $c_i = \min(m_i, e_i)$. The vector c formulates the agreement of the two contents by taking the minimum appearance of a word in both contents. The calculation of recall and precision can be done by summing the number of words which appear in the vectors:

$$r = \frac{\sum_{i=1}^n c_i}{\sum_{i=1}^n m_i} \quad , \quad p = \frac{\sum_{i=1}^n c_i}{\sum_{i=1}^n e_i}$$

Set of Words: Ignoring further how often the words appear in the contents leads to modelling the content as a set of words. The IR interpretation of CE is accordingly reflected by retrieving from a set of words the relevant ones, i.e. those words which

5.2 Measures for Evaluating Content Extraction

appear in the main content. This approach corresponds most closely to an application background in which the main focus is on indexing the terms in the documents, e.g. for building an inverted index data structure.

The recall and precision measures in this case do not need to be adapted, as they are defined on sets anyway. Thus, if m is the set of words in the main content, e the set of extracted words, the intersection of relevant and retrieved words is the normal intersection of sets and recall and precision are accordingly given by:

$$r = \frac{|m \cap e|}{|m|} \quad , \quad p = \frac{|m \cap e|}{|e|}$$

The four above ways to model the main and the extracted content and accordingly how to measure recall and precision are all suitable to evaluate CE. The level of granularity becomes coarser in small steps from the character sequence model to the set of words model. Based on the definitions of recall and precision all four models can be used to calculate the F1 measure as well.

However, it is possible to artificially construct cases in which those measures will fail to provide a correct evaluation of the performance of a CE algorithm. One case is a document which contains twice exactly the same text, once as main and once as additional content. If a CE algorithm extracts wrongly the additional content, none of the described measures will be able to notice this mistake and will attest a perfect recall and precision rating.

The implications arising from this problem can however be neglected for several reasons. First, from a semantic point of view the question arises, why the same text should appear twice in a document, once as main content and once as additional content. There might be rare cases where such kind of redundancy can occur in a reduced way, for example, due to a document which mentions itself via its title and its teaser text in a related links list. But even then, the additional content would be so closely related to the main content that it can be said to actually belong to the main content and the definition of the gold standard is questionable. Second, from a practical point of view most applications will not suffer if the correct text is extracted but from the wrong place in the document. In the most extreme case where the two texts are simply concatenated and located at the same place in a document it is actually even impossible to decide which one finally has been extracted, when simply looking at the results. And last, from a realistic point of view, experience in analysing web documents suggests that there simply are no such documents.

While the measurements of recall, precision and F1 are certainly the most important indicators for the performance of a CE algorithm, there are a few additional measures we will employ in the comparison. They are intended to estimate stability and time performance of the algorithms.

The stability criterion implies the idea that a CE method should achieve a similar performance on similar documents. In other words, the criterion is supposed to measure the

5 Evaluating Content Extraction

reliability of a method. So, for testing the stability we have to look at a collection of similar documents. A method is employed to extract the main contents and its results are compared with the gold standard for the main content. Distilling the F1 measure from this comparison we look at how much the performance differs between the documents. To do so, we consider the F1 scores of the single document extraction as results of a probability experiment and use them to calculate an estimate for the standard deviation. Given n documents for which the i-th document has an F1 value of f_i and the average F1 value is $\bar{f}$, then the standard deviation σ can be estimated by:

$$\sigma = \sqrt{\frac{1}{n-1}\sum_{i=1}^{n}\left(f_i - \bar{f}\right)^2}$$

The standard deviation can be calculated for each of the different document models corresponding to the different levels of granularity.

Obviously, the smaller the standard deviation is, the more stable is the CE method. Note, that a high stability on its own does not say anything about the quality of an algorithm. An algorithm scoring always an F1 value of 0 is extremely stable, but performs particularly poor. On the other hand, a high standard deviation indicates fluctuations in the performance of a method. Thus, even if it scores relatively high F1 ratings on average, it might deliver very bad results even for similar documents.

As all the algorithms discussed in this thesis are at least conceptually generic enough to work with any website and can be realised as a non intrusive system, we have to consider for their comparison only the last quality aspect mentioned by Rahman, Alam and Hartono [RAH01]: the algorithm has to be fast. For those algorithms described in literature with enough detail it is possible to analyse their time complexity from a theoretical point of view and determine their runtime behaviour. However, not for all algorithms the descriptions are detailed enough and not always the worst case complexity reflects the behaviour in practice. To be further able to also evaluate algorithms that come as a black box, we will in all cases take a look at the time performance by simply measuring the time needed to process a document.

The time aspect is particularly important for systems that need to do the extraction on-the-fly in time critical applications. If CE is, for example, employed as a pre-processor for a screen reader or a small screen device the users are certainly not willing to wait too long for the results. The extraction process has to be fast enough for not delaying the transmission of web documents to the final browser too much.

As the document length will most likely influence the time needed to find and extract the main content, we need to normalise the processing time with respect to the document length in order to get comparable results. This normalisation can be achieved by braking down the processing time to seconds per kB. Even though, none of the methods we will deal with operates on a byte level, it is the most neutral dimension to normalise the processing time for documents with different length. However, the assumption does not seem too far fetched that the number of HTML elements, tags, words, blocks or whatever other structures are used as basis for the extraction process increase more or less linear with the byte length of the document.

Summarising our evaluation measures we have: the recall, precision and F1 measure to evaluate the quality of a CE algorithm, the F1 standard deviation to measure its stability and the normalised processing time to measure the time performance. To determine recall, precision and F1 we will use different underlying models to cover different levels of granularity in the evaluation process.

5.3 Implementation of an Evaluation Framework

The evaluation framework we will discuss in this section provides all functionalities necessary to evaluate and compare CE systems. We will briefly discuss some decisions made about the design of the framework and some aspects of its implementation. The most fundamental decision is to incorporate the CE systems as HTTP proxy servers. While this approach might seem a bit cumbersome at the first sight, we will see that in this way we are very flexible in evaluating different kinds and architectures of CE systems.

5.3.1 Design Decisions

To keep the implementation of the evaluation framework as simple as possible, the idea is first of all not to provide a full evaluation environment, but rather an API which allows to quickly draft programs for creating and managing sets of test documents, running evaluation tests with different CE algorithms and storing the results in a simple format which can be analysed with other tools. As CE systems and applications might appear on different platforms and as in the future other evaluation measures might be developed, platform independence and extensibility of the framework are the main issues for the design.

In more detail: the platform independence has to have two qualities. First and most important, the framework must be independent from the evaluated CE algorithm. Implementations of CE systems can come along in different programming languages, for different operating systems and in different environments. Separating the evaluation framework from the CE systems under these aspects is strictly necessary simply for being able to evaluate as many different CE configurations as possible. This also requires – as demanded for the CE systems themselves – a non intrusive design. CE systems might be black boxes with no possibility to access their functionality via an API. The evaluation framework is intended to be able to integrate virtually any application which operates on HTML documents.

The second independence quality to aim for is the possibility to keep the evaluated and the evaluating application physically separated on different machines. The intention behind this requirement is that a high demand of system resources due to the operations of the evaluation framework should not interfere with the time performance of the CE system.

The solution for realising platform independence is to involve Internet technologies. Given the fact that we are working with web documents the approach to use web techniques is nearly a self-evident solution. Modelling all the interactions between the evalua-

5 Evaluating Content Extraction

tion framework and CE systems via standard network protocols is, in fact, the solution for both independence issues. Obviously when communicating over a network, the CE system and the evaluation system can be physically separated. Furthermore, as most modern programming languages and operating systems provide the means for network communications, the platform independence under this aspect is achieved as well.

Some of the existing applications for CE already come along as a proxy server (e.g. the Crunch framework), others can easily be wrapped into such a server. Accordingly we use the HTTP protocol [FGM$^+$99] for the communication with the CE systems. The evaluation framework is then using the proxy with CE capabilities to retrieve documents and thereby locate their main content. We will get to the implementation details of this approach later on. The point is, that this concept separates the framework entirely from the CE implementations, guaranteeing a maximum freedom on both sides.

Another, further platform independence aspect, though of minor importance, is achieved by using the platform independent Java programming language to finally implement the framework. In this way the platform independence goes even beyond the connection with the CE systems and allows to use the evaluation framework on different operating systems.

The requirement for extensibility comes in two variations as well: extension of the employed evaluation measures and extension of the used evaluation data. The first issue bears in mind the development of other evaluation measures which can then be incorporated easily. This demands a modular design for the framework. A subdivision into three relatively independent components should be sufficient: an evaluation component, a document management component and a component for interacting with the CE systems. The interfaces between these components can be kept quite simple and be restricted to the necessary interactions. By subdividing the tasks so clearly, the mutual interdependence between evaluation, document management and communication with the CE system is at an absolute minimum. For example it would be no problem to modify the communication component in order to use the API of a CE system directly. For the evaluation this change would be entirely irrelevant. Likewise, an exchange or extension of the evaluation measures does effect neither the document management nor the communication component.

The second extensibility focuses on the possibility to extend, rearrange and manage the set of documents used for the evaluation process. A simple but yet powerful way to organise the test documents in *evaluation packages* is the answer to this requirement. The organisation of documents in packages allows to easily configure test scenarios which can even be run in a batch mode to evaluate the performance of different CE applications.

The simplicity of the package concept should also allow to easily create different applications for creating evaluation data. Following the remarks in 5.2.1 on how a gold standard can be obtained, it should be possible to create the packages in both ways: automated and via a user interface for human experts.

Therefore, the data formats used by the evaluation framework for input and output are kept as simple as possible. A package of test data simply consists of a description file and the files for the evaluation process. Those files comprise the source code of the HTML documents, an expert's notion of their main content in a plain text format and the meta information. To link a document with its additional files, they all share the same name using solely different extensions. This simple file based format allows an easy and, if necessary, even manual recompilation and adaptation of test packages. As the collections of data can become quite large very quickly, the files are additionally compressed using the standard zip-format[1].

Measuring the performance of a single CE system on all the documents in one of the evaluation packages is what we will consider from now on as an *evaluation run*. In other words, an evaluation run can basically be compared to a test of the behaviour of a certain system in a given scenario.

To store the results of an evaluation run, the measures taken for each document in a package of the processing time, precision, recall and F1-measure, we use again a simple and platform independent format. As the downstream evaluation and also the presentation of the results should be possible with other applications, we save the results of each evaluation run in a CSV (comma separated values) file format. This text based format is a very wide spread format for storing tabular data in a platform independent way. Several applications, in particular for data analysis, are capable of handling CSV files.

5.3.2 Implementation Characteristics

The design decisions outlined already the three big components which characterise the implementation and are visualised in the overview in figure 5.1: management of the data packages, communication with the CE systems and evaluation. The data package component provides all the necessary functionalities for creating and handling the document collections which represent single test scenarios. The communication component, instead, takes care of the interaction with the CE systems via the HTTP protocol. Both these components are intensively used by the evaluation component. The latter, being the heart of the evaluation process, controls how the different kinds of data are handled, orders the extraction process, computes the evaluation measures and stores the results.

Going more into the details, the data management component provides all the functionalities necessary to work with the test data packages. Aside from the data structures for the packages themselves, it also contains structures for the evaluation documents. Each test document consists of the source code of the web page, the main content as plain text according to the gold standard and some additional meta data. Among the meta data of the documents is the language and the URL of the original web document. Several functionalities are arranged around these central data structures to work with them as shown in figure 5.2.

The creation of packages is supported by the options to compile packages from the exports created by a Firefox extension. This extension is meant to support a human expert in defining a gold standard for web documents and is described in more detail in

---

[1]The decision to use the zip-format was based on the general availability of tools for this format on all common operating systems and the possibility to handle the file format quite easily via interfaces provided by the standard Java API.

5 Evaluating Content Extraction

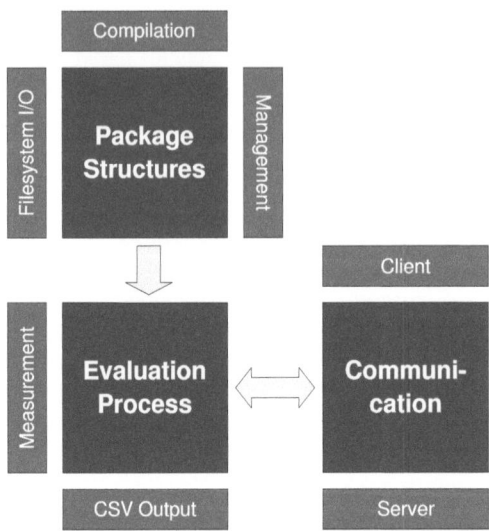

Figure 5.1: Overview of the components of the evaluation framework.

5.4.1 in the context of actually creating evaluation packages. Another option to create packages is to gather the results of specialised content extractor programs, which can be used to generate large packages. Finally, new packages can be created by selecting documents from existing packages and recombining them in a new test scenario. A reliable and simple mechanism to save an entire package to the file system of a computer is an essential functionality. As the collected data of the source code of the document and the gold standard for the main content can easily become quite large[2], the saving and loading process contains a transparent layer for compressing the data in a zip file format. The management functionality for a package, instead, comprises methods to add, remove and change documents in a test package. An important feature for the evaluation process is the possibility to easily iterate over all the single documents in a package.

As figure 5.3 shows, the communication component is simpler. Because we assume the evaluated CE systems to be wrapped in an HTTP proxy server, the component contains only two main elements: a client and server implementation. This is necessary as the evaluation framework takes both roles. On one hand, it provides a document as a web server, and on the other hand it requests the CE system to retrieve it. Only in this way it has full control of the original document and of the version it retrieves from the CE proxy. Client and server are always handling one document at a time.

---

[2]Hardly any of the HTML files in the test packages has a size of less then 30 kB. The average files size for storing only their source code is already somewhere between 50 and 70 kB. Hence, the mere source codes for one package of 1000 documents makes up around 50 to 70 MB of data.

5.3 Implementation of an Evaluation Framework

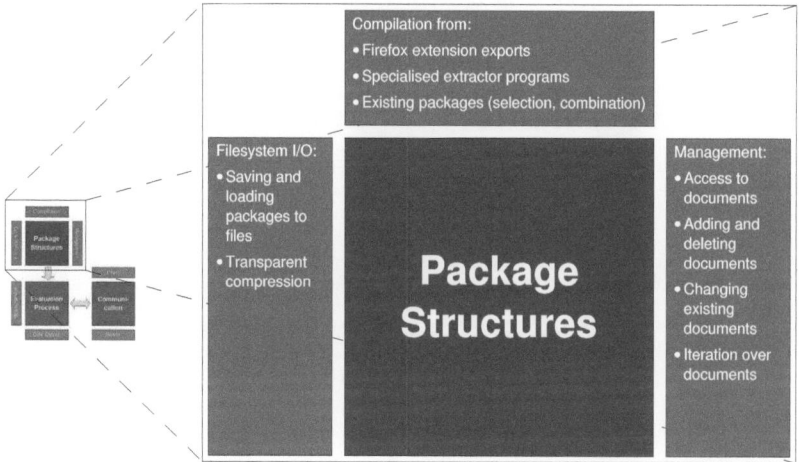

Figure 5.2: Details of the component for managing the evaluation packages.

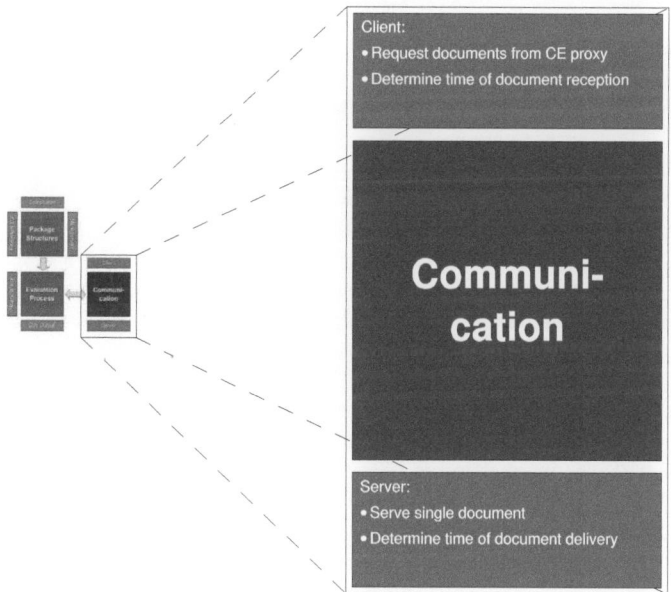

Figure 5.3: Details of the communication component.

5 Evaluating Content Extraction

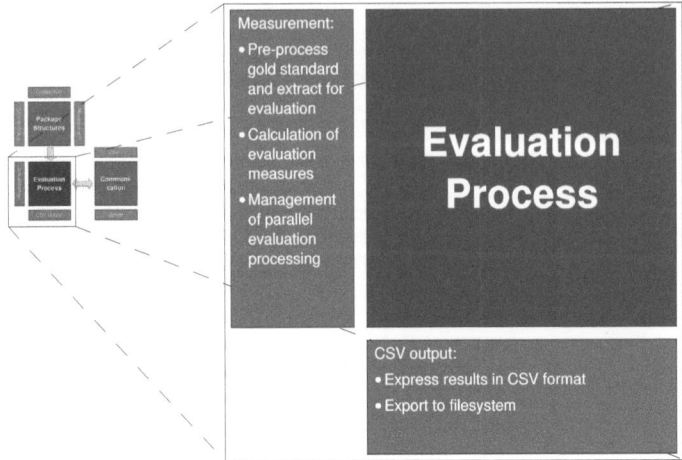

Figure 5.4: Details of the evaluation component.

Which documents the communication component has to serve and request via the CE system is controlled by the evaluation component. Apart from controlling all the processes in an evaluation run, this component is responsible for calculating the evaluation measures and saving the results to CSV files. These two main functions are depicted in figure 5.4.

As the proposed evaluation measures are based on unstructured text, the first step before the actual evaluation is to strip off all tags, comments, style and script elements. After resolving further the HTML entities into Unicode characters and reducing superfluous whitespace[3] we have a string representation of the extracted content, which is equivalent to the plain text format of the expert's main content.

The next step taken by the evaluation component is to prepare the text for the different evaluation measures. For the word based measures it splits both the extracted and the main content into word tokens. To calculate precision and recall it is essential to find the intersection of the extracted and the main content for defining the extracted relevant elements. To determine this intersection for the methods based on the character and the word sequence, we calculate the LCS using the algorithm of Hirschberg [Hir75]. The intersection for the measures based on a set of words is based on the set structure provided by the Java API, the intersection of bags of words can be calculated based on vectors as described above.

As the evaluation of a single document is independent from the evaluation of all other documents, the process is suitable for parallelisation. Hence, the evaluation component makes massive use of parallel threads: each document is evaluated in a single thread. As

---

[3] As cumulative whitespace is ignored in the presentation of HTML documents it is usually used to layout the source code. As such, it does not affect the content and accordingly we ignore it.

5.3 Implementation of an Evaluation Framework

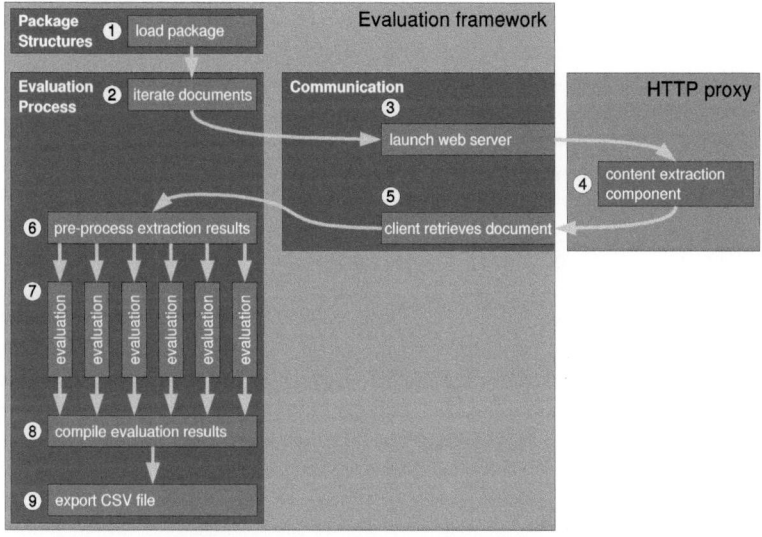

Figure 5.5: Process of an evaluation run.

the main issue of computing the evaluation measures is to find the LCS for words and characters, CPU usage is the bottleneck of the process. The parallel approach can make optimal use of the ability of modern computers to handle several processes in parallel due to multi-core or hyperthreading technologies. However, for not interfering with the communication process with the CE system or causing delays in the network transactions and thereby influencing the measurement of time, the parallel processes for calculating recall and precision are not started before all documents have been passed through the CE system.

The results of the parallel computation of the evaluation measures are collected and handled again by a central part of the component. The results are then formulated in a CSV format and written to the file system for downstream processing with other applications.

5.3.3 An Entire Evaluation Run

To explain how the components work together in detail, it is best to follow a step by step example of an entire evaluation run. As said above, an evaluation run is the process of evaluating the performance of a single CE system on all the documents in a single evaluation package. The overall process is visualised in figure 5.5. The single steps are numbered to follow more easily the course of the entire process.

The first step (①) is to load the data for the evaluation scenario, i.e. the package of documents. Afterwards the evaluation component takes over control and starts to iterate over the documents in the package ②. Each single document has to be passed through the extraction process. To do this, the communication component launches a minimal web server ③, which serves exactly the one document that has to undergo extraction, before the server shuts down itself. In the next step the framework issues the proxy capable of CE to retrieve and implicitly filter ④ the document from the previously launched server. During this process the time between the completion of serving the document on the side of the web server till the completion of receiving it from the proxy at the side of the client ⑤ is measured to estimate the time needed for the extraction. The filtered document is passed back to the evaluation component together with the time measured for the extraction process.

Once all documents have been filtered, the results are pre-processed ⑥ to create the detagged content, resolve HTML entities and reduce superfluous white space. Now the gold standard and the extracted content have the same form and can be compared with each other. The comparison and computation is done for each document in a separate thread to use efficiently the resources of multi-core processor architectures. Each thread ⑦ tokenises the text content into words for the word based evaluation measures. Afterwards it computes the LCS for the word and the character sequences, the common word appearance for the bag of words based measure and the intersection of the set based document representation. These values are used to determine recall, precision and the derived F1 measure for all the different document models. As soon as a thread has finished all the calculations, it reports its results to a central instance controlling the parallel processes. And once all threads have reported that they completed their task, the results are compiled ⑧ into a single data structure and exported to a CSV file ⑨.

5.4 Comparison of Existing Single Document Algorithms

The first application for which we use the evaluation framework is to compare several of the existing single document CE algorithms we have mentioned in the related work chapter. This comparison has three main goals. First, to develop some realistic and interesting test scenarios, second, to establish an objective ranking of the existing algorithms under the developed evaluation criteria, and third, to estimate how well the evaluation measures reflect the performance of CE systems.

Especially the last goal is a tricky issue, as there is no reliable reference measure for comparison. Hence, the approach we will take is to use the simplest way of human evaluation and check that the evaluation results obtained by the evaluation framework do not contradict the subjective impression of the extraction performance.

5.4.1 Creating Test Data

To generate test data, we need to collect HTML documents and have an expert to determine their main content. We will take both of the described above ways for creating a

5.4 Comparison of Existing Single Document Algorithms

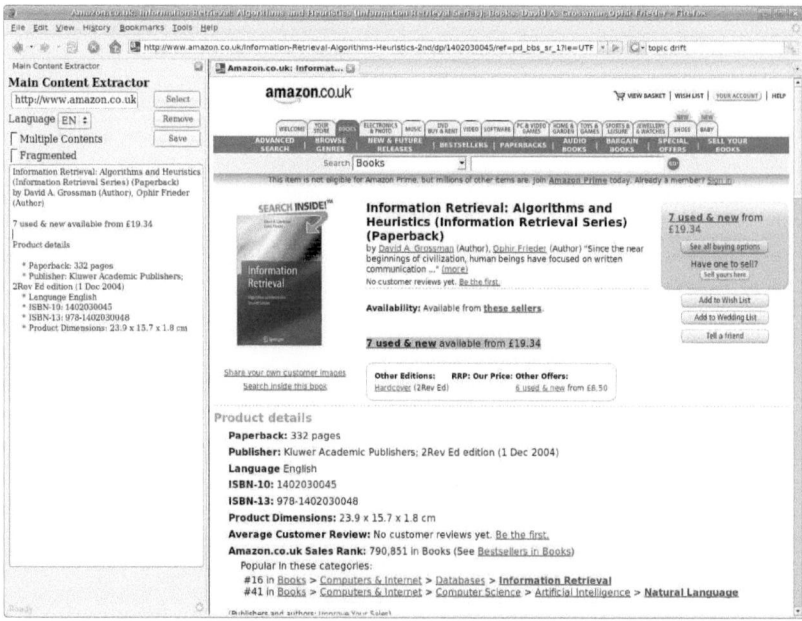

Figure 5.6: The Firefox browser with the activated extension for outlining the main content.

gold standard for the main content: employing a human user and constructing specialised extractor programs.

The human expert is asked to look at different web documents and outline the main content. A self implemented extension to the Mozilla Firefox browser supports the user in the task and allows him or her to save an HTML document together with its meta information and the selected text of the main content. As can be seen in figure 5.6, the extension is located in a sidebar and consists of a large text editor component for the main content and several controls to handle the meta data. The user can repeatedly select text in the web document by highlighting it with the mouse and copy it into the editor component. Once the main content has been completely transferred into the editor and the meta data settings of language etc. have been made, the browser extension provides the functionality to store the HTML source code of the original document, the outlined main content and the meta data to the file system. A separated Java program is used to compile the single files into a package structure as used by the evaluation framework.

This approach was used to create a very diversified test package. It consists of a collection of 65 documents from a variety of web sites with different backgrounds. Including e-commerce online shops, newspapers portals with short news flashes and full articles, manuals and references, the collection covers a wide range of different web pages containing

5 Evaluating Content Extraction

Table 5.2: Overview of the automatically generated test packages.

Package	Web site	URL	Language	Documents
bbc	BBC online	http://news.bbc.co.uk	English	1000
chip	Chip online	http://www.chip.de	German	361
economist	Economist.com	http://www.economist.com	English	250
espresso	L'espresso	http://espresso.repubblica.it	Italian	139
golem	Golem	http://golem.de	German	1000
heise	heise online	http://www.heise.de	German	1000
repubblica	La Repubblica.it	http://www.repubblica.it	Italian	1000
slashdot	Slashdot	http://slashdot.org	English	364
spiegel	Spiegel online	http://www.spiegel.de	German	1000
telepolis	Telepolis	http://www.telepolis.de	German	1000
wiki	Wikipedia	http://de.wikipedia.org	German	1000
yahoo	Yahoo! news	http://news.yahoo.com	English	1000
zdf	ZDF heute.de	http://www.heute.de	German	422

textual main contents. To reduce the impact of making an unlucky choice of documents which represent outliers caused by extreme forms of single articles, five typical pages from each website were included in the package, if possible relating to different topics.

The specialised extractors for particular web sites are based on the Java networking API, the SAX oriented HTML parser mentioned in 2.1.2 and the package management functionality of the evaluation framework. They are basically equivalent to hand coded wrappers for locating the main content in web documents. To build the packages it is then sufficient to download several documents from the according web sites and extract the main content. Also the meta data of the documents can be harvested or extracted automatically. Packages created in this way allow massive testing of a CE method on documents with different contents but similar structure, thus, they provide a good base for evaluating the stability of the method.

The packages created with this approach are listed in table 5.2. All the web sites used to create the packages have in common that they provide textual main contents; the kind, the style and the length of this content, instead, varies. The documents also cover a large range of different layouts and web design techniques to reflect several different scenarios: the documents of some the web sites are quite rich in additional contents, others consist of little more than the main content; some have a quite structured or fragmented main content, in others the main content consists of a single block of text; some are rich in graphics, others contain only few images; some documents are written are in English, others in German and yet others in Italian.

In most cases the main content is quite obvious to spot. The only tricky case is represented by the documents of the slashdot package. As already mentioned in 4.1, the main article of those documents is always extended by a rather lengthy discussion thread created by the slashdot users. We will consider the discussion not to be part of the main content.

This test data of manually and automatically created gold standards forms altogether 14 packages with a total of 9,601 documents available for the evaluation of CE algorithms. Appendix A contains more details about the packages and how the gold standards were obtained.

5.4.2 Algorithms

Not all single document CE algorithms have been developed to an extent that they are ready to be used. Some of the papers we found dealing with CE remain vague about implementing the proposed concept, even less provide a reference implementation. The more developed algorithms were already presented in 3.2, accordingly our comparison of algorithms takes into consideration only those approaches, namely Crunch, BTE, DSC, LQF, FeatureExtractor and K-FeatureExtractor.

But even most those algorithms are presented only in theory and it was impossible to find an implementation. Only the Crunch framework can be downloaded and run as an independent application [KGB05]. For BTE exists a publicly available reference implementation in Python [Fin05]. The other algorithms had to be implemented from scratch, following as close as possible the descriptions in literature. Where description details were missing, small gaps were filled at best knowledge to follow the ideas of the algorithms. In the case of the FeatureExtractor and K-FeatureExtractor algorithms it was necessary to contact the authors to clarify some open questions.

The CE algorithms were implemented in Java. Beyond having a very rich standard API, especially in the field of web technologies, this allowed to reuse some of the code written for the evaluation framework. Furthermore, there are several available libraries for standard tasks: the JTidy program, for instance, to correct syntactical errors in HTML documents and to build DOM tree representation.

So, while the theoretic background of the algorithms has been described in detail in chapter 3 about related work, here we will take a look at the algorithms from a practical point of view. We will describe a few implementation details and give an example of how they find the main content of a web document using the news article from the Yahoo web site shown in figure 5.7. This web page is certainly not representative for a general evaluation, but can help to get a subjective impression of the performance and to possibly discover some weak points of the algorithms. For this purpose we will always take a look at the general shape of the web document and in detail how the upper part of the main content is affected.

The evaluation framework was designed to incorporate the CE filters as proxy servers in a network environment. Hence, it is necessary to provide a simple proxy server, which needs to be capable of modifying web documents when forwarding them. The option of modifying a document will be used by the CE filters to remove the additional contents.

Under this aspect, Crunch is the easiest application to test as it is designed as a ready to use proxy server itself. We use version 2.0 with standard settings. The output of Crunch for our example web page from Yahoo is shown in figure 5.8. The changed layout and

5 Evaluating Content Extraction

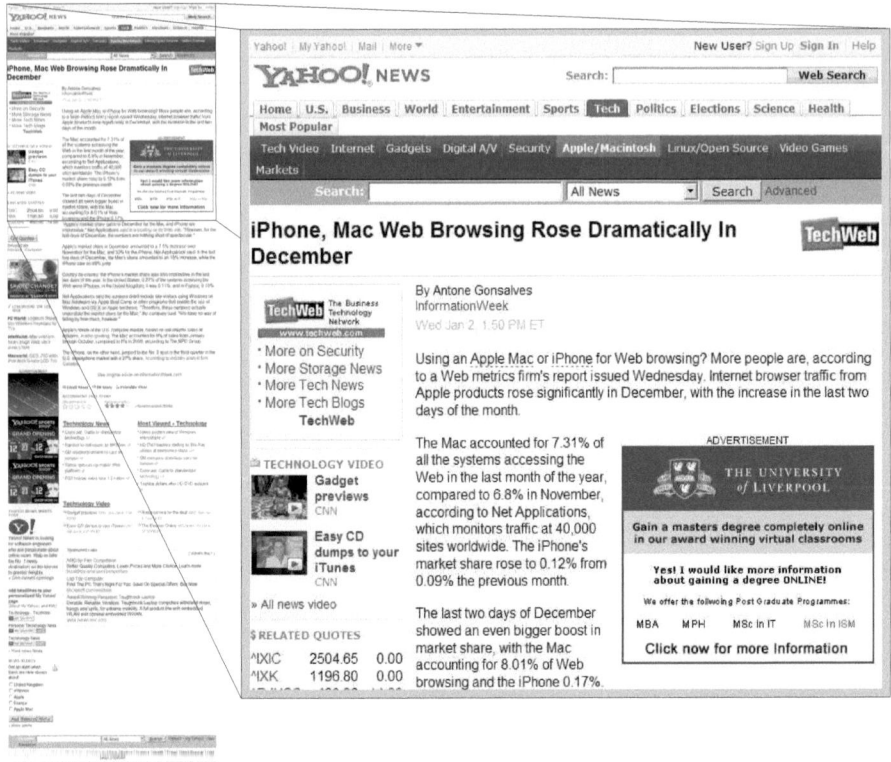

Figure 5.7: Original form of the Yahoo news article prior to any CE.

the removal of images are due to the rewriting and restructuring that is part of Crunch's extraction process. Beyond this, the example shows clearly how Crunch removes text lists and link lists with its internal LQF. Concerning the other kinds of content Crunch is quite conservative and rather removes too little than too much of them.

For the other algorithms we will use a very simple, self implemented and Java based HTTP proxy with a standardised interface for content filters. The CE algorithms are communicating with the proxy via this interface. For an easier incorporation with this proxy we use a reimplementation of the BTE algorithm in Java which follows exactly the Python reference implementation. This has the additional advantage that all algorithms are realised in Java. Hence, none of them should have particular advantages or disadvantages in time performance due to the underlying programming language. The tokenisation of a web document in word and tag tokens as required for BTE or DSC is based on the HTML

5.4 Comparison of Existing Single Document Algorithms

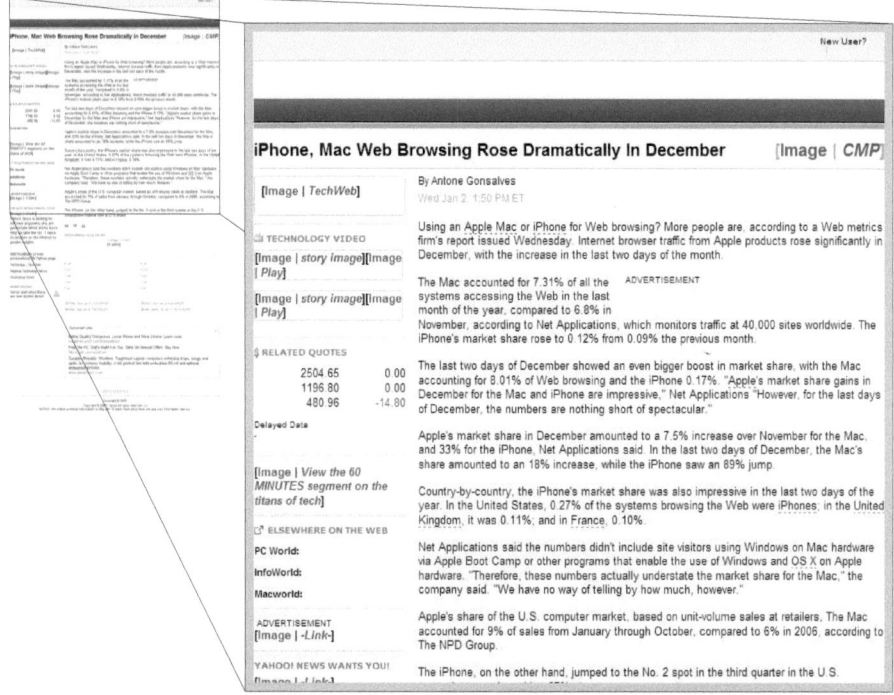

Figure 5.8: The Yahoo news article filtered with Crunch.

parser mentioned in 2.1.2 for locating tags and a function to split up strings at white space characters for distinguishing single words.

The result of the BTE extraction of our example document can be seen in figure 5.9. It extracts far too much; only the navigation menu at the top of the page has been removed. Optimising the extract to contain most words while excluding most tags seems not to work very well with the Yahoo page. The additional contents are probably too rich in words and contain relatively few tags.

Unlike the publications on Crunch and BTE, the paper introducing the DSC algorithm mentions no reference implementation. Further, the approach was originally not intended for CE at all but served solely for distinguishing between documents which contain a text article as main content versus those which do not. Hence, we have to provide an implementation of the algorithm ourselves. To do so, we can exploit the document tokenisation developed for BTE and use it to build the document slope curve. Following precisely the description of the algorithm as in 3.2.3, the extract generated by DSC on the Yahoo article looks like in figure 5.10. It seems DSC tends to extract too little of the main content as the

5 Evaluating Content Extraction

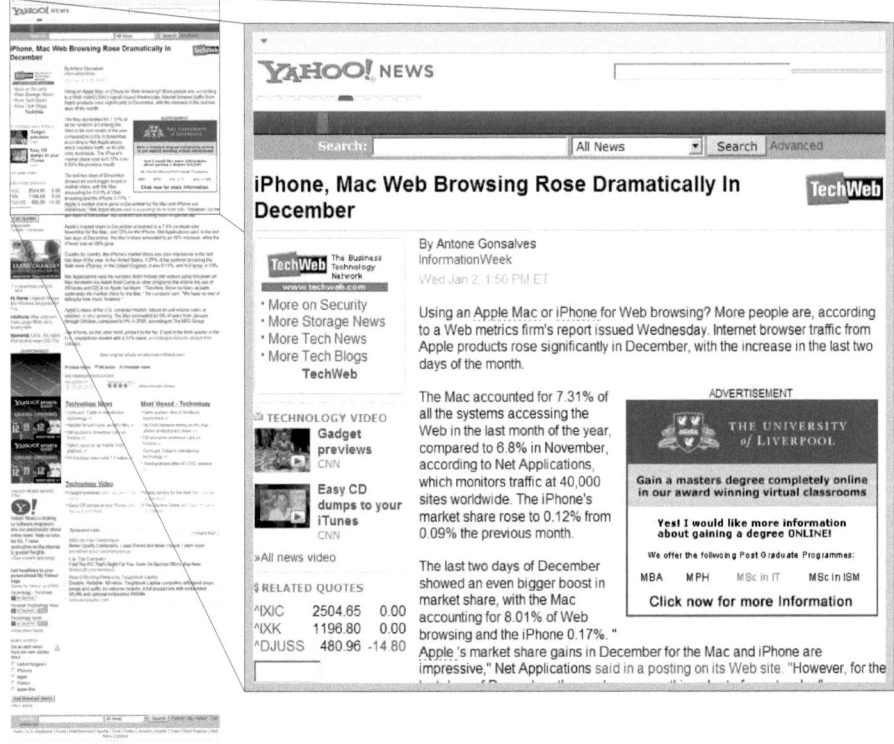

Figure 5.9: The Yahoo news article filtered with BTE.

headline and the first paragraph are missing. However, the result is very precise – most of the additional contents have been removed as well.

Also for FeatureExtractor and K-FeatureExtractor we have to implement the algorithm based on the description in the related literature [DMG05b] alone. The DOM access to a document is realised via the according functions of JTidy. An e-mail exchange with Sandip Debnath, one of the authors of the algorithm, clarified a few open questions about the web page segmentation and that the employed k-means clustering algorithm has to be used with a setting of $k = 3$, i.e. to form three clusters. Therefore, following the descriptions closely and using the original setting of forming three clusters, the performance of our implementation should correspond quite closely to the one of the original paper. In figure 5.11 the extract of the K-FeatureExtractor algorithm is shown. Applied to our example document, it seems to perform quite well as it extracts the entire article body. The headline is missing, though, and also some additional contents in the footer remained undetected.

5.4 Comparison of Existing Single Document Algorithms

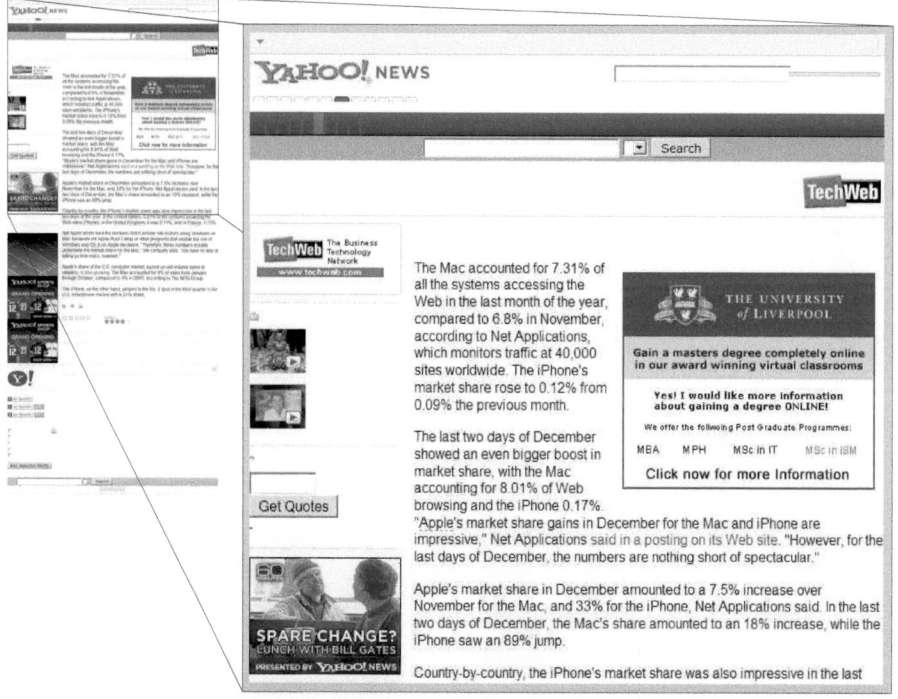

Figure 5.10: The Yahoo news article filtered with DSC.

As the LQF extractors may have several variations, we will use only one representative, general algorithm which follows the formal description as given in 3.2.4. The extraction is based on a block local link/text removal ratio, which does not take into consideration nested blocks. If this ratio of links is above a certain threshold the entire block is discarded as not being part of the main content. As threshold we use ratios of 0.25, 0.5 and 0.75 to evaluate different settings. This corresponds to removing those regions in a document for which more than a quarter, more than half or more than three quarters of the text resides in hyperlinks. The effect of LQF on the example web page can be seen in figure 5.12. As expected, it eliminates navigation menus and link lists very well but it fails to remove any additional content which is not characterised by a high rate of hyperlinks.

Except the above mentioned CE algorithms we will further use a proxy which serves the documents unchanged. This "plain" method for CE will always score a perfect recall as it certainly extracts all relevant contents, but it will perform poorly considering the precision as it extracts all irrelevant contents as well. This pseudo-method corresponds to

5 Evaluating Content Extraction

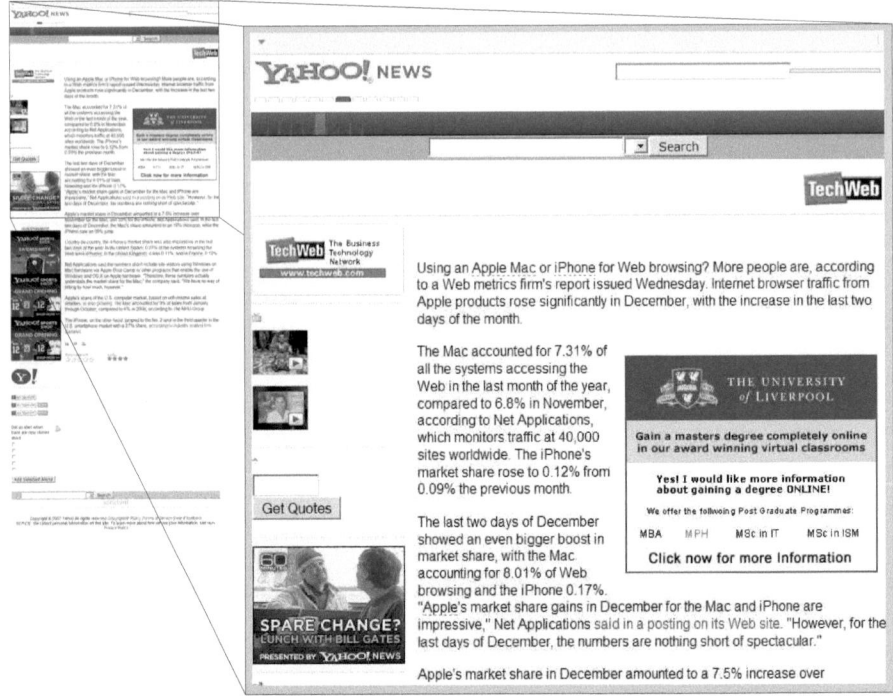

Figure 5.11: The Yahoo news article filtered with K-FeatureExtractor.

not using CE at all and allows to claim from any CE algorithm to perform better than this alternative, hence, it will serve as a baseline in the evaluation process

So, with Crunch, BTE, DSC, FeatureExtractor, K-FeatureExtractor, LQF with the three threshold settings and the plain method as baseline, we will evaluate altogether nine different methods for CE.

5.4.3 Evaluation Process

The evaluation process is set up as follows. We conduct an evaluation run for all possible combinations of packages and algorithms. Hence, we create a total of $9 \cdot 14 = 126$ CSV files containing altogether all the results for each single document.

Those results are then compiled into a graphical presentation to allow an easier analysis and comparison of this huge amount of data. To do so, we compute for each evaluation run an average value for recall, precision and F1 separately for all levels of granularity, as well as an average for the processing time per kB and the estimate for the standard deviation of F1 over all the documents. Further, to allow the direct comparison of the performance of

5.4 Comparison of Existing Single Document Algorithms

Figure 5.12: The Yahoo news article filtered with LQF and a threshold of 0.25.

the different methods, we integrate the average values of each measure across all methods concerning the same package. That is, we take, for example, the F1 performances of all methods on the same package and plot them in a single diagram, to see how the methods perform in direct comparison. To see the influence of the different levels of granularity, the performance values based on the character sequence, the word sequence, the bag of words and the set of words are displayed in the same graph. Continuing our example of the F1 performance, we will obtain as a result the characteristic curve of the F1 scores for each CE method. The combination of the curves of several CE algorithms in one chart shows the relative and absolute performance of the methods at all levels of granularity.

The chart in figure 5.13 shows an example of how these curves look like for the F1 performance of all of our nine CE methods concerning all levels of granularity. The chart is read as follows: the title of the diagram tells that the chart in this case plots the F1 performance on the heise package. Each CE method is represented by a line with a different colour; the assignment of colours to the extraction algorithms is indicated in the legend. FeatureExtractor and K-FeatureExtractor are abbreviated by *fe* and *kfe* respectively; the

5 Evaluating Content Extraction

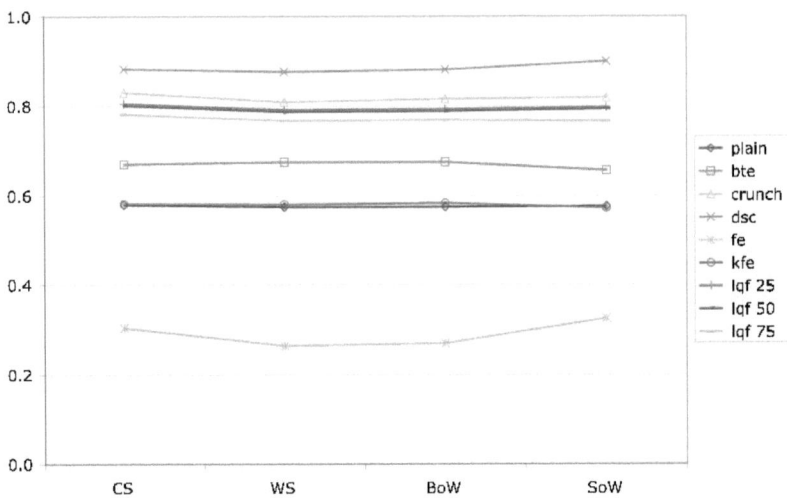

Figure 5.13: F1 performance of the CE algorithms on the heise package.

other methods are abbreviated as before. The granularity of the performance measures can be read from the labels on the x-axis: CS for the character sequence, WS for word sequence, BoW for bag of words and SoW for the set of words model underlying the document representation. The y-axis shows the actual performance and ranges from 0 to 1 according to the possible values of F1.

5.4.4 Results

Having explained how to read the charts of the evaluation results, we can now focus the attention on the actual performance of the CE methods. Most of them perform in a comparable manner across the mayor part of the evaluation packages. The results for the heise package shown in figure 5.13 are quite typical and representative for most other packages. So, the considerations that follow can be observed in the heise chart but are valid for nearly all the samples.

Looking at the results in general, the first thing to notice is that the different levels of granularity do not influence the resulting performance very much. On the heise package in particular, the relative performance of the CE algorithms remains unchanged under all document models: the algorithms are always ranked in the same order independently of the granularity. With few exceptions this behaviour can be observed in most cases – at least for the average F1 scores.

124

5.4 Comparison of Existing Single Document Algorithms

Table 5.3: Word sequence F1 scores for all packages and CE algorithms.

	bbc	chip	economist	espresso	golem	heise	manual	repubblica	slashdot	spiegel	telepolis	wiki	yahoo	zdf
bte	0.676	0.262	0.736	0.835	0.532	0.674	0.409	0.842	0.113	0.749	0.927	0.853	0.602	0.875
crunch	0.756	0.342	0.815	0.810	0.837	0.810	0.382	0.887	0.123	0.706	0.910	0.725	0.738	0.772
dsc	0.937	0.708	0.881	0.862	0.958	0.877	0.403	0.925	0.252	0.902	0.859	0.594	0.780	0.847
fe	0.147	0.015	0.002	0.035	0.273	0.264	0.141	0.099	0.067	0.002	0.143	0.236	0.109	0.015
kfe	0.677	0.276	0.697	0.035	0.200	0.580	0.357	0.097	0.077	0.689	0.823	0.593	0.673	0.491
lqf-25	0.834	0.502	0.732	0.667	0.926	0.791	0.387	0.826	0.135	0.790	0.906	0.690	0.708	0.579
lqf-50	0.826	0.502	0.720	0.666	0.806	0.787	0.381	0.816	0.127	0.775	0.906	0.752	0.670	0.578
lqf-75	0.798	0.473	0.694	0.665	0.735	0.767	0.374	0.816	0.118	0.749	0.906	0.785	0.644	0.571
plain	0.595	0.173	0.613	0.624	0.502	0.575	0.371	0.704	0.106	0.549	0.858	0.823	0.582	0.514

Also the ranking of the algorithms itself is quite typical and is confirmed by the results on most other packages, in particular the result that DSC scores the highest F1 values. While the figures 5.13 to 5.21 illustrate some the evaluation results graphically for the more significant packages, table 5.3 gives a very compact but complete overview of the word sequence based F1 performance of all methods on all packages. It can be seen in this table, that the telepolis, wiki and zdf packages are the only ones where DSC is outperformed by other methods[4]. However, on the telepolis package DSC is obtaining very good results and is inferior to the other CE methods merely because they perform extraordinarily well. Also on the documents taken from ZDF heute it is second to BTE only by a narrow margin. So, the wiki package is the only one, where DSC shows significant drawbacks. But as we will see soon, wiki pages are problematic in general in a CE context.

In the performance ranking of the algorithms, the second position after DSC is not as clear. BTE, LQF and Crunch show their weak and strong sides, depending on the package. We will now take a closer look at these algorithms. As on the heise package Crunch is better than LQF, which is in turn better than BTE, we will look at the algorithms in this order.

Crunch achieves good results not only on the heise but also on most other packages. However, on some documents the performance seems to drop remarkably, e.g. on the chip package. An explanation for this outlier in performance could be that Crunch is slightly outdated in version 2.0. The incorporated heuristics are based on assumptions about how web pages are designed and coded – but design and coding guidelines have changed since the publication of Crunch and its latest update in 2004. Another observation is that Crunch performs better than LQF on the major part of the test packages. This is

---

[4]Looking at the figures, BTE seems better also on the manual package. However, a difference in F1 scores of 0.006 is so small, that the two methods can be considered of equivalent quality for this package.

not very surprising, as Crunch involves an LQF implementation itself. The additional heuristics might then slightly improve the results in most cases. The observation that the additional heuristics do not always lead to an improvement might be ascribed to fact that the assumptions underlying those heuristics do not fit the documents in these cases. A reason for the failure of the heuristics might be once more the changes in web design.

The different versions of LQF, instead, are doing usually a quite reliable job. Their performance is pretty good on all of the test packages. The threshold setting, remarkably, influences the results surprisingly little. Quite often there is hardly any difference between the F1 values for the thresholds of 0.25, 0.5 and 0.75. If a difference occurs it is usually the 0.25 threshold which performs slightly better. Higher settings probably prevent additional contents with some but not too many links from being removed. The biggest drawback of LQF is its incapability to recognise those additional contents which do not consist mainly of hyperlinks.

Also the BTE algorithm usually delivers good results, though not always at the same height as Crunch. In few packages it even outperforms DSC, on others instead it is falling far behind. On average BTE achieves the same ranking as LQF in relation to the other methods. When looking at the individual packages, instead, the performance of the two approaches varies noticeably. The reason that sometimes it is LQF and sometimes it is BTE obtaining better results is very likely found in the two very different approaches for locating the main content. BTE effectively looks for a long text, while LQF excludes parts of the document which contain too many links. Accordingly, it depends on the kind of document which one of the algorithms performs better.

All of the so far mentioned methods score good results. Leaving aside the wiki package, they are in particular always achieving better F1 scores than the plain method. Hence, they more or less really do manage to locate the main content. This observation cannot be made in general for the FeatureExtractor and K-FeatureExtractor.

FeatureExtractor in particular shows a remarkably bad performance. It achieves nearly always the worst results, except for one case where K-FeatureExtractor performs still worse. And while K-FeatureExtractor apart from this one exception seems a much better approach, it still has quite often an F1 score below the one of the baseline of the plain method.

These results seem quite confusing, given the observations of Debnath et al. when evaluating their algorithm in [DMG05b]. They calculated very high scores for the block based recall and precision measures in most test cases for both of their algorithms. Also the performance of K-FeatureExtractor on our example Yahoo web page seemed better.

Looking at the details of the algorithms and the evaluation method of Debnath et al. explains the divergence between the observed results. Both algorithms look for blocks in the document which are particularly "pure" with respect to a certain desired feature. For a textual main content, as in our case, the desired feature is text. So, the algorithms need to look for those blocks containing preferably only text. Now, while short blocks, like headlines or teaser texts, usually contain no other content beside text and not even other HTML elements, the article body – and thus the major part of the main content –

5.4 Comparison of Existing Single Document Algorithms

is frequently a bit more structured. It very likely consists of several paragraphs, contains hyperlinks or uses simple formatting instructions like changing the font style to bold or italic writing. These small structures cause the main article block to be less pure than the headline or teaser and, thus, might cause it to be discarded. This effect occurs actually quite often in practice and FeatureExtractor eliminates all contents from a document except the headline. The block clustering mechanism in K-FeatureExtractor partly counterbalances this behaviour. However, this balance is not very stable and can easily be tipped to the wrong side. If the 100% pure text blocks form a cluster on their own, while the slightly less pure blocks of the article body form another cluster, the same results can be observed as for FeatureExtractor: headline and teaser remain, all the other contents are deleted.

The fact, that Debnath et al. observed nevertheless a good performance is probably due to their evaluation method and an unlucky choice of test documents. In the motivation for new evaluation measures we have already seen an example of when block based IR measures like F1, recall and precision can cause distorted and deceiving results. While the example we used then was constructed and not based on an existing document for the sake of simplicity, the described problem is very real for the two FeatureExtractor algorithms. Both algorithms very likely classify most blocks correctly into additional and main content, but simply fail on the largest block of main content. Additionally it seems that the documents used for evaluation in [DMG05b] consisted of one pure text block for the main content only, so the sample fitted perfectly to the algorithm. But for some few, other web documents, also the evaluation in the paper of Debnath lists some extreme drops in F1 performance, which correspond more to the results we can see here. So, FeatureExtractor and K-FeatureExtractor really do have a bad CE performance and our evaluation measures reflect this very well.

When choosing a CE algorithm for a particular application, for which the impact of missing or superfluous data is known, it is also interesting to take a closer look at precision and recall separately. After all, precision gives the ratio of superfluous data in the result and recall provides information about the ratio of missing data. Using again the heise package as quite representative for all packages, we look at the respective recall and precision charts in figure 5.14 and 5.15.

The precision performance is quite interesting. All methods are more precise than the baseline of the plain method. And the ranking under F1 seems to correspond to the gain in precision – except for FeatureExtractor and K-FeatureExtractor. As already explained above, those two algorithms might be quite precise, but tend to extract far too little.

This behaviour is also reflected in the charts in 5.15 showing the recall scores. Especially FeatureExtractor falls far behind the other methods. DSC and Crunch loose points under the recall measure as well, but not of the same magnitude. This observation clearly shows the tradeoff between precision and recall. A method scoring high in recall usually is poor in precision, a common problem in the field of IR. However, it seems that with little loss in recall the methods usually achieve a quite good improvement in the precision rating. And DSC seems – in the light of the F1 measure – to strike the best balance between a loss of recall and the gain in precision.

5 Evaluating Content Extraction

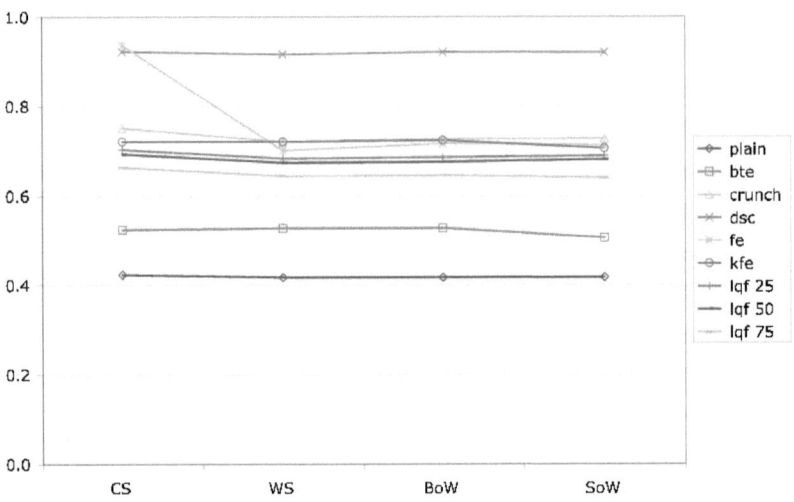

Figure 5.14: Precision performance of the CE algorithms on the heise package.

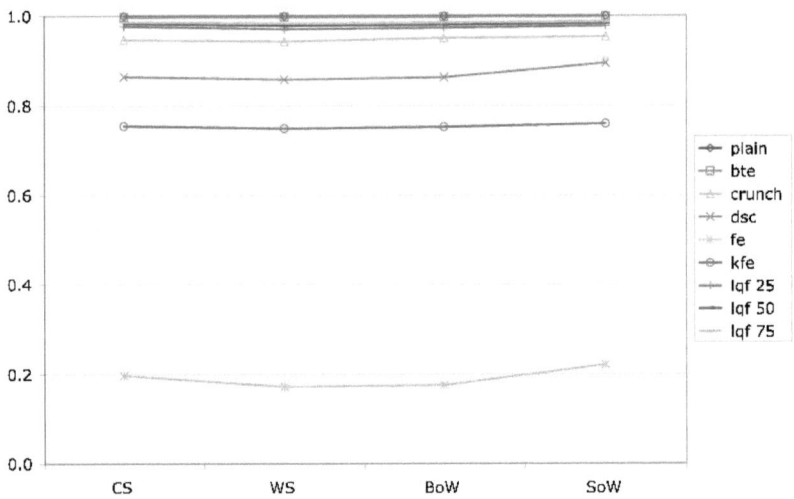

Figure 5.15: Recall performance of the CE algorithms on the heise package.

5.4 Comparison of Existing Single Document Algorithms

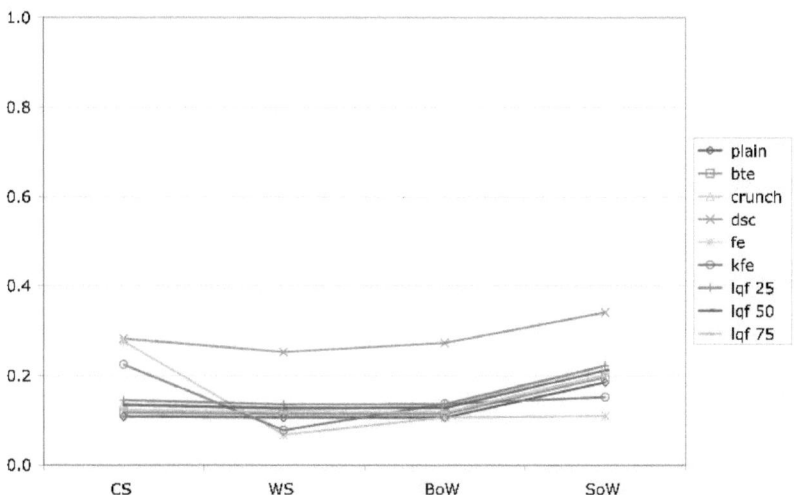

Figure 5.16: F1 performance of the CE algorithms on the slashdot package.

So far we looked mainly at the evaluation results on the heise package. Referring again to table 5.3 above, we can say that most other packages are comparable, with slight variations in the order of the CE algorithms coming second to DSC. In addition to the relative performance of the algorithms, also the absolute scores for F1, recall and precision are similar – in particular the extraction performance of DSC is settled on a constantly high level. In appendix B the evaluation results for all packages, all CE methods and all evaluation measures under the different document models are listed with all details in tabular form.

However, it is worth take a look at two particularly interesting packages in detail: slashdot and wiki. They are of particular interest, because they reveal some of the typical problems of CE algorithms.

Figure 5.16 shows, that the F1 performance of the CE methods on the slashdot package is in general much lower than on all other packages. This is due to the fact that we excluded the users' discussion and remarks on the original news article from the main content. Under the aspect of style and appearance, these discussions and remarks fit very well the description of the main content and as the news article is additionally very short its appearance does not dominate the web page. All heuristics which look for a longer text will accordingly tend to extract also the user discussion, if not even exclude the short main content. Hence, we can deduce that short main contents are difficult to retrieve, especially if the documents are polluted with additional contents containing longer texts.

5 Evaluating Content Extraction

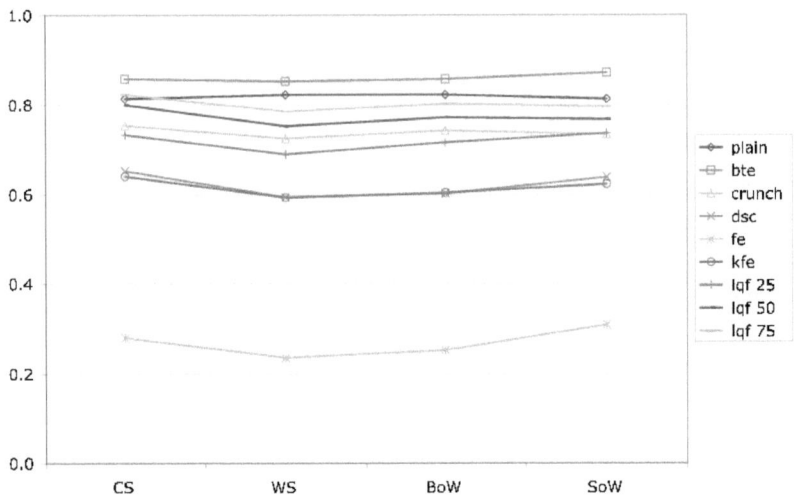

Figure 5.17: F1 performance of the CE algorithms on the wiki package.

The F1 scores concerning the packages built from Wikipedia documents are presented in figure 5.17. Also the wiki package turns out to be very tricky for all the algorithms and, at least in the light of the F1-measures, it nearly seems best not to use any CE method at all. Only BTE achieves better results than the plain method. Taking into account that basically all methods try to identify parts in a document with little links or long texts with no tags, it becomes obvious, that a wiki article with its structured and, thus, fragmented content and its usually high rate of in-text-links is the worst scenario possible.

The problem of the methods with the wiki package becomes obvious when looking at recall and precision separately, as shown in the figures 5.18 and 5.19. While precision, in comparison to the baseline, improves only a little or even decreases for some algorithms, the recall rate drops drastically. So, here the usually observed tradeoff between recall and precision does not seem to apply.

It remains to look at the stability of the algorithms, i.e. the estimates for the standard deviation concerning the F1 values within each package. We see those values in figure 5.20 for the heise package. In addition to being representative again, this is one of the largest packages as well. Accordingly it provides a large base of experiments to estimate the standard deviation.

The chart shows that the standard deviation of the F1 measure roughly ranges from 0.1 to 0.15 for all methods. An observation which can be made in all automatically created

5.4 Comparison of Existing Single Document Algorithms

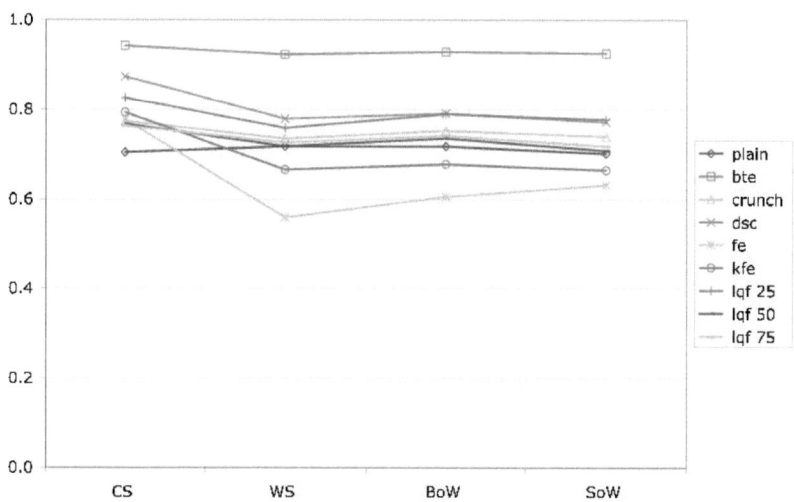

Figure 5.18: Precision performance of the CE algorithms on the wiki package.

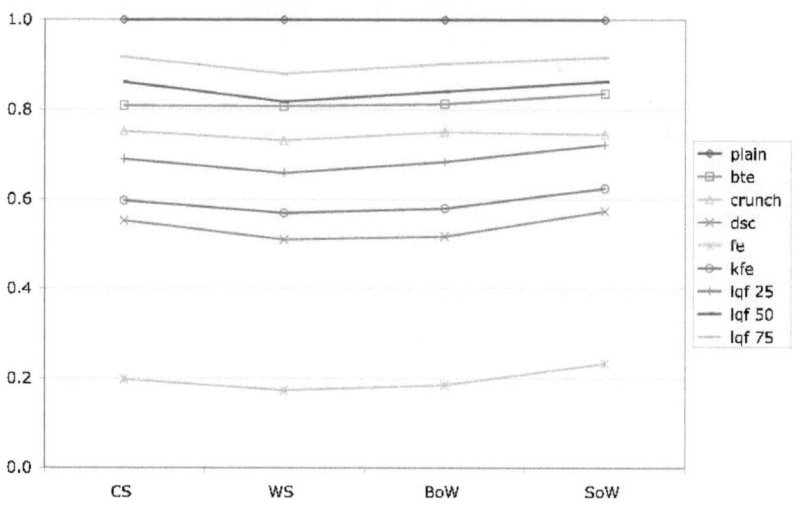

Figure 5.19: Recall performance of the CE algorithms on the wiki package.

5 Evaluating Content Extraction

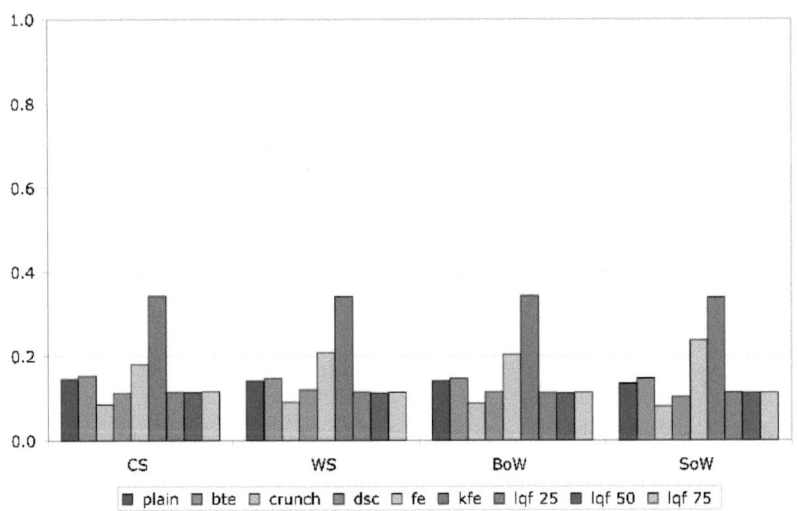

Figure 5.20: Stability of the CE algorithms on the heise package.

packages[5]. Concerning stability, the generally bad performing FeatureExtractor and K-FeatureExtractor are an exception again. Especially the instable behaviour of the latter underlines the remark of above on the fragile outcome of the clustering of blocks according to their purity. This could explain as well, why the performance of K-FeatureExtractor seemed different for our example Yahoo document: it might simply be one of those cases where the unstable algorithm delivered quite good results.

Looking lastly at the time performance of the algorithms in figure 5.21, we can say that DSC and FeatureExtractor are the fastest, though the differences with other methods are negligible. Only BTE peeks out, by being on average much slower in processing a document. On some packages the processing time of BTE is even beyond one second per kB. Considering an average document size of 50 to 70 kB, BTE will take about a minute to locate the main content. Its incorporated approach of formulating CE as an optimisation problem and finding a solution to it turns out to be expensive for long documents. This renders BTE unsuitable for use in an on-the-fly system.

---

[5]The standard deviation in the manual package is higher as the documents have a much more varied form.

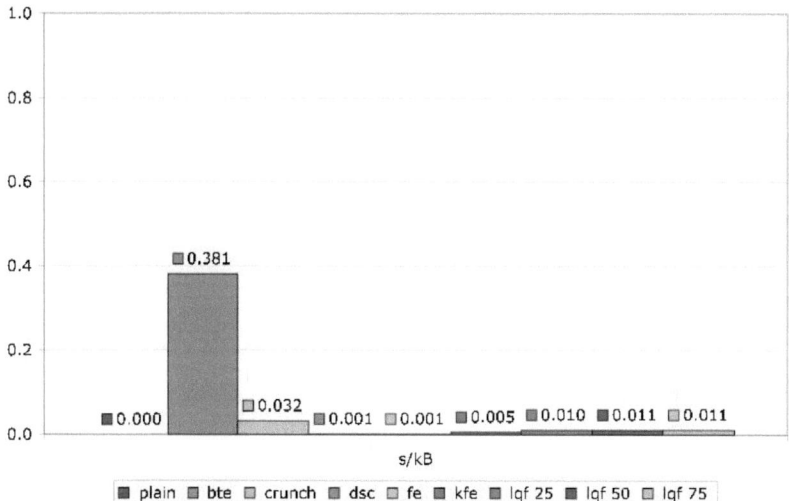

Figure 5.21: Time performance of the CE algorithms on the heise package.

5.5 Summary

The evaluation framework and the incorporated evaluation measures have proved to work as intended and the results correspond quite well to the subjectively perceived performance of the CE algorithms. The different levels of granularity used for evaluation measures showed to be more or less equivalent. However, in comparison with the block based evaluation measures, they reflect far better the real performance of CE algorithms and are less prone to deliver misleading results.

Considering the existing CE methods, it is ironically DSC which is the best performing CE algorithm, as it originally was not even intended to be used for CE. The results of Crunch are very good as well, but demonstrate in some cases how the heuristics underlying a single document CE algorithm can become outdated and cause the system performance to drop significantly under certain circumstances. The LQF extractors on the other hand revealed to be relatively stable and surprisingly tolerant to the threshold setting.

The performance of the two FeatureExtractor algorithms is quite disappointing. Given the observations and evaluations in the original paper of Debnath et al. one would have expected far better results. This demonstrates quite impressively, how important the development of new evaluation measures was in order to obtain reliable results. Finally, BTE is a good algorithm but it is too slow for being incorporated in time critical systems.

5 Evaluating Content Extraction

Beyond the performance of the algorithms it turned out that short or very fragmented textual main contents are difficult to locate, as shown by the documents taken from the Slashdot and Wikipedia web site.

In the next chapter we will develop three new single document CE algorithms. In doing so, we will pay attention to the observed problems in order to overcome some of the difficulties.

6 New Single Document Algorithms

In this chapter we will develop, describe and finally evaluate three new CE algorithms: *largest pagelet*, *largest size increase* and *content code blurring*. The first two algorithms are based on work in the related fields of wrapper generation and TD. They represent a variation of the original CE task. The aim of this variation is to locate the smallest DOM sub-tree which contains all of the main content fragments, even if this sub-tree contains some additional contents as well. Before going into the details of those algorithms, we will motivate this concept of modifying the search for the main content to finding a single DOM sub-tree. For this purpose we will describe a few application scenarios where this slightly modified version of CE can be of interest.

Content code blurring, the third algorithm presented, is instead a classical CE algorithm which is again aiming at outlining the main content as good as possible. It is an entirely novel algorithm, based on the idea to find those parts in a web document which have a uniform format as a homogeneous format is quite characteristic for the main content. It also incorporates some techniques which particularly aim at helping with the problematic documents we have seen in the last chapter. We will develop three variants of this algorithm and see that on most documents it performs better than the methods we have seen so far.

6.1 Locating the DOM Sub-Tree of the Main Content

The first two algorithms we will develop in this chapter try to find the smallest possible DOM sub-tree which still covers all of the main content. The aim of finding this main content sub-tree seems, at first sight, contradictory to the observations made in the last chapter. After all, the results in chapter 5 reveal that the CE approaches which perform better, are those capable of locating also split up and distributed main contents. The best example is the comparison between DSC and BTE, which are both based on the same data structure and conceptual idea: DSC being able to deal with fragmented and distributed main contents is in general the better CE solution.

We will now describe four scenarios to elucidate this apparent contradiction of introducing the variation of the CE task of finding a single DOM sub-tree. In these scenarios the process of locating a particular node in the DOM tree which is the root of all of the main content fragments can be interesting or even more important than outlining the main content as precisely as possible.

Exchange of the underlying template framework: The templates used by WCMS quite often provide a single slot for the main content. Even though the content in this slot might later on be enriched on-the-fly and extended with commercials or related information, the article or text which makes up the main content is usually not fragmented or split up to anticipate this modification. Hence, the main content usually resides in a single DOM sub-tree. Extracting contents from one template based document and including them in another template structure gives rise to the need of identifying the root node of the main content slot in the first document. Copying contents from one document into another one while maintaining the structure of the content is much easier when dealing with DOM sub-trees, as there is no need to pay attention to the resulting document having a syntactically correct HTML structure. Personal information management and e-learning suites are examples of applications that can benefit from this scenario of information integration. These applications can include the main content of a document and its structured DOM sub-tree into their own repository without having to bother about the additional contents.

Discovery of regions for editing: In 3.2.6 we mentioned the IsaWiki system. It allows to personalise and edit arbitrary web pages in a Wiki style. To preserve the general structure of the web pages, editing is restricted to those regions which contribute to the content and do not serve structural purposes. To find these regions the rule-based elISA algorithm classifies document blocks into categories like content, navigation, commercial, etc. The document blocks correspond to DOM sub-trees. Hence, providing additional information about the sub-tree which contains the main content or at least which part of the document has to be analysed more carefully for the presence of the main content supports this task and might improve the performance of elISA and related systems.

Pre-processor for other CE method. Locating a DOM node which most certainly contains the main content can also be suitable to aid other CE methods. By narrowing the focus of downstream CE methods on certain parts of the document, the extraction process might be faster and more reliable.

Template analysis: The last scenario we describe in this context is the analysis of the template that underlies an HTML document. As the main content certainly contributes most data for the final document, finding and outlining the root node of the main content slot allows deeper insights into the structures of a template. It might allow e.g. to recognise the structures outside the main content sub-tree as being most likely template induced. This application might serve TD tasks and is, in a certain way, complementary to the pre-processing scenario for CE applications.

In all these applications it is useful to pin-point a DOM node which is a common ancestor to all main content fragments and for which none of its child nodes satisfies this requirement. The algorithms we will describe in 6.2 and 6.3 are promising to fulfil this task. Given the specified scenarios we demand from such algorithms to achieve a high if not even perfect recall. Under this constraint they should also improve the precision scores in comparison to the alternative of not using CE at all, i.e. the plain method in our previous experiments. A high recall and an improved precision correspond exactly to fulfilling the described task of narrowing the focus on those parts of a document which certainly contain the main content.

6.2 Largest Size Increase

The XWRAP elite system of Han, Buttler and Pu [HBP01] has already been mentioned earlier during the discussion of related work in 3.1.2. It was said to be of particular interest in the context of CE as it comprises a pre-processing phase to locate the primary content. While finding the primary content in XWRAP is supposed to help the system focussing on certain HTML source code regions for building a wrapper, it is itself a variation of CE. We will now take a closer look at how the pre-processing phase of XWRAP is working and turn it into a CE filter.

6.2.1 Concept and Idea

Han et al. developed three heuristics to find the main or primary content in a document: *largest tag count* (LTC), *highest fanout* (HF) and *largest size increase* (LSI)[1].

The first two heuristics aim particularly at finding structured or semi-structured data in web documents, as this is the type of data wrappers search for. LTC counts the number of tags contained in a DOM sub-tree; a large number of tags corresponds to a highly structured content. HF slightly refines this approach by comparing the number of immediate child nodes. A DOM sub-tree with more direct children is more likely an immediate root node to the highly structured contents. For classical CE applications, those two approaches are not very useful, as a textual main content is usually not very structured. Quite opposite, the additional contents very likely will be much more structured.

The third heuristic instead, namely LSI, is intended to find a single node containing the textual main content. In order to find a part of the document containing the most and, presumably, main content, Han et al. calculate for each node in the DOM tree how much visible text content the node adds to the document. By looking at this increase relatively to the overall visible content of the parent node, it is possible to find the node which contributes more strongly to the contents of the document. For the content location phase of XWRAP, this information is important in combination with LTC and HF, as otherwise the primary content location phase might result in finding highly structured DOM sub-trees which do not contain any text content.

For us it is instead interesting to analyse the suitability of LSI to support CE. Interpreting the node with the largest size increase as the root node of the main content, allows turning the LSI algorithm into a CE method.

---

[1]Note that the largest size increase algorithm is entirely different from the concept of latent semantic indexing which is commonly abbreviated by LSI as well.

6.2.2 Adaptation and Implementation

There is not much adaptation work to do in order to use LSI for CE tasks. The algorithm, as it is shown in 6.1, can straight away be used for locating the DOM node with the largest size increase. The only gap to fill in the work of Han et al. is the way how to measure the amount of visible content in a sub-tree, i.e. to define how exactly the function `getText()` works. With this detail missing in the original publication, we will take the straight forward approach of counting the number of characters in the visible text nodes in the entire sub-tree. Superfluous white space characters will obviously not be taken into consideration, in the same way as texts in `style` and `script` nodes will be ignored.

Algorithm 6.1: LSI: finding the node with the largest size increase

Input: D: DOM representation of a document
Output: n: DOM node with the largest size increase
begin
$\quad N \leftarrow \text{nodes}(D)$;
$\quad lsi \leftarrow 0$;
$\quad n \leftarrow \text{rootNode}(D)$;
$\quad$ **foreach** $m \in N$ **do**
$\quad\quad v_m \leftarrow \text{length}(\text{getText}(m))$;
$\quad\quad C \leftarrow \text{descendents}(m)$;
$\quad\quad v_c^{\max} \leftarrow 0$;
$\quad\quad$ // Find largest child size
$\quad\quad$ **foreach** $c \in C$ **do**
$\quad\quad\quad v_c \leftarrow \text{length}(\text{getText}(c))$;
$\quad\quad\quad$ **if** $v_a^{\max} < v_c$ **then**
$\quad\quad\quad\quad v_c^{\max} \leftarrow v_c$;

$\quad\quad$ // Determine size increase of node
$\quad\quad si \leftarrow v_m - v_{c^{\max}}$;
$\quad\quad$ **if** $lsi < si$ **then**
$\quad\quad\quad n \leftarrow m$;
$\quad\quad\quad lsi \leftarrow si$;

$\quad$ **return** n
end

Once the node which adds most visible content to the document is found, the extraction process corresponds to deleting all visible text contents which are not contained in the according DOM sub-tree. The easiest way to realise this is to traverse the DOM tree and remove all text nodes. When coming across the main content root node as indicated by LSI, the traversal does not descent into this sub-tree. Accordingly the texts in this sub-tree are not removed.

The algorithm can easily be implemented in Java by using the DOM tree functionality for HTML documents, which is provided by the JTidy package [GTG+08]. In this way, the

CE adaptation of LSI can easily be incorporated into the proxy framework developed in the last chapter, thereby allowing to evaluate and to compare LSI with other approaches.

6.3 Largest Pagelet

We are now going to use another algorithm from the related work chapter as a basis for CE. The Page Partitioning [BYR02] of Bar-Yossef and Rajagopalan was discussed in 3.3.1 and is intended to locate pagelets. Pagelets are described as self-contained regions in a web document, i.e. regions which encapsulate a content, a navigation menu, a function or another atomic element. Looking at this informal description, also the main content represents one of those self-contained regions. As it usually will be the largest of them, we create a single document CE filter based on extracting the largest pagelet (LP).

6.3.1 Concept and Idea

The Page Partitioning algorithm was developed in the context of discovering template structures. Bar-Yossef and Rajagopalan understand templates as collections of recurrent, self-contained regions, i.e. the pagelets. So, in their notion pagelets are somehow the building bricks of a web page as they can be reused on different documents and provide thereby a template characteristic.

In order to discover templates – which was the original intention of the approach – it is accordingly necessary to locate the pagelets in a web document. This in turn requires a formal description of pagelets. To describe what makes up a pagelet from a syntactical point of view, Bar-Yossef and Rajagopalan use the following definition: a pagelet is a DOM node which does not have a pagelet as ancestor node and does not contain any child node with at least k links. The requirement that a pagelet has no pagelet node as an ancestor formulates a kind of maximality criterion. Otherwise all child nodes of a pagelet would be pagelets as well, as they certainly will not contain any children themselves which have k or more links.

Using the number of hyperlinks contained in child nodes as a characterisation for self-contained regions seems at first sight a strange approach. In particular, navigation menus can be considered a pagelet from the semantic description. But, given the syntactic definition, they will very likely be split up in smaller fragments.

However, for the concept of textual main content, the pagelet description seems to fit quite well. Hence, detecting the pagelets in a single HTML document and looking for the one which contains the most text is an interesting approach to find the main content.

6.3.2 Adaptation and Implementation

Based on the syntactic definition of pagelets, Bar-Yossef and Rajagopalan developed the Page Partitioning algorithm as shown in 6.2. Starting from a queue containing the root node of a document, they check for each pagelet candidate node in the queue, whether it has child nodes with at least k links. If this is the case, the current node is discarded as a pagelet and all its child nodes are added to the queue as new pagelet candidates. Otherwise, if no child node has k or more links, the node is classified to be a pagelet itself.

Algorithm 6.2: Page partitioning of Bar-Yossef and Rajagopalan

Input: D: HTML document, k threshold of number of hyperlinks per pagelet.
Output: P: set of pagelet nodes.
begin
    // Start with root node in queue
    $q.\text{append}(\text{rootNode}(D))$;
    $P \leftarrow \varnothing$;
    while $\neg\text{isEmpty}(q)$ **do**
        $n \leftarrow q.\text{pop}()$;
        $C \leftarrow \text{descendents}(n)$;
        if $\exists c \in C : \text{countLinks}(c) \geq k$ **then**
            foreach $c \in C$ **do**
                $q.\text{append}(c)$;
        else
            $P \leftarrow P \cup \{n\}$;
    return P
end

The Page Partitioning algorithm does not need to be adapted for using it in the CE environment. The only additional work is to find the largest among the pagelets determined by the Page Partitioning algorithm. As we are again interested in text, we search once more for the DOM sub-tree which contains most visible text in terms of characters. Just as for the LSI implementation, script and style contents and white space characters are ignored when determining the amount of content. Also the extraction process can be realised, as done for LSI, by using a tree traversal to remove the text from all DOM nodes which are not children of the node that represents the largest pagelet.

An important parameter for the Page Partitioning algorithm is k, the number of links in child nodes which causes a pagelet candidate to be split in smaller pagelets candidates. Bar-Yossef and Rajagopalan used a value of $k = 3$, but did not motivate this decision further. Hence, we will also take a look at other settings during evaluation.

6.4 Content Code Blurring

After LSI and LP, which have been adaptations and translations of other algorithms for CE purposes, content code blurring is an entirely novel algorithm. Further, it is a "traditional" CE algorithm in the sense that it focuses on outlining the main content as good as possible – not necessarily fixing it to the sub-tree of a particular DOM node.

6.4 Content Code Blurring

The idea underlying content code blurring is to take advantage of the visual impression a web page is supposed to achieve. Additional contents such as commercials, navigation menus, functional and design elements are usually highly formatted and contain little and short texts. The main content on the other hand is commonly a long and homogeneously formatted text. As in the source code of an HTML document any change of format is indicated by a tag, we will accordingly try to identify those parts of a document which contain a lot of (visible) text and few or no tags[2], i.e. areas with a lot of content and little code.

To give an example, figure 6.1 shows a fragment of an HTML document as it is rendered by a web browser and its source code form. Even in this quite small fragment we can see a main content and several additional contents. The main content is the text in the paragraph and reports about a list of alternative search engines. Additional contents appear in the shape of meta information about the date and time of publication, an image logo and a functional element to add user comments. The source code of the documents reflects quite clearly how the additional contents consist of much shorter texts and, at the same time, are much richer in markup code.

6.4.1 Concept and Idea

So, the idea and aim of content code blurring is to locate those regions in a document which contain "a lot of content and little code". To formalise this task we first of all need to formalise what is a region in a document, what exactly we mean by content and by code and how to measure the amount of content or code in the regions.

The question of what is content and what is code can be answered quite easily. Generally speaking, all the tags in the source code correspond to code while everything else corresponds to content. The tags after all provide the structure, the layout and the formatting of a web document, the text outside the tags makes up the content. There are, however, a few exceptions from this simple rule:

- HTML comments are ignored for obvious reasons, even though they form a part of the source code.

- White space like blanks, linefeeds and tabulators may be part of the text in their function to separate single words. But in the major part of currently found HTML documents they are also used to layout and prettyprint the source code. Commonly, the intention behind this white space is to improve the readability and maintainability of the code. In this function blanks, linefeeds and tabulators are neutral characters which are neither content nor code, accordingly we will ignore them.

- The data in `script` and `style` elements is usually encapsulated in comments and, as such, will be ignored as stated above. But even if this behaviour is considered

---
[2]We will not differentiate between the different kinds of tags, even if certain kinds of tags have a stronger influence on the layout than others.

6 New Single Document Algorithms

> **Posted by Hemos on Monday January 29, @09:12AM**
>
> ReadWriteWeb writes "Search Engine Optimizer (SEO) Charles S. Knight has compiled a list of <u>the top 100 alternative search engines</u>. The list includes Artificial Intelligence systems, Clustering engines, Recommendation Search engines, Metasearch, and many more hidden gems of search. People use four main search engines for 99.99% of their searches: Google, Yahoo!, MSN, and Ask.com (in that order). But Knight has discovered, via his work as an SEO, that in the other .01% lies a vast multitude of the most innovative and creative search engines around."
>
> [+] *(tagging beta)*

```
<div class="details">
  <b>Posted by
  <a href="http://everything2.com/index.pl?node_id=322">Hemos</a>
    on Monday January 29, @09:12AM</b><br>
</div>
<div class="body">
  <div class="topic">
    <a href="http://slashdot.org/search.pl?tid=95">
    <img src="http://images.slashdot.org/topics/topicinternet.gif"
         width="70" height="73" alt="The Internet"
         title="The Internet" ></a>
  </div>
  <div class="intro">
    <a href="http://www.readwriteweb.com/" rel="nofollow">ReadWriteWeb</a> writes
    <i>"Search Engine Optimizer (SEO) Charles S. Knight has compiled a list of
    <a href="http://www.readwriteweb.com/archives/top_100_alternative_search_engines.php">
        the top 100 alternative search engines</a>.
    The list includes Artificial Intelligence systems, Clustering engines,
    Recommendation Search engines, Metasearch, and many more hidden gems of
    search. People use four main search engines for 99.99% of their searches:
    Google, Yahoo!, MSN, and Ask.com (in that order). But Knight has discovered,
    via his work as an SEO, that in the other .01% lies a vast multitude of the
    most innovative and creative search engines around."</i>
  </div>
  <div class="ad6"></div>
</div>
<div id="tagbox-07:01:29:1134241" class="tags">
  <div id="tagbox-title-07:01:29:1134241" class="tagtitleclosed"> 
    <a href="//slashdot.org/login.pl">
    <span class="tagsheader" id="toggletags-button-07:01:29:1134241">[+] </span></a>
    <i>(<a href="/faq/tags.shtml">tagging beta</a>)</i>
  </div>
</div>
```

Figure 6.1: A fragment of an HTML document and its source code.

best practice not all web pages follow it. In the latter cases the style definitions or the script code do look like content, while in fact they are not. Neither can they be considered code concerning our notion as they usually do not affect the layout of the document at the same location as they are defined in the source code. Therefore,

6.4 Content Code Blurring

even if they are not encapsulated in comments, `script` and `style` elements and their contents are disregarded in the process[3].

- HTML entities are basically some kind of code, though they do represent content. Trickier even, several characters are finally meant to be resolved to one single character when the document is displayed in a browser application. Accordingly we will resolve them to single characters prior to further operations on the document.

Having treated those special cases and stripped off the ignored parts, we now have a version of the document in which we can determine clearly and for each part of it whether it is content or code.

The next question we posed is, how to turn the document into a structure for which we can define the concept of regions. We will take two different approaches here. The first approach is to strike a new path for document representations in the CE context by determining for each single character whether it is content or code. It is this character based concept of regions which requires in particular the above mentioned handling of white spaces and HTML entities. So, a document is turned into a sequence of code and content characters. The second approach is based on a token sequence like the one underlying BTE and DSC. Each tag and each word correspond to a token. The whole document is accordingly represented as a sequence of tag and word tokens.

In the end, both ways lead to a representation of a document as a sequence of elements which are either content or code. The sequence can be characterised as a vector of atomic content or code elements. We will refer to this vector from now on as the *content code vector*. An advantage that comes along with this document representation is the robustness to invalid or badly formatted HTML code. Indeed, as long as the tags can be identified, the creation of the content code vector will succeed.

Now, based on this vector of atomic elements, we need to define our regions and the way to calculate the amount of content and code therein. The windowing approach of DSC could be a solution, but the problem with moving a window of fixed width by always the same offset is that the window positions do not take into consideration any document structure. The window might be positioned in an unlucky way and slice off parts of the main content which are then grouped together with parts that are mainly code. Thus, we will adopt a more flexible approach.

We will form regions, which are based themselves on the criteria of consisting mainly of content or of code. Accordingly, it is immediately clear whether to retain or to discard a region in an extraction process. To determine these regions, we will calculate for each atomic element a ratio of how much it is surrounded by other content or code elements. So, we determine for each character or each token how many content and code characters or tokens surround it. If the *content code ratio* is high for several atomic elements in a row we can say that we have found a part of the document with a relatively uniform format,

---

[3]This also means that content code blurring – like all other CE and TD algorithms – is incapable of dealing with content dynamically created by client side JavaScript.

as a high ratio implies that there are few tags in a part of the document which mainly consists of text.

How much an element is surrounded by content or code depends on the appearance of content or code elements in its neighbourhood. The neighbourhood is defined individually for each atomic element and corresponds to a symmetric range of entries in the content code vector. To further relax the sharp boundaries of this neighbourhood and to allow an influence even beyond neighbourhood borders, we will use an iterative process inspired by the blurring filters in image processing applications.

6.4.2 Blurring the Content Code Vector

Before starting the process of determining the content code ratio we will transform the representation of the content code vector into a more suitable format. We will represent it as a vector of floating point values. Each entry in the vector is initialised with a value of 1 if the according element is of type content and with a value of 0 for code. These initial ratios can be interpreted as the content code ratio of the elements prior to being influenced by their neighbourhood. A value of 1 means that 100% of the considered elements are content, a value of 0 means that 0% of the elements are content.

To obtain the actual ratios which incorporate also the surrounding element values we calculate a weighted and local average of the values in the neighbourhood of each entry, i.e. for each atomic element. Based on these local average values, we create a new vector which represents for each element the individual ratio of content and code in the neighbourhood. If all the elements in a neighbourhood had a content code ratio of 1, also the neighbourhood average will be 1. The same is valid for neighbourhoods with an initial ratio of 0. In a mixed neighbourhood the value for a single entry will be somewhere in the interval between 0 and 1. The precise value depends on the values of the surrounding elements. If they are mainly content, the ratio will be high, if they are mainly code, the ratio will be low – exactly the effect that we intended to achieve.

The weights in the average calculation are used for modelling a stronger influence of near elements and a weaker influence for those located further away. We choose the weights according to a Gauss distribution with parameters $\mu = 0$ (reflecting the pivot element as the centre of the distribution) and $\sigma = \frac{1}{2}\delta$, where δ is the range of the neighbourhood. Roughly speaking, it can be said that the range δ indicates the direct influence of an element.

The influence of elements beyond the neighbourhood boundaries is achieved by iteratively repeating this process of calculating weighted, local neighbourhood averages. In each iteration we use the resulting vector of content code ratios as input for the next step. The iteration is stopped as soon as the values start to settle.

Visually the whole process corresponds to constructing a one dimensional image from the atomic elements, in which each pixel represents a single element, initially being coloured white if it represents content and black if it represents code. The iterative calculation of the content code ratio corresponds to applying repeatedly a Gaussian blurring filter –

6.4 Content Code Blurring

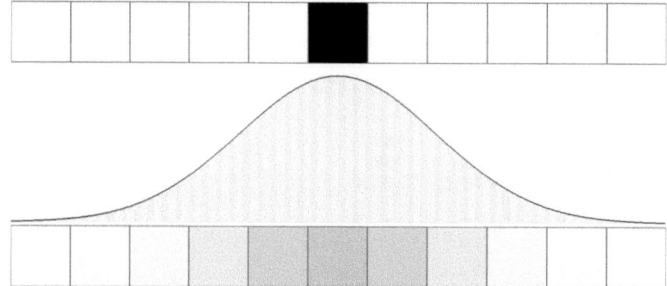

Figure 6.2: A Gauss filter blurs an image by spreading the colour information of a pixel to its neighbour pixels according to a Gauss distribution.

hence the name content code blurring. Gaussian filters can be found in nearly all image processing programs. They achieve the blurred effect in an image by spreading the colour value of a pixel to its neighbour pixels according to a Gauss distribution. The effect is demonstrated in figure 6.2: the upper image represents a very simple one dimensional image with one black pixel surrounded by white pixels. The Gauss curve plotted beneath this image determines how the colour is spread across the neighbour pixels and the result is the blurring effect which can be seen in the lower image.

Figure 6.3 demonstrates the same blurring effect on a more complex image which was generated in the described above way from the source code of the HTML fragment of our initial example from figure 6.1. The first image corresponds to the original vector and is a sequence of black and white pixels. A black pixel represents a code element in the content code vector, a white pixel a content element. The region of the long text of the main content can be recognised quite clearly by the longer white region which is interrupted only by black pixels for the few tags inside the main content[4]. The second image in figure 6.3 demonstrates what happens when blurring the image: the abrupt transitions between black and white are smoothed into shades of grey. The parts of the image which were initially mainly black end up being coloured in darker shades, those which have initially been mainly white will remain in lighter shades. Translated into the content code ratio, the bright areas have a high ratio of content to code and, accordingly, are rich in content, the dark ones have a low ratio and are rich in code. However, the effect, as can be seen in the last three images in figure 6.3, is less strong with every iteration and shows a convergence of the shades.

The shades of the image after the last application of the blurring filter can be interpreted as the final content code ratio. The brighter the shades, the higher is the ratio of content to code. Translating the shades back again into numeric values, we have a value of 1 for content and 0 for code. A brighter grey corresponds to value closer to 1, a darker grey will be closer to 0.

---

[4]the longest interruption corresponds to the tag of the hyperlink and its attribute for the URL.

6 New Single Document Algorithms

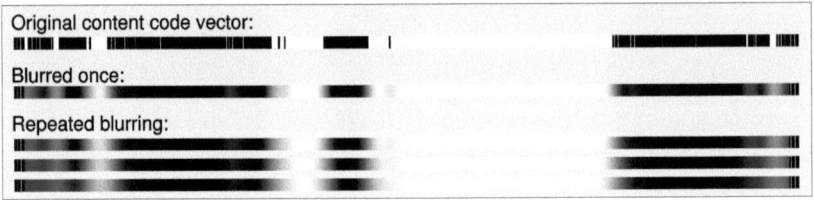

Figure 6.3: Blurring a character vector interpreted as greyscale image.

Finding the regions in a document which contain mainly content then corresponds to selecting those elements which have a high content code ratio, i.e. values closer to 1. We will use a fixed threshold for this ratio and select all elements of the document which have a content code ratio above this threshold as being part of the main content.

Looking again at our example in figure 6.3: the bright areas in the last image have a high content code ratio, the dark ones have a low ratio. Due to the repeated blurring, the pixels which correspond to the short texts in the additional contents became very dark. On the other hand, the pixels representing the few tags which appeared in the main content became quite bright. If now we extract only those texts, which have a high content code ratio value, we get exactly the main content we were looking for in our example.

Altogether, the iterative blurring process has all the properties we want: each element is assigned its own, individual content code ratio and it is influenced by the surrounding elements, while conversely influencing them as well. Additionally, the elements that are closer to the pivot element have a stronger influence than those being further away.

6.4.3 Adaptation and Implementation

Though the visual interpretation of blurring a black and white image is very descriptive, our implementation of the content code blurring algorithm performs the calculations of blurring the content code vector without the overhead of creating an image representation. Instead, it uses the vector representation of floating point numbers as described above and assigns the content elements an initial value of 1 and the code elements an initial value of 0. The operations of the blurring filter are then applied to this vector.

As soon as a certain stop criterion is met, we stop the iteration of the blurring process. The stop criterion we will use is a low rate of changes in the finally extracted text. This means, we determine, after each step of the iteration, the content which would be declared main content given the current content code ratio of the atomic elements. And if this content extract is becoming stable, the iteration is stopped. Other possible stop criteria could be to fix an absolute number of iterations or to require the changes in the content code ratio to become small.

The extraction itself is based on the final values of the content elements. If their value is above a certain threshold t they are considered main content, otherwise additional content

6.4 Content Code Blurring

and are replaced with a previously defined character r, usually a blank[5]. Algorithm 6.3 outlines the formal definition of content code blurring and includes the creation of the character based content code vector. We will refer to this initial form of the algorithm as CCB.

This basic content code blurring algorithm is then further extended by a few downstream refinements, in order to be able to handle special cases. The first adaptation is to extract for each content element with a content code ratio above the threshold all surrounding content elements as well. This extension of the extraction ranges till the next code elements and it is intended to maintain continuous text blocks between tags. It is particularly necessary for the character based CCB, as otherwise it might happen that words are extracted only partially, if some characters are above the threshold while others are below.

This adaptation is also intended to support the recognition of short main contents – a task which was problematic for most CE algorithms. In fact, due to this modification, it is enough if only a single element of a short text is considered main content to extract the entire text block.

Another problem we discussed in chapter 5 was the one of the wiki package: highly fragmented contents which additionally contain a lot of in-text hyperlinks contradict most CE heuristics. We will introduce a variation of CCB to cope with this problem as well.

The most prominent feature of Wikipedia articles is the high number of in-text hyperlinks. They contribute most strongly to the fragmentation, which is problematic also for the attempt of CCB to find areas with few tags. Thinking of our initial idea of text blocks with uniform layout, we create an *adapted CCB* (ACCB) which ignores anchor-tags entirely. After all, hyperlinks are not influencing the format intentionally. The visual influence they have on the document is more a side-effect of the necessity to reference another document.

At the first glance, this approach might seem too specialised, overfitted for the Wikipedia pages and even counterproductive for other kinds of HTML documents. LQF for example uses the presence of hyperlinks as a sure sign for additional contents. Hence, ignoring the hyperlinks might weaken the general performance of the CCB approach. For this reason we will compare the performance of ACCB with the original CCB. We will not make this differentiation for the token based document representation, though, as it is much less affected by the change of a single token.

So, for evaluation we will consider three variations of content code blurring: the character based version in its original form (CCB), the one with the adaptation of ignoring hyperlinks (ACCB) and the token based version (TCCB), which ignores hyperlinks as well.

---

[5]The option of replacing the additional contents with any other character can be used to get a visual impression of the removed content when looking at a filtered document in a web browser.

6 New Single Document Algorithms

Algorithm 6.3: CCB

Input: D: HTML document with resolved entities, where $D[i]$ is the i-th character, w: weight vector of length $2\delta + 1$, SC: stop criterion, t: threshold, r: replacement character

Output: D' HTML document, where all characters in additional contents are masked by r

begin

  // Creating the content code vector
  $k \leftarrow 1$;
  for $i = 1 \ldots |D|$ **do**
    if $\neg($isComment $(D[i]) \vee$ isWhiteSpace $(D[i]) \vee$ isScript $(D[i]) \vee$ isStyle $(D[i]))$ **then**
      if inTag $(D[i])$ **then**
        | $c[k] \leftarrow 0$;
      else
        $c[k] \leftarrow 1$;
      $k \leftarrow k + 1$;

  // Iterative blurring
  repeat
    for $i = 1 \ldots |c|$ **do**
      $c_{tmp}[i] \leftarrow 0$;
      for $j = -\delta \ldots +\delta$ **do**
        $c_{tmp}[i] \leftarrow c_{tmp}[i] + c[i+j] \cdot w[j]$;
    $c \leftarrow c_{tmp}$;
  until *stop criterion SC is met* ;

  // Extraction process
  $k \leftarrow 1$;
  for $i = 1 \ldots |D|$ **do**
    if $\neg($isComment $(D[i]) \vee$ isWhiteSpace $(D[i]) \vee$ isScript $(D[i]) \vee$ isStyle $(D[i]))$ **then**
      if inTag $(D[i])$ **then**
        | $D'[i] \leftarrow D[i]$;
      else
        if $c[k] > t$ **then**
          | $D'[i] \leftarrow D[i]$;
        else
          $D'[i] \leftarrow r$;
      $k \leftarrow k + 1$;
    else
      $D'[i] \leftarrow D[i]$;

  return D'

end

6.5 Evaluation

Now that the adaptation of LSI and LP for CE purposes and the new content code blurring method and its variations have been developed and described from a theoretical point of view it is time to evaluate their performance. For evaluation we will use again the evaluation framework developed in the last chapter. For comparability the evaluation will be made on exactly the same data and using the same evaluation measures.

During evaluation we will have to differentiate between the performance of LSI and LP on one hand and CCB, ACCB and TCCB on the other. As mentioned already above, we would wish and expect LSI and LP to provide very good results under the recall measure, while the F1 performance is of secondary importance – as long as it is above the baseline of the plain method. This would correspond to an extraction in which the algorithms locate the main content very well, even if some additional contents have not been removed. For the content code blurring algorithms, instead, the primary aim is to deliver good F1 results – especially in comparison with DSC, which is so far the best among the evaluated CE algorithms.

6.5.1 Fixing the Parameters

Before proceeding to the evaluation, we need to fix the parameters for LP, CCB, ACCB and TCCB. For this purpose we use the evaluation framework as well. Using a small set of documents we look at the performance for different parameter settings and choose the one which provides on average the best results.

The parameter in LP corresponds to the number k of links in nested structures which is required to split up pagelet candidates into smaller structures. In detail: if a DOM node which is analysed for being a pagelet contains a child node which in turn contains at least k hyperlinks, the node is discarded as possible pagelet and all its child nodes become pagelet candidates. Bar-Yossef and Rajagopalan used a setting of $k = 3$. However, since the publication of the Page Partitioning algorithm some time has passed and the web has always shown quick changes in design principles and habits. Therefore, the number of links in documents might have increased and accordingly also the characteristic number of links in a pagelet. Hence, we evaluate the LP content extractor with different settings for k between 3 and 11 in the Page Partitioning algorithm.

The results obtained for LP are very irregular. For some documents, high settings for k achieve better results, on other documents, instead, low settings of k are better. Worse even, if high settings for k perform well, low settings seem to fail and vice versa. Choosing $k = 7$ is a good balance, which on average performs best.

The content code blurring algorithms have two main parameters: the range of the neighbourhood and the threshold value. The range defines the direct influence of the atomic elements on their neighbourhood; the threshold provides the minimum content code ratio an element has to reach for being declared part of the main content.

6 New Single Document Algorithms

Table 6.1: Evaluation results of new single document algorithms: average F1 (WS).

	bbc	chip	economist	espresso	golem	heise	manual	repubblica	slashdot	spiegel	telepolis	wiki	yahoo	zdf
accb-r40	0.924	0.703	0.890	0.875	0.959	0.916	0.419	0.968	0.177	0.861	0.908	0.682	0.732	0.929
ccb-r40	0.923	0.716	0.914	0.876	0.939	0.841	0.420	0.964	0.160	0.858	0.913	0.403	0.742	0.929
tccb-25	0.914	0.842	0.903	0.871	0.947	0.821	0.404	0.918	0.269	0.910	0.902	0.660	0.758	0.745
crunch	0.756	0.342	0.815	0.810	0.837	0.810	0.382	0.887	0.123	0.706	0.910	0.725	0.738	0.772
dsc	0.937	0.708	0.881	0.862	0.958	0.877	0.403	0.925	0.252	0.902	0.859	0.594	0.780	0.847
lsi	0.886	0.070	0.842	0.838	0.554	0.645	0.376	0.877	0.076	0.722	0.942	0.764	0.781	0.574
lp-7	0.954	0.698	0.835	0.863	0.319	0.603	0.322	0.918	0.177	0.893	0.931	0.574	0.060	0.623
plain	0.595	0.173	0.613	0.624	0.502	0.575	0.371	0.704	0.106	0.549	0.858	0.823	0.582	0.514

During the evaluation it became evident quite soon, that a threshold of 0.75 is a good setting for all neighbourhood ranges and all variations of the algorithm. Keeping the threshold fixed allows an easy exploration of settings for the range. Here a range of 40 empirically showed to be a good choice for the character based algorithms CCB and ACCB, while for the token base TCCB a range setting of 25 results in a good performance.

6.5.2 Results

After having fixed the parameter settings based on a few experimental runs, we can evaluate and compare the new algorithms with the ones we have evaluated in the last chapter. Table 6.1 provides a quick overview of the average F1 results for the word sequence based evaluation. The table also lists the results for DSC and Crunch, as DSC was the best performing CE algorithm and Crunch achieved quite good recall values. Hence, we will compare CCB, ACCB and TCCB with DSC and the LP and LSI algorithms with Crunch.

We will first look at the performance of the LSI and LP algorithm, before considering the content code blurring implementations. The results in the table highlight immediately that LSI and LP have extreme problems under certain circumstances. LSI shows a very bad F1 performance on the chip package, LP, instead, fails on the documents of the yahoo package. This clearly shows the problem with heuristic based, single document CE approaches. The assumptions about how to locate the main content do not always hold and in these cases the extraction process fails entirely.

Looking at the structure of the document, the reasons for the failures become quite obvious in both cases. As shown in figure 6.4, the chip documents usually comprise a not too long main content and some quite verbose additional contents in a side bar. Both regions are DOM sub-trees which split up quite early in the DOM tree. Hence, the sub-tree of the additional contents increases remarkably the amount of text in its parent node. LSI quite often makes the mistake of simply selecting this wrong branch of the DOM tree

6.5 Evaluation

Figure 6.4: A document from the chip web site in its original form.

as main content, because it contributes largely to the visible text. The result of such a mistake is shown in figure 6.5: the main content, in this case, has been removed entirely.

Figure 6.6 outlines the two sub-trees in the DOM tree of a chip document which contain the additional and the main content region. The figure illustrates quite clearly that both sub-trees contribute strongly to the visible content. For other algorithms, these additional contents are not as problematic. Even though they are quite rich in text, they are also rich in hyperlinks and other formatting instructions. Accordingly, the other algorithms recognise these nodes as additional contents quite easily.

The problem of LP with the yahoo package has another reason. However, also in this case the bad performance is caused by a particular structure of the DOM trees. The main content and a list of related links are settled together as sibling nodes in a `div` element. Figure 6.7 shows such a yahoo document. The high number of links in the related links list

6 New Single Document Algorithms

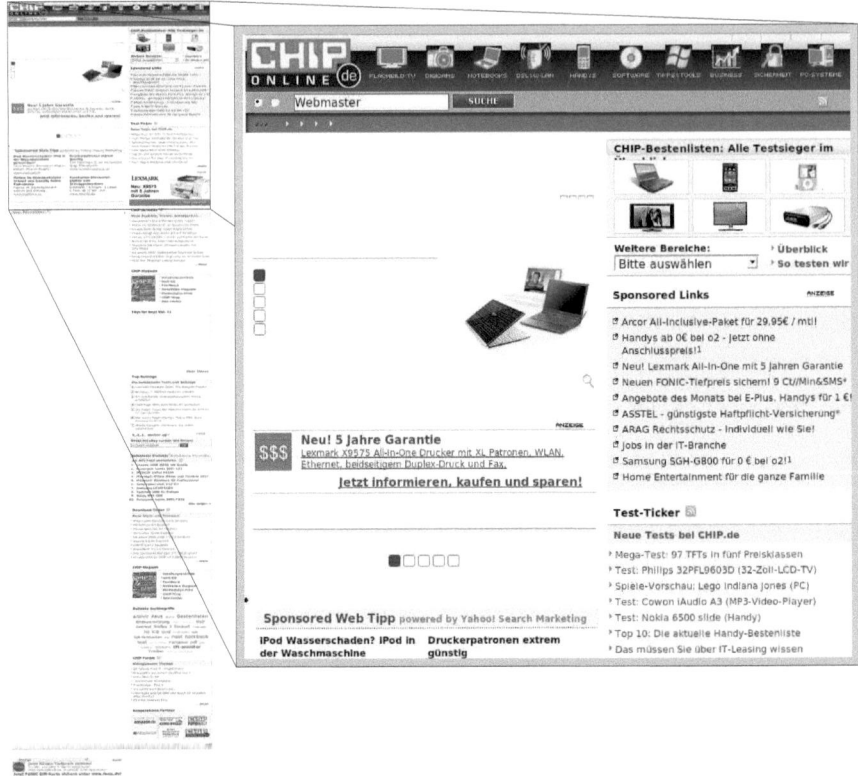

Figure 6.5: LSI often extracts the content rich side bar of chip documents.

causes this `div` element to be discarded as a pagelet candidate and it is split up by the Page Partitioning algorithm. Unfortunately this splits also the main content. As the main article is subdivided into several paragraphs which are direct children of the `div` node, the text is segmented into several pagelets. The LP algorithm then selects the largest pagelet which accordingly corresponds to the longest paragraph of the main content, as demonstrated in figure 6.8. The longest paragraph, however, represents only a small fraction of the main content, hence, LP obtains a very low recall score. This problem will always occur whenever a pagelet structure is nested in the pagelet candidate containing the main content.

But even apart from those two heavy failures of LSI and LP, the concepts do not convince in general. Their attempt to achieve a high recall value and to possibly restrict the search for the main content to certain DOM sub-trees is not very successful either. While the methods in general do reach a quite high recall value, there are better solutions under this aspect. In table 6.2 we compare the average recall of LSI and LP with Crunch, which was

6.5 Evaluation

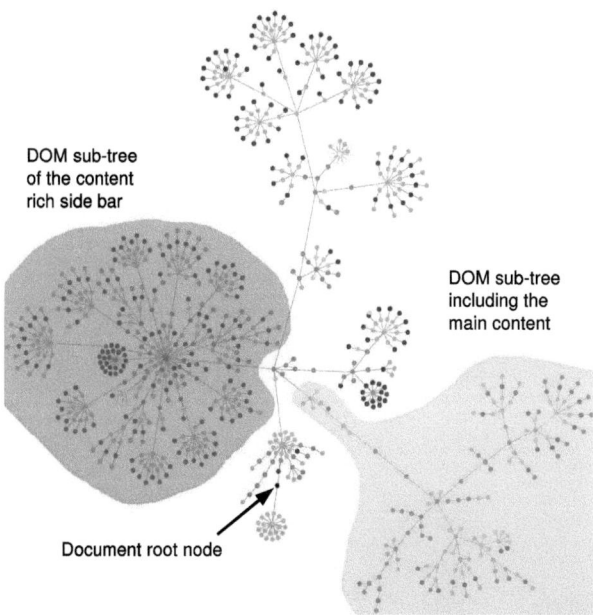

Figure 6.6: DOM tree of a chip document with the two sub-trees of the main content region and the content rich side bar.

already said to be quite conservative and careful in removing additional contents. It can be seen, that Crunch is significantly outperformed only on the wiki package and merely by LSI. In all other scenarios, Crunch delivers better or equivalent recall results. Therefore, Crunch is a better candidate for a pre-processor to reduce the search for the main content. Certainly, it does not attach the main content to a particular DOM sub-tree as needed for some other applications mentioned in 6.1, but LSI and LP seem too unreliable and fragile. Finding suitable algorithms for the scenarios we described above and which do require a single DOM sub-tree as input will need some further research.

The results obtained for the content code blurring algorithms look much more promising. First of all, when looking at the average F1 values in table 6.1, we can notice that ACCB does not show a significant drawback in comparison to CCB. So, the adaptation of ignoring hyperlink tags during the construction of the content code vector does not cause a drop in the performance of the content code blurring approach. We can deduce that ACCB – though also improving the F1 performance on the wiki package significantly – is not overfitted for Wikipedia documents. ACCB is actually performing better for some of the other packages as well. So, the adaptation, which was specifically introduced for the

6 New Single Document Algorithms

Figure 6.7: A document from the yahoo web site in its original form.

particular case of a main content with a high ratio of in-text links is useful for other scenarios as well.

Secondly, we can say that ACCB in general performs better than DSC. The results in figure 6.5.2 on the heise package are quite typical under this aspect as the F1 performance curve of ACCB is well above the one of DSC for all document models. CCB and TCCB, instead do not show a clear advantage or disadvantage in comparison with DSC. On the documents of the heise package they actually obtain a lower F1 score. This is not always the case and on average CCB, TCCB and DSC have a comparable performance.

6.5 Evaluation

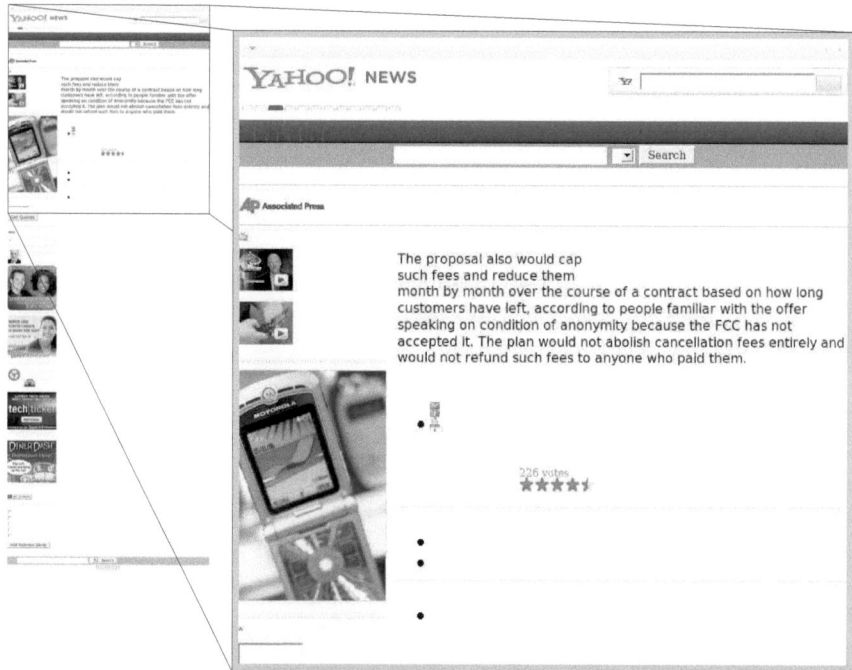

Figure 6.8: Due to the DOM structure LP extracts only one paragraph of the main content of a yahoo document.

Table 6.2: Recall for LSI, LP and Crunch in direct comparison

	bbc	chip	economist	espresso	golem	heise	manual	repubblica	slashdot	spiegel	telepolis	wiki	yahoo	zdf
accb-r40	0.927	0.913	0.952	0.894	0.929	0.930	0.717	0.962	0.905	0.902	0.911	0.566	0.838	0.921
ccb-r40	0.925	0.875	0.948	0.894	0.890	0.806	0.706	0.954	0.748	0.889	0.911	0.295	0.838	0.921
tccb-25	0.914	0.833	0.949	0.878	0.913	0.882	0.681	0.892	0.908	0.897	0.898	0.557	0.866	0.669
crunch	0.993	0.988	0.982	0.963	0.981	0.944	0.815	0.996	0.911	0.978	0.998	0.731	0.996	0.999
dsc	0.900	0.902	0.909	0.860	0.936	0.859	0.601	0.938	0.750	0.924	0.822	0.510	0.887	0.803
lsi	0.975	0.272	0.968	0.901	0.988	0.755	0.816	0.991	0.521	0.934	0.996	0.907	0.985	0.858
lp-7	0.982	0.952	0.895	0.937	0.303	0.640	0.522	0.963	0.315	0.843	0.985	0.494	0.038	0.686

6 New Single Document Algorithms

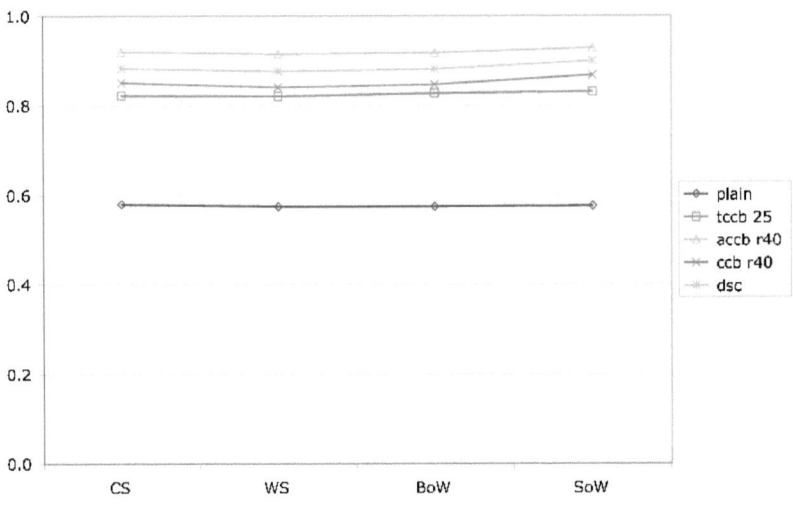

Figure 6.9: Average F1 performance of CCB, ACCB and TCCB on the heise package in comparison with DSC.

Looking at the total of our 14 evaluation scenarios, ACCB obtains significantly higher F1 scores than DSC for five packages, comparable results on six packages and worse results only for three packages. Further, on four of the comparable packages ACCB has slightly higher F1 scores, which might underline its tendency to perform better. Among the packages where ACCB is inferior to DSC is the anyway problematic slashdot package. Though ACCB achieves better recall values for slashdot documents, it is much less precise. The problems with the short main content and long additional text contents seems to affect the character based content code blurring stronger than DSC. Interesting is, that on the same package, DSC itself is coming second to the TCCB when considering the F1 performance. This is also the case for the spiegel package, where ACCB is outperformed by DSC, but TCCB is better than DSC. So, the question arises whether in these cases the character based approach has exceptional drawbacks in comparison to a token based approach. This might be a hint that a more sophisticated construction of the content code vector could improve the results of the content code blurring idea. A solution somewhere between the character and token based construction of the vector might deliver still better results. Reducing the influence of long words and attribute values in tags could be an approach worth pursuing.

When looking in more detail at the packages where ACCB performs better than DSC, the results in table 6.2 show that the key to the success of ACCB is a better recall. It is usually slightly less precise than DSC, but it achieves better recall values and, as a result,

6.5 Evaluation

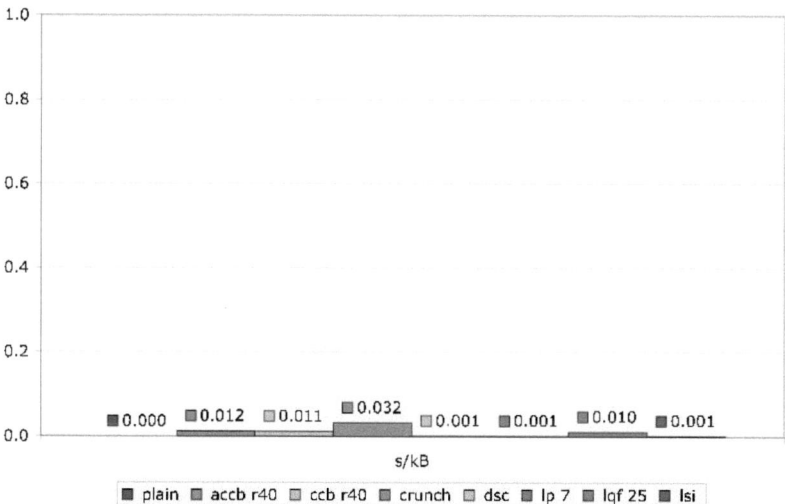

Figure 6.10: Time performance of LP, LSI, CCB, ACCB and TCCB on the heise package in comparison with DSC, LQF and Crunch.

in the light of F1 it reaches a better tradeoff between recall and precision. This explains also the observations for the slashdot package: ACCB extracts the user comments better and more completely than DSC. But as they are not considered to be part of the main content, ACCB is punished for this extraction in the precision measure.

However, the recall of ACCB is not perfect either. If parts of the main content are highly formatted, i.e. marked up with any kind of tags, they might not be recognised as main content, especially if they are positioned close to other highly structured additional contents. This problem affects all content code blurring implementations and is a phenomenon which can typically be observed for the headlines of news articles. They usually follow a section of additional contents, have a short text themselves and are separated from the rest of the main content by some other formatting instructions. However, it is worth to note that DSC suffers from the same problem, even to a higher degree. The improvements of ACCB in recall are also due to a better performance exactly in these tricky cases. The adaptation of always extracting continuous content element sequences entirely seems to help in some of the cases.

Looking at the processing time in figure 6.10, the token based approaches DSC and TCCB are comparably fast. ACCB and CCB need longer to process a document, simply due to the much longer content code vector. However, both ACCB and CCB are reasonably

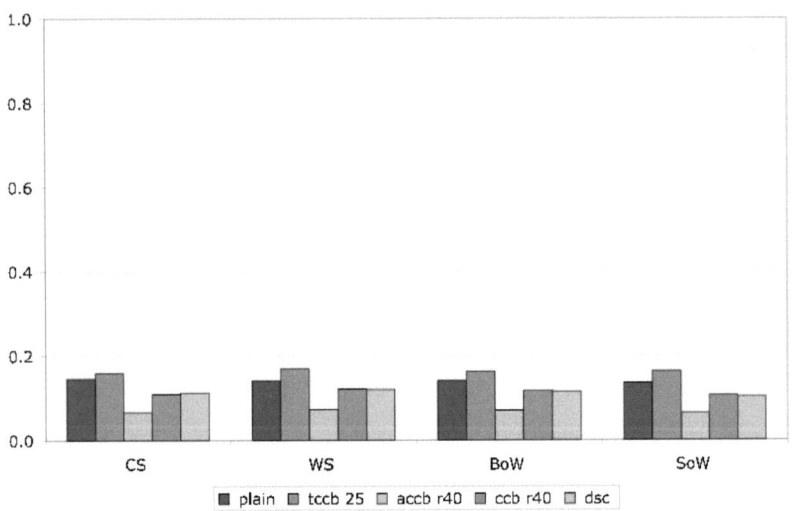

Figure 6.11: Stability of CCB, ACCB and TCCB on the heise package in comparison with DSC.

fast. Their time performance is similar to the LQF filters and still faster than Crunch which have also been included in the graph of figure 6.10 for completeness of comparison.

Finally, also under the aspect of stability, the content code blurring algorithms are competitive with DSC. As shown in figure 6.11, on the heise package ACCB is even slightly more stable than DSC, and this tendency is confirmed by most other packages.

6.6 Summary

In this chapter we looked at several new algorithms. Two of them, namely LSI and LP, were deduced from existing algorithms in other application scenarios in order to locate the DOM sub-tree containing the main content. One motivation for this CE variation in our context was the idea to restrict the search for the main content to a certain part of the document.

However, the empirical results showed that those two algorithms are not suitable for this task. We observed situations and document structures where LSI or LP might fail entirely to locate the main content. Even when looking at the general recall performance, the Crunch framework seems to perform far better in situations where a restricted part of the document is needed for further downstream CE algorithms.

A question arising from these results is how suitable LSI and LP are in their original context. If LSI might indicate wrong DOM sub-trees for building a wrapper upon their contents, or if LP fragments a web page too much also XWRAP and Bar-Yossef and Rajagopalan's TD algorithm might have problems under certain scenarios.

Different from LSI and LP, the variations of the content code blurring algorithm are designed as a classical CE algorithm. They are based on the idea of finding those parts in the document which have a homogeneous format, using the ratio of content and code in the neighbourhood of atomic elements. We used source code characters as atomic elements for the CCB and the ACCB implementations and word and tag tokens for the TCCB realisation of the content code blurring concept. In an iterative process we employed a technique comparable to blurring filters in image processing for calculating the content code ratio, and finally extracted those parts which contain mainly content. Some additional adaptations were made to ACCB and TCCB to cope in particular with the observed problems of documents with a high rate of in-text hyperlinks.

Looking at the evaluation results, ACCB can be said to be the best performing general CE algorithm to date. On most of our evaluation packages it is superior or at least equal to DSC, which in the previous chapter obtained the best results. In particular, on the Wikipedia documents ACCB achieves better results, thanks to the incorporated adaptations.

6 New Single Document Algorithms

7 Template Clustering and Detection

In the last chapter we have developed some new single document algorithms. Even though the ACCB algorithm improves the performance of single document CE in comparison with the existing approaches analysed in chapter 5, it still suffers from the drawback that it needs to make assumptions about how the main content looks like. Therefore, if those assumptions do not hold, the extraction of the main content will very likely fail. The behaviour of LSI on the chip documents and of LP on the yahoo package demonstrated this problem of single document algorithms quite impressively.

TD approaches, based on multiple documents, do not suffer from this problem. They discover the main content indirectly by first deducing a common template structure of the documents in a training set and then, by using this knowledge, locate the main content. The need for a training set, though, is their biggest drawback. The training set is a problem for two simple reasons: first of all, it needs to be created, and second, it needs to be of good quality.

In most publications on TD the creation of training sets is a manual process. A human user selects documents which he judges to be based on the same template. The judgement is usually made on the basis of the visual impression of the documents and/or an analysis of the source code. This approach might be suitable for cases where only few templates have to be analysed. However, the biggest drawback is that it cannot be automated and that it is too time consuming for a large scale application where very many or continuously new templates have to be detected.

Another, alternative approach is to download a large amount of files from the same origin, i.e. a particular web site. The idea of this approach is to assume that all the documents on this web site are based on the same or at least very similar templates. This assumption, however, does not always hold and the training set is very likely containing noisy or polluted data – polluted in the sense that it includes documents based on entirely different templates or on no template at all.

Naturally, this noise influences the quality of the training set. If the training set comprises documents build on different underlying templates, the TD algorithms will almost certainly deduce wrong template structures. Another tricky issue is the presence of duplicate or near duplicate documents in the training set. Those algorithms which are based on an entropy calculation for discovering redundant contents, will suffer from duplicate documents as they distort the document frequency of the contents. So, for a TD algorithm to work without problems, the training set should consist only of documents, which are all mutually different, but which are based on the same template. Such a purity of the

7 Template Clustering and Detection

training set is actually expressly assumed for most TD algorithms described in literature, e.g. by Lin and Ho for InfoDiscoverer [LH02].

In this chapter we will start with developing a way to create high quality training sets automatically by detecting different templates underlying the documents. This aim is achieved by incorporating a cluster analysis based on distance measures for the structural similarity of web documents. Once that this step is taken, we will bridge the gap between CE and TD by describing a way in which it is possible to turn virtually any multi document TD algorithm into a single document CE algorithm. This process comprises building a training set from a single seed document and cleaning it via the cluster analysis approach. We will confirm the applicability of this approach by using a basic entropy based TD algorithm to build a CE filter.

7.1 Clustering Template Based Documents

Discovery and removal of duplicate or near duplicate documents is a topic which has been analysed already in other works and the methods developed in this context obtain quite reliable results by now [CFGM02, BGMZ97, BDGM95]. Cleaning a training set from documents with different underlying templates, instead, has hardly ever been dealt with. As mentioned in 3.3.5, Reis et al. [RGdL04] proposed to cluster the documents in the training set using a distance measure based on the RTDM tree edit distance algorithm. They never tested the success of this approach for the support of TD, though. Ma et al. [MGCC03] proposed a clustering of the training set documents as well. After some attempts they discarded their approach altogether, as it showed to be too unreliable to create clean data sets. In the end, they created the training sets in a manual fashion. Given these experiences, the automatic creation of high quality training sets remains a challenge.

We will now tackle this challenge and analyse several ways to cluster documents in a training set according to their underlying template. The first step we will take is to describe, develop and compare different distance measures. Then we will use the distance measures in combination with different clustering algorithms to see which combination reflects best the detection of the templates underlying the documents.

7.1.1 Distance Measures for Template Structures

Some distance measures were already described in 3.5 in the chapter about related work. We will mention them here again and describe them more formally to provide an overview of all the distance measures we are going to employ in the cluster analysis later on. In addition to these existing distance measures, we will also develop two new ones. These new distance measures are based on an evaluation of tag sequences and we will include them in the comparison with the existing measures.

With the approaches which we present here, the list of distance measures for web documents is far from being complete. But with the presented measures we cover several different aspects of how to capture the structure of a document and how to compare the

7.1 Clustering Template Based Documents

structural similarity of two documents. Hence, for our purpose the number of illustrated approaches will be sufficient.

The focus of the following part will be on describing roughly the computation of the distance measures and their computational complexity. For the formulas in the definitions we will always assume D_1 and D_2 to be two HTML documents containing t_i tags and n_i nodes of which l_i are leaf nodes, with $i = 1, 2$ respectively. However, the number t_i of tags can roughly be estimated to be $2 \cdot n_i$, as in most cases a node in the DOM tree will correspond to a pair of an opening and a closing tag in the source code of the document.

Tree Edit Distances: Any tree edit distance measure is based on calculating the cost for transforming a source tree structure into a target tree structure. For this purpose elementary operations like inserting, deleting, replacing or moving nodes or entire sub-trees in the tree structure are associated with certain costs. The distance between two documents corresponds to the minimal cost for changing one tree into another.

The hierarchical top-down tree matching algorithm RTDM of Reis et al. [RGdL04] was mentioned already in 3.3.5 as a solution which is specifically tailored for HTML documents and which has proven to perform quite well in practice. Further, the authors report the time performance of the RTDM algorithm to be good in practice. Anyway, it remains of quadratic order in the worst case.

We use a slightly modified version of the original algorithm, which requires only linear space of degree $O(n_1)$, whereas the original algorithm needs quadratic space. The improvements correspond to computing the *Levenshtein distance* [Lev65] with linear space. The algorithm in 7.1 shows how the modifications are incorporated into the RTDM algorithm. For particularly large documents it turned out that this modification remarkably sped up the distance calculation in the final application. In fact, the original algorithm easily requires a lot of memory space and causes the operating system to swap some of the runtime memory to the hard disk – a process which is extremely time consuming.

Common Paths: Another way to compare the structure of web documents is to look at the paths leading from the root node to the leaf nodes in the DOM tree. A path is denoted e.g. by concatenating the names of the elements it passes from root to leaf. It is then possible to represent each document D by the set $p(D)$ of paths it contains. A distance measure is derived from the overlap of the path sets of two documents – the common paths (CP). The approach we use to compute the distance is based on the intersection of the two path sets:

$$d_{CP}(D_1, D_2) = 1 - \frac{|p(D_1) \cap p(D_2)|}{\max(|p(D_1)|, |p(D_2)|)}$$

Computing the paths for the documents can be done in linear time of degree $O(n_1 + n_2)$ with respect to the nodes. Using hashing, the intersection of two resulting sets

7 Template Clustering and Detection

Algorithm 7.1: RTDM (linear space)
Input: Two DOM (sub-)trees T_1 and T_2 with direct child nodes $t_1[i]$ and $t_2[j]$, threshold ε
Output: Tree edit distance for (T_1, T_2)
begin
    $m =$ length (t_1);
    $n =$ length (t_2);
    $M[0] = 0$;
    for $i = 1 \ldots m$ **do**
        $C_{(1,i)} \leftarrow$ descendents $(t_1[i])$;
    for $j = 1 \ldots n$ **do**
        $C_{(2,j)} \leftarrow$ descendents $(t_2[j])$;
        $M[j] \leftarrow M[j-1] + \sum_{k \in C_{(2,j)} \cup \{j\}}$ insert $(t_2[k])$;
    for $i = 1 \ldots m$ **do**
        $tmp \leftarrow M[0]$;
        $M[0] \leftarrow M[0] + \sum_{k \in C_{(1,i)} \cup \{i\}}$ delete $(t_1[k])$;
        for $j = 1 \ldots n$ **do**
            $del \leftarrow M[j] + \sum_{k \in C_{(1,i)} \cup \{i\}}$ delete $(t_1[k])$;
            $ins \leftarrow M[j-1] + \sum_{k \in C_{(2,j)} \cup \{j\}}$ insert $(t_2[k])$;
            $sub \leftarrow tmp$;
            if $sub > \varepsilon$ **then**
                $sub \leftarrow \infty$;
            else if identicalSubTrees $(t_1[i], t_2[j])$ **then**
                $sub \leftarrow sub + 0$;
            else
                if isLeaf $(t_1[i])$ **then**
                    $sub \leftarrow sub +$ replace $(t_1[i], t_2[j])$;
                    $sub \leftarrow sub + \sum_{k \in C_{(2,j)}}$ insert $(t_2[k])$;
                else if isLeaf $(t_2[j])$ **then**
                    $sub \leftarrow sub+$ replace $(t_1[i], t_2[j])$;
                    $sub \leftarrow sub + \sum_{k \in C_{(1,i)}}$ delete $(t_1[k])$;
                else
                    $sub \leftarrow sub+$RTDM $(t_1[i], t_2[j], \varepsilon)$;
            $tmp \leftarrow M[j]$;
            $M[j] \leftarrow \min(del, ins, sub)$;
    return $M[n]$
end

7.1 Clustering Template Based Documents

can be computed in expected linear time as well, this time with respect to the number of paths which corresponds to the number of leaf nodes.

Common Path Shingles: A combination of the paths distance with a shingling technique was proposed by Buttler in [But04], as already mentioned shortly in 3.5.2. The idea of this measure is not to compare the complete paths but rather breaking them up in smaller pieces of equal length – the shingles. The distance is then based on the common path shingles (CPS). The advantage of this approach is that two paths which are differing only for a small part, but are quite similar for the rest, will have a large "agreement" on the shingles. The shingling can be realised in a way that it does not add any substantial cost to the computation in comparison with the CP distance.

So, if $ps(D)$ provides the path shingles for a document D, the CPS distance can be computed similarly as above by:

$$d_{CPS}(D_1, D_2) = 1 - \frac{|ps(D_1) \cap ps(D_2)|}{\max(|ps(D_1)|, |ps(D_2)|)}$$

Buttler suggested a shingle length between one and four path elements. As we are particularly interested in the structure of a document we will use the maximum recommended setting and use shingles of length four.

Tag Vector: Thinking of the occurrence of tags as a typical feature of a document – in particular of a template based document – leads to the tag vector distance measure (TV). As the number of possible (i.e. complying with W3C's HTML recommendation) tags is limited, the idea is to convert a document D into a vector $v(D)$ of fixed dimension N by counting how many times each tag appears. This approach entirely ignores the order of the tags, but has the advantage that we can use the standard Euclidean distance to measure distances in the vector space of $v(D)$:

$$d_{TV}(D_1, D_2) = \sqrt{\sum_{i=1}^{N}(v_i(D_1) - v_i(D_2))^2}$$

A critic often mentioned when using the Euclidean distance for classification or clustering tasks is that it sensitive to vector length. When it comes to measuring templates of HTML documents this might instead be a desirable effect. The vector length corresponds to the number of tags, which itself might be quite characteristic for a template after all. The computational cost corresponds mainly to creating the tag vector and calculating the sum and is of order $O(t_1 + t_2)$.

Longest Common Tag Subsequence: The tag vector approach neglects the order of the tags in the document. To overcome this drawback, we interpret the structure of a document as a sequence of tags. The distance of two documents can then be expressed based on their longest common tag subsequence (LCTS). The LCTS is – equivalently

7 Template Clustering and Detection

to the definitions for character or word sequences – the longest but not necessarily continuous sequence of tags which can be found in both of the documents. If $|D|$ denotes the number of tags in a document, the LCTS of two documents D_1 and D_2 can be turned into a distance measure by:

$$d_{LCTS}(D_1, D_2) = 1 - \frac{|lcts(D_1, D_2)|}{\max(|D_1|, |D_2|)}$$

Unfortunately, the computation of this distance is expensive, as finding the longest common subsequence has quadratic complexity of $O(t_1 \cdot t_2)$.

Common Tag Sequence Shingles: To overcome the computational costs of the previous distance measure we utilise again the shingling technique. Breaking up the entire sequence into a set of shingles $ts(D)$ allows to maintain a certain context for each tag without having to look at the complete document. The distance measure is once again based on the overlap of sets and corresponds to finding the common tag sequence shingles (CTSS): thus, we apply shingling to reduce the computational costs for this distance to $O(t_1 + t_2)$. The distance can then be computed similarly to the CPS distance:

$$d_{CTSS}(D_1, D_2) = 1 - \frac{|ts(D_1) \cap ts(D_2)|}{\max(|ts(D_1)|, |ts(D_2)|)}$$

The length of the shingles will need to be different from the CPS approach, as we have a very different underlying model to represent the template structure. As the document model has similarities with the tokenisation of web documents discussed used by BTE and DSC, we will use shingles of length eight. This was the minimum window length in the DSC algorithm, which in our tests performed quite well.

7.1.2 Clustering Techniques

Cluster analysis is a vast field of ongoing research. The aim of a cluster analysis is to form groups of similar objects, i.e. of objects which lie close to each other according to some distance measure. We will apply three different techniques to analyse how well the HTML document distance measures of above reflect the underlying template structures. The techniques will now be described briefly and by settling them straight away in our context of grouping web documents according to the templates they are based on.

Multidimensional Scaling: Multidimensional scaling (MDS) is a technique used to find a configuration of data points in a (possibly low-dimensional) vector space which represents best a given distance matrix. In our case, this means the documents are mapped onto points in a vector space and the Euclidean distances between these points resemble the distances between the documents as good as possible. MDS

7.1 Clustering Template Based Documents

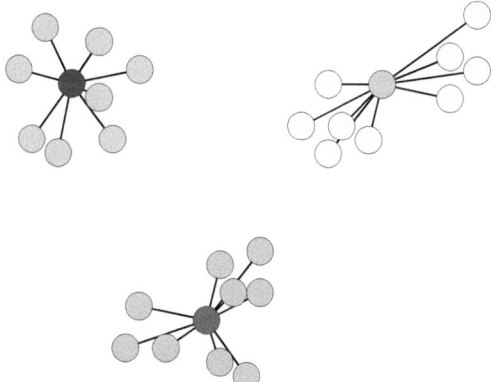

Figure 7.1: The k-means algorithm is using centroids to form clusters.

comes in two general variations: metric for a distance matrix which is in fact based on a (usually Euclidean) metric and non-metric if the distances are computed in a different way or even estimated. It is commonly used to reduce the dimensionality of data to the essential dimensions. The aim is often to obtain a 2D or 3D representation of the data which allows a visual analysis.

The latter is our aim as well, when we are going to apply MDS on the distance matrices computed for the template based documents. As the distances are not all fulfilling the requirements of a metric[1] and certainly cannot be represented by an Euclidean distance in a 2D space, we apply non-metric MDS. Starting with the result of a metric principal component analysis [Pea01] as initial configuration we use Kruskal's algorithm [Kru64] to obtain a stable configuration.

K-Median Clustering: k-means clustering is a classical approach for clustering data. The basic idea is to start with a configuration assigning randomly each of the documents to one of k cluster. For all the clusters a centroid is computed, i.e. a document in its centre. In an iterative process each document is now assigned to the cluster whose centroid is closest. This creates new clusters and thereby new centroids for the next step of the iteration. The iteration process is stopped if the configuration is not changing any more or the changes of the centroids become minimal. Figure 7.1 shows the result of a k-means clustering for 3 clusters. The darker points represent the centroids of each cluster and it can be seen quite clearly how all items have been assigned to the correct cluster.

In k-means clustering the mean of the data items in each cluster is computed and used as centroid. As in our case it is difficult to define a mean document, we use a

---

[1] It is e.g. possible, that two documents have zero distance, though they are not identical.

7 Template Clustering and Detection

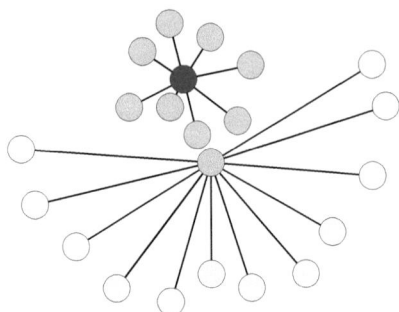

Figure 7.2: A cluster configuration which has too complicated shapes for k-means clustering.

common adaptation of the method which uses the median document as centroid – hence the name k-median clustering. The median document is the document which has the overall minimum distance to all other documents in the same cluster.

Though a standard method for clustering, k-means clustering, and likewise k-median, is known to have three mayor drawbacks. First, the number k of clusters is a parameter, implying a certain knowledge of the data as it has to be fixed a-priori. In our experiments where the number of templates will be known this is not a problem. In an arbitrary set of documents, instead, it might not be possible to predict the number of different templates occurring in the set, neither the number of clusters to be formed. Secondly, the result depends on the initial random configuration. This drawback is usually overcome by clustering the data items several times and averaging the evaluations over all solutions. And thirdly, due to the use of centroids, the clusters cannot have complicated "shapes". The example in figure 7.2 shows such an example, where the centroid of one cluster lies too close to the data items of another cluster. Hence, in the next step of the iteration the correct clusters would be destroyed and rearranged.

Single Linkage: Unlike the previous method, *hierarchical clustering* methods do not require to fix the number of clusters a-priori as parameter. They start with each document forming a cluster on its own. The clusters are iteratively merged until only one cluster remains which contains all documents. The information on which clusters have been merged at which step during the iteration is represented as a tree structure – the *dendrogram*. This tree structure can be examined to determine different cluster configurations, e.g. due to cluster size, average distance or number of clusters. An example of a dendrogram is given in figure 7.3 starting from the data items A to H. It shows the iterative merging of clusters and their thereby created hierarchy. To obtain from such a dendrogram a cluster configuration of, for example, three clusters it is enough to "undo" the last two merges. These correspond to the

7.1 Clustering Template Based Documents

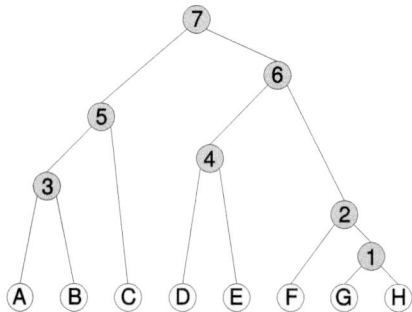

Figure 7.3: Example of a dendrogram.

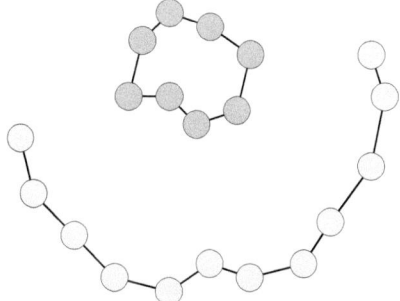

Figure 7.4: Single linkage clustering can handle also tricky shaped clusters.

two tree nodes labelled ⑦ and ⑥. Removing these nodes, the process results in the three sub-trees containing the elements $\{A, B, C\}$, $\{D, E\}$ and $\{F, G, H\}$ which represent the three clusters.

There are several ways to decide which clusters are merged in each step and thereby to compute the dendrogram. The single linkage approach looks at all the distances which appear between documents from different clusters and merges those two clusters which feature the smallest inter-cluster distance of two documents. This allows the method to capture also quite fancy shaped clusters, as long as they are connected by documents close to each other. In figure 7.4 we revisit the example of a cluster configuration which was impossible to detect for k-means. The single linkage method can handle this example perfectly well.

However, we can easily give an example where single linkage will have problems, while the k-means approach will have good chances to succeed. In figure 7.5 we see two clusters which have a series of a few documents that connect the clusters. This is a classical example where single linkage might deliver strange results, as the largest

7 Template Clustering and Detection

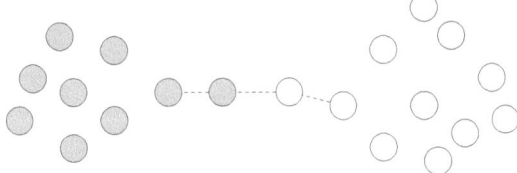

Figure 7.5: A cluster configuration which might be difficult for single linkage clustering.

intra-cluster distance might easily be greater than the smallest inter-cluster distance. So, the clusters might get merged at an early stage in the dendrogram because of the short distances of the data items which are connected with the dashed line.

The two very different approaches for building clusters in k-means and single linkage are in a certain way complementary to each other. Hence, the motivation to employ them in our case is to find out, which of these different concepts works better for template clustering.

7.1.3 Experiments

To evaluate the different distance measures and the two clustering algorithms we will use a corpus of 500 documents collected from five different German news web sites. The online versions of Frankfurter Allgemeine Zeitung (FAZ), Focus, Frankfurter Rundschau (FR), Spiegel and Stern served as source for this document collection. As shown in table 7.1, each of these web sites contributes 20 documents from five different topical categories. As far as possible, the topics of the categories are chosen to be similar across the web sites. The topics comprise news about national politics, international politics, sports, business and Internet or IT related matters. The only exception to this rule is the web site of the FR, which does not subdivide the category of politics into national and international. Hence, in this case we will use 20 documents about politics in general and 20 documents from the news about travelling and foreign countries.

The idea for taking into the corpus not only documents from different web sites but to cover also different sections within the sites is to see how well the distance measures can cope with the slight changes in the templates which usually occur within the documents of different categories. Further, to use similar topics across the web sites allows to see how well the distances can separate documents with similar contents, but different layouts.

While computing the distance matrices for the 500 documents, we use the occasion to take a look at the time needed to compute the matrix for an increasing number of documents. The graph in figure 7.6 shows the time in seconds needed for computing (symmetric) distance matrices depending on the number of documents involved and using the different distance measures. While obviously the RTDM and the LCTS approaches

7.1 Clustering Template Based Documents

Table 7.1: Web documents used for evaluating template clustering approaches.

Web site	Topic	Category on web site	Documents
FAZ (www.faz.de)	national politics	Politik – Bund	20
	foreign politics	Politik – Ausland	20
	sports	Sport – Fußball	20
	business news	Wirtschaft	20
	IT news	Computer	20
Focus (www.focus.de)	national politics	Politik – Deutschland	20
	foreign politics	Politik – Ausland	20
	sports	Fußball	20
	business news	Boerse – Aktien	20
	IT news	Digital – Internet	20
FR (www.fr.de)	politics	Politik	20
	travelling	Reisen	20
	sports	Sport	20
	business news	Wirtschaft	20
	IT news	Multimedia	20
Spiegel (www.spiegel.de)	national politics	Politik – Deutschland	20
	foreign politics	Politik – Ausland	20
	sports	Sport – Fußball	20
	business news	Wirtschaft	20
	IT news	Netzwelt	20
Stern (www.stern.de)	national politics	Politik – Deutschland	20
	foreign politics	Politik – Ausland	20
	sports	Sport – Fußball	20
	business news	Wirtschaft – Unternehmen	20
	IT news	Computer	20

are very time consuming already for small document collections, the other measures can be computed reasonably fast. CTSS sequence shingling is on average taking twice as long as the CPS approach, which itself is slower than the CP distance measure by a factor of about 1.5. The TV distance is the fastest to be computed, probably because there is no need to handle sets and determine their intersection.

The resulting matrices for all 500 documents are shown in figure 7.7 through a graphical interpretation. The documents are arranged in the same order from left to right for the columns and top down in the rows. The arrangement groups together documents from the same web site and within each site from the same topic category. Each pixel in the image represents the distance between two documents. The closer two documents are to each other, the brighter the pixels are coloured. Dark colours, accordingly, represent large distances between documents. In all cases the distances have been normalised to convert a distance of 0 to white pixels and the largest distance to black pixels.

7 Template Clustering and Detection

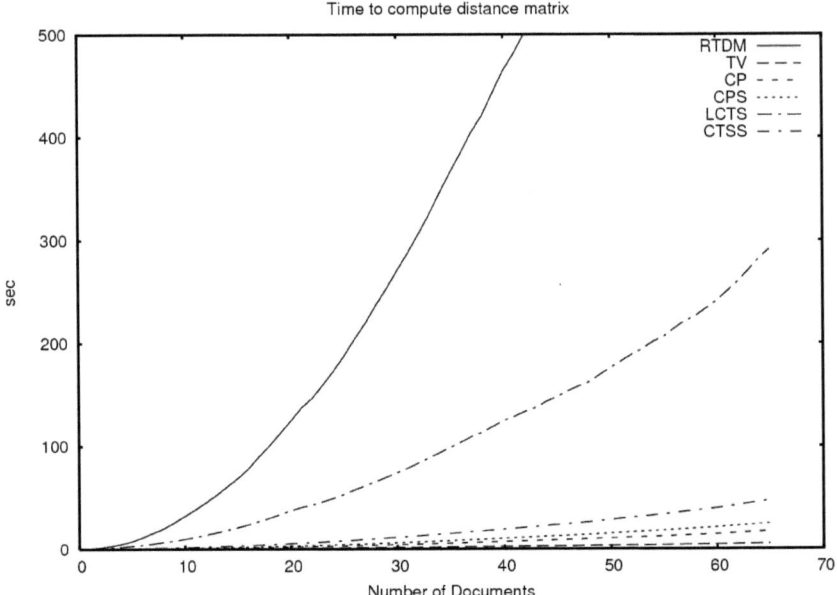

Figure 7.6: Time needed to compute the distance matrix with the different distance measures, depending on the number of documents.

The five brighter large squares along the diagonal of the images confirm quite well that under all distance measures the documents based on the same template tend to have smaller distances than the documents from different web sites. These bright squares correspond to the similarity entries of the matrix for documents which are coming from the same web site. Also the substructures of the different topic categories can be seen more or less clearly for most distance measures and web sites. They appear as a series of 25 smaller and still brighter squares along the diagonal of the matrix.

However, not for all measures the differentiation between the five web sites is equally clear. Especially the matrix based on the TV distance measure shows very bright colours also for documents based on different templates. As this might be an artefact of the necessary normalisation of the colour range, we will also look at other indications for how well the templates have been separated.

One instrument for such an analysis is the *Dunn index* (see e.g. [SMW03]). The Dunn index, in our case, compares the maximum distance d_{max} occurring between documents based on the same template with the minimum distance d_{min} occurring between documents based on different templates and is defined as:

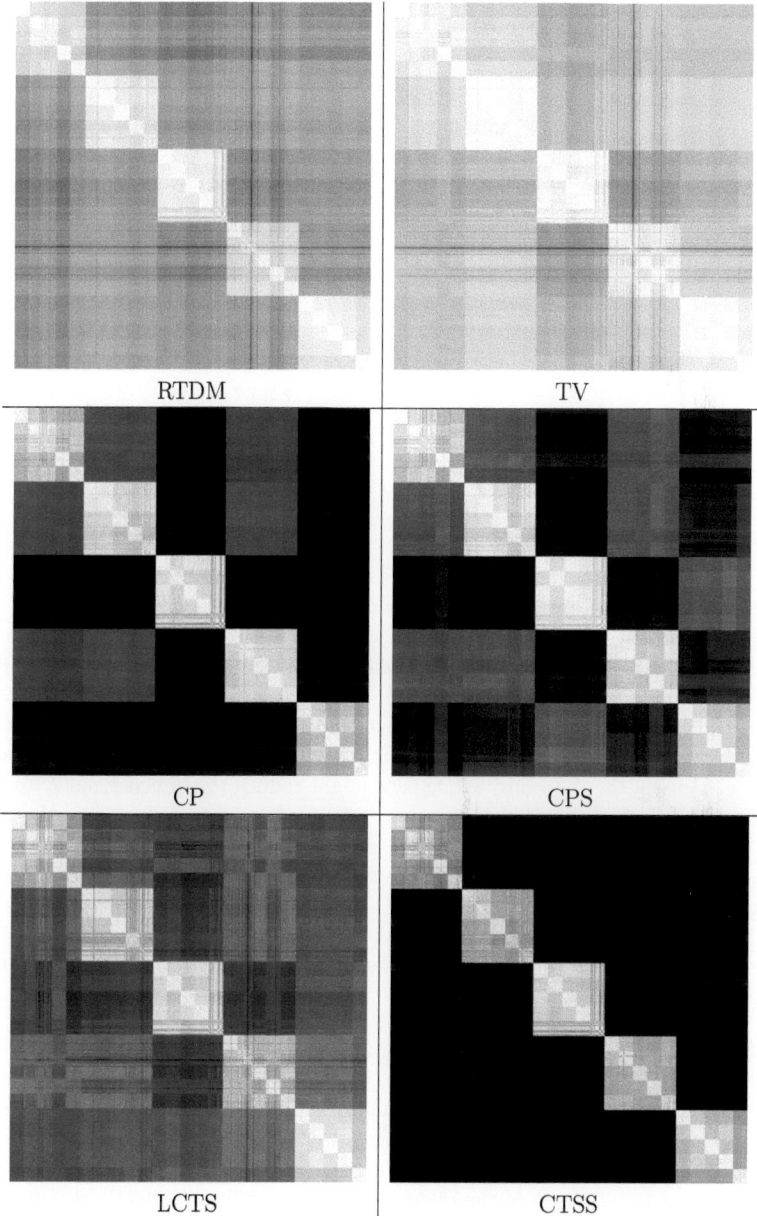

Figure 7.7: Visual interpretation of the distance matrices for 500 template based documents from five web sites.

7 Template Clustering and Detection

$$I_{Dunn} = \frac{d_{min}}{d_{max}}$$

The higher the value of I_{Dunn}, the better the distance measure separates the documents based on different templates. In table 7.2 we see the Dunn index for all distance measures on our set of 500 documents. The best results are achieved by the two shingling measures and the CP method. The TV distance measure instead scores the lowest value. So, the impression of the visual matrix interpretation is reinforced also by the Dunn index: the TV distance does not reflect very well the underlying template similarities.

Table 7.2: Dunn index I_{Dunn} for all distance measures.

Distance Measure	I_{Dunn}
RTDM	0.4657
TV	0.1031
CP	1.1691
CPS	1.2272
LCTS	0.6726
CTSS	1.2901

Now that the distance matrices have been computed and analysed, it is time to apply the different cluster analysis methods. To get a first idea on how the documents could be located relatively to each other in a 2D vector space, we use the MDS method as described above. The resulting 2D mapping of the distance data is shown in figure 7.8. Here the clusters of the different templates can be determined quite clearly as well, but it becomes even more obvious that their separation is not always as distinctive as it could be expected. However, mapping the data into a 2D space might reduce the dimensionality too much to allow more than a first visual analysis on how the data might be clustered. Hence, we will now apply first the k-median and then the single linkage clustering algorithm.

To evaluate the clusters computed by the two algorithms we use three different measures: the *Rand index* [Ran71], the *cluster purity* and the *mutual information* (as explained e.g. in [SGM00]). We will first take a short look at these measures and explain and formulate them, once again, directly in terms of how they translate into the context of web documents and their underlying template structures.

Rand Index: Given a ground truth providing a "correct" clustering of the documents according to their underlying templates, the Rand index measures how often a computed cluster configuration "agrees" with the ground truth. In our case an agreement corresponds to the cluster analysis either claiming correctly two documents to be based on the same template (i.e. being grouped together in the same cluster) or to claiming correctly two of the documents having different underlying templates (i.e. putting them in different clusters). A disagreement accordingly corresponds to either putting documents together in a cluster which have different underlying templates or

7.1 Clustering Template Based Documents

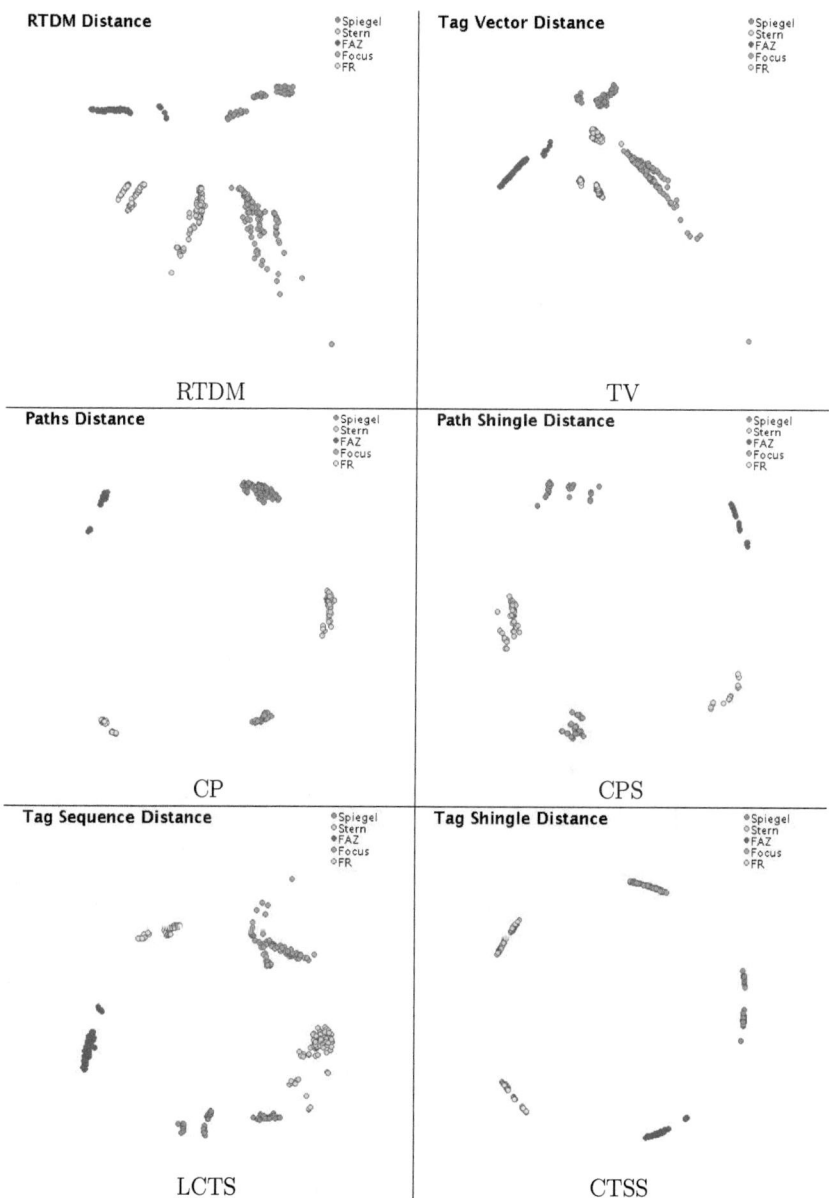

Figure 7.8: Using MDS to map the documents into a two dimensional space while maintaining the distances.

to separate them in different clusters though they are based on the same template. Therefore, if A and D are the numbers of agreements and of disagreements, the Rand index I_{Rand} is:

$$I_{Rand} = \frac{A}{A+D}$$

Purity: The purity of a single cluster compared with a ground truth provides a measure of how many documents based on the same template are lying within the cluster. Given a cluster c_l and the number $n_l^{(i)}$ of documents in cluster l which according to the ground truth actually belong to cluster i, the purity is:

$$P(c_l) = \frac{1}{\sum_i n_l^{(i)}} \cdot \max_i n_l^{(i)}$$

Purity is a measure to evaluate one cluster only. So, for an entire cluster analysis it is necessary to compute some kind of aggregation, e.g. the average purity.

Mutual Information: Mutual information is another common measure to evaluate the consensus of a clustering with a ground truth. Given a collection of n documents based on g different templates, which were grouped by the cluster analysis into k different clusters, the mutual information is:

$$MI = \frac{1}{n} \sum_{l=1}^{k} \sum_{h=1}^{g} n_l^{(h)} \log_{g \cdot k} \frac{n_l^{(h)} \cdot n}{\sum_{i=1}^{k} n_i^{(h)} \cdot \sum_{j=1}^{g} n_l^{(j)}}$$

As the results of the k-median algorithm depend on the random initial configuration, we apply this algorithm 100 times and take the average performance for comparison with the single linkage algorithm. Table 7.3 shows the results for a clustering with k set to 5. RTDM provides the best results, followed by the CP measure. However, no distance measure, not even the RTDM tree edit distance algorithm, allows the centroid based k-median approach to generate a perfect cluster configuration.

Single linkage clustering performs far better. Extracting from the resulting dendrogram five clusters allows a perfect clustering under some measures as shown in table 7.4. All measures except RTDM and TV group together exactly the documents based on the same templates. We can deduce that for those measures, single linkage is a better way to form clusters for template based documents.

As mentioned above, it is usually not known how many different templates occur within a set of documents. Hence, k-median clustering is in general unsuitable for this task. Neither can a hierarchic clustering algorithm use a fixed number k to deduce k clusters from the dendrogram. It needs a different criterion to form the clusters. A typical approach in this case is to define a threshold distance for which the clusters are not merged any more.

7.1 Clustering Template Based Documents

Table 7.3: Evaluation of k-median clustering based on the different distance measures for $k = 5$ (Average of 100 repetitions)

Distance Measure	I_{Rand}	Avg. Purity	MI
RTDM	0.9608	0.9613	0.1444
TV	0.9399	0.9235	0.1354
CP	0.9560	0.9535	0.1432
CPS	0.9140	0.9057	0.1302
LCTS	0.9157	0.8629	0.1250
CTSS	0.9293	0.9218	0.1350

Table 7.4: Evaluation of single linkage clustering for five clusters

Distance Measure	I_{Rand}	Avg. Purity	MI
RTDM	0.9200	0.9005	0.1287
TV	0.9200	0.9005	0.1287
CP	1.0000	1.0000	0.1553
CPS	1.0000	1.0000	0.1553
LCTS	1.0000	1.0000	0.1553
CTSS	1.0000	1.0000	0.1553

To find such a threshold, we take a look at the distribution of distances within each distance matrix. The graphs in figure 7.9 show the histograms of the distance distributions using a logarithmic scale for the y-axis. Some of the measures show gaps (distances which never occur) between higher and lower distances. In particular the CPS and the CTSS measures show clear gaps, the CP distance measure even two gaps. LCTS, RTDM and the TV distance do not show such a clear gap in their distance histogram, which corresponds to their lower scores for the Dunn index and the more problematic 2D configuration retrieved when using MDS.

Assuming these distributions to be typical, we will use clustering thresholds which correspond to the gaps. As the CP, the CPS and the CTSS measure are normalised to produce distances in the interval $[0, 1]$, we can translate the gaps in the histograms directly into thresholds. We will employ thresholds of 0.6 for the CPS measure, a threshold of 0.85 for the CTSS measure and thresholds of 0.7 and 0.9 for the CP measure. Based on the threshold we can now apply again single linkage, but this time without the need of providing a priori the number of clusters to be formed.

The 0.9 threshold for the CP measure turns out to be unsuitable and results in three clusters only. However, table 7.5 shows that, apart from this exception, the gaps do really correspond to a separation of the ground truth clusters. So, choosing the distance threshold accordingly for a single linkage clustering results in perfect groups of documents which are based on the same template. Given this results, we have achieved our aim of clustering web documents with respect to their underlying templates.

7 Template Clustering and Detection

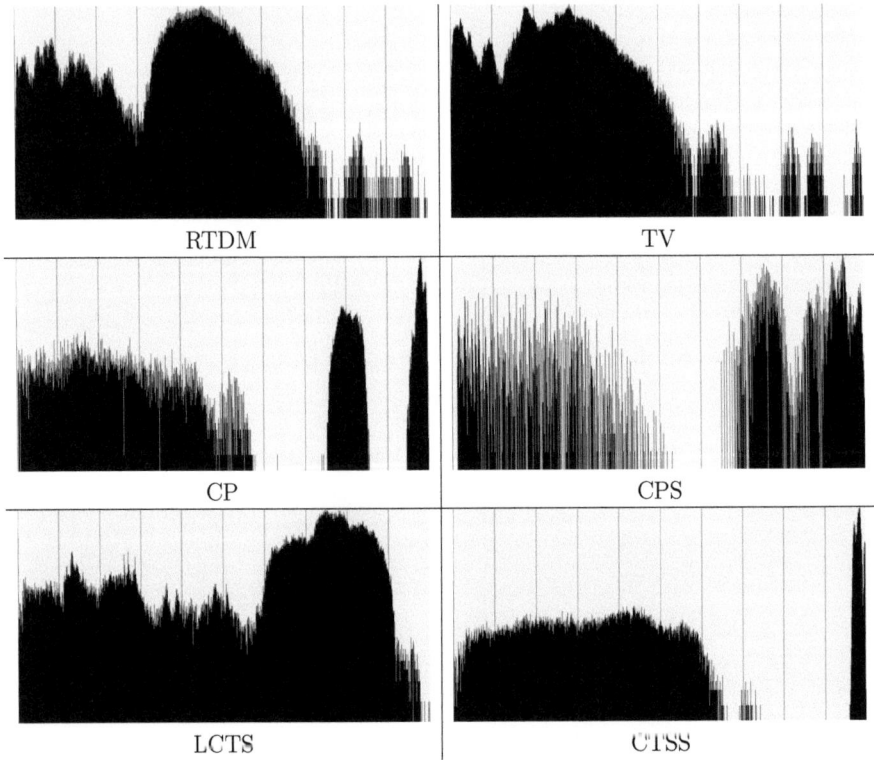

Figure 7.9: Distribution of distances for all distance measures (logarithmic scale)

7.1.4 Preliminary Results of Template Clustering

The chosen thresholds should certainly be confirmed on a larger set of documents and templates. It is too early to generalise the threshold values to be suitable for all template based documents. However, the template clustering experiments provide some very interesting results.

The first thing to notice is, that the tree edit distance measures – though often referred to as the most suitable measures to compare HTML documents and here represented by the RTDM measure – are not the best approach for clustering templates. For this purpose, some simpler measures perform significantly better. The CP, the CPS and the CTSS measure in combination with a single linkage clustering deliver perfect results.

An explanation for this better performance could be that the simpler measures are more tolerant towards particular changes in the DOM structure of a document. If a structure appears repeatedly but possibly in a variable number (e.g. the entries in a related links

Table 7.5: Evaluation of single linkage with a distance threshold chosen according to the gaps in the distance histograms.

Distance Measure	CP	CP	CTSS	CPS
Threshold	0.7	0.9	0.85	0.6
Clusters	5	3	5	5
I_{Rand}	1.0000	0.7600	1.0000	1.0000
Avg. Purity	1.0000	0.7778	1.0000	1.0000
MI	0.1553	0.1296	0.1553	0.1553

list) or if the same blocks of template generated content appear in a different order, the distances of CP, CPS and CTSS are affected only little or not at all. A tree edit distance like RTDM, instead, will detect relatively big changes in the DOM tree. The distance measure will accordingly be affected much more.

Considering the computational cost of the simple measures, the CTSS approach is slightly more expensive than the other two. The larger gap in the distance histogram, the MDS analysis and the Dunn index, instead, hint to a better separation of the clusters when using the CTSS distances.

In any case, the most interesting and important result is that template clustering is feasible. The observation of Ma et al., that their template clustering approach was not reliable was probably due to an unlucky and unsuitable combination of distance measure and clustering algorithm. The observations made here confirm that single linkage clustering based on some simpler distance measures allows to separate documents based on different templates very well.

7.2 Automatic Training Set Creation

Having solved the problem of clustering web documents according to their underlying template structure allows to detect different templates within a training set for a TD algorithm. Further, by knowing these clusters, it is actually possible to clean the training sets automatically.

A particular application of this automation is to convert a multi document TD algorithm into a CE algorithm which can operate on a single document as input. The idea of this approach is, that we create a training set online and automatically whenever confronted with a web document. In this way we can virtually apply TD on a single document. This allows to combine the advantages of the two worlds of TD and CE. We will now describe such a method to bootstrap TD.

This process of bootstrapping consists of two phases. Provided an initial single document for which the main content should be extracted, we collect in the first phase a set of documents which are likely to be based on the same template. By clustering the collected documents according to their underlying templates, we distinguish in the second phase

7 Template Clustering and Detection

between the different template structures present in this set. Using the cluster which has been formed around the initial document as the training set for a TD algorithm allows to detect the very template we are interested in, namely the one of the initial document. We will now look at this process in more detail.

7.2.1 Bootstrapping Template Detection

So, starting from the single document of a classical CE algorithm we have to provide a set of training documents for a TD algorithm automatically and without any user interaction. To bridge the gap between TD and CE algorithms, we already identified the two steps of finding a set of documents which are likely to be based on the same template as the initial document and of filtering out those documents which are not based on this template.

To realise the first task we simply download the web documents referenced from the initial document via its hyperlinks. Recalling our remark from the introduction on the increased use of WCMS motivates this approach. Web pages created by the same WCMS usually have a high number of intra-site links which connect them. Furthermore, the documents originating from the same web site are a good starting point for building a training set as they are very likely based on the same or at least similar templates. Collecting the referenced documents corresponds to a limited crawling process. A simple crawler is fed with the initial document, parses it for all anchor elements a and downloads the documents referenced via their `href` attribute.

This set of documents will most certainly contain documents, which are based on different templates. Hyperlinks to external web sites, to internal pages which use a different layout (e.g. a printer friendly layout for the same main content) or to pages which serve as navigation pages (e.g. the TOC pages as described by Kao et al. in [KCLH02]) cause this collection of documents to contain several different template structures. To clean the document set from this noise, we apply a suitable cluster analysis like the ones introduced in 7.1. Clustering all referenced documents including the initial document groups the web pages according to their underlying templates. Selecting the cluster which contains the initial document provides a clean training set of documents based on the same template. The single steps of the overall process of crawling and clustering the linked documents and building a TD training set for an initial document automatically is summarised in figure 7.10.

A similar approach of clustering documents to purify training sets is taken by Reis et al. in [RGdL04]. They use the top-down hierarchical tree matching algorithm RTDM to calculate the similarities and form clusters with a similarity threshold of 80%. As they already start with a given collection of training documents, they do not need to build training sets on-the-fly. They note, however, that crawling and downloading all documents from the domain of a web site is a common way to build training sets. Aside from the problems of RTDM to form reliable clusters – as we have observed above – this approach causes an additional problem. The document set to be cleaned becomes large very quickly,

7.2 Automatic Training Set Creation

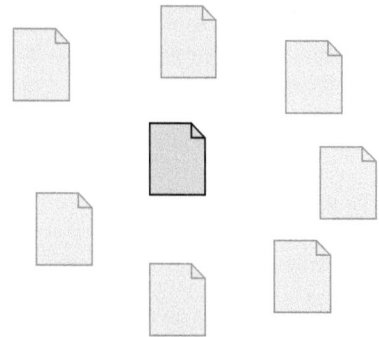
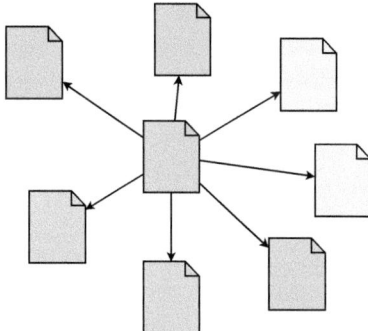

(a) The process starts from a single seed document for which the main content has to be extracted via a TD algorithm.

(b) In a first step, all documents referenced via hyperlinks are downloaded. These documents might be based on different template structures.

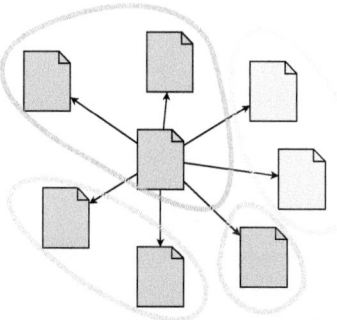
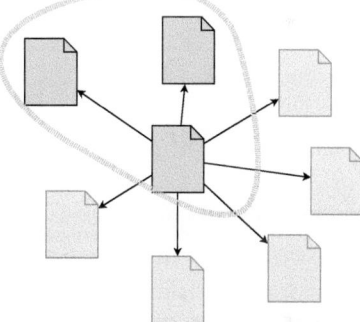

(c) Comparing all of the documents and calculating a distance for their structural similarity allows to cluster the documents according to their underlying template.

(d) The cluster which forms around the initial seed document can then be used as training set for the TD algorithm.

Figure 7.10: The process of building a clean TD training set for a single seed document.

hence, the whole process will take very long. Further, the paper of Reis et al. does not mention any evaluation of how well this clustering approach works.

7.2.2 Entropy Based Template Detection

In 3.3 we already referred to several publications discussing TD algorithms. Some of them – namely InfoDiscoverer, ContentExtractor and to a certain degree also the pagelet based approach of Bar-Yossef and Rajagopalan – are segmenting the pages to find redundant pieces of information. For this purpose all approaches calculate the entropy or a similar

7 Template Clustering and Detection

measure for each of the segments found in the training set. Segments which appear too often across several documents are considered redundant and are declared to be part of the template framework or some other automatically generated content.

We use a simplified version of the algorithm of Ma et al. [MGCC03] to confirm that the idea of training set generation for TD is working and to complete the link to the CE world in practice. Given the background of CE, we analyse only the texts appearing in the web documents of the training sets. We base the segmentation of a web document on its DOM tree representation: each text node in the DOM tree is considered a segment of the web page. Counting in how many documents the fragments appear in exactly the same form we calculate the document frequency of the texts. If the document frequency for a text fragment of the initial document is too high, we remove it from the document. In this way, all redundant texts are removed and the content which remains should be the main content. This corresponds to the functionality of a CE algorithm.

In our context, the algorithm of Ma et al. has an advantage beyond being well and fully described and its simplicity to implement it. It does not really make use of the structures of the web documents – the algorithm is based solely on the text contents. Hence, it should be unbiased towards the structures detected and used by the distance measures.

For evaluation purposes, the algorithm has been implemented and wrapped into a proxy server as all the other CE algorithms. Thus, from a logical aspect of interaction it is not different from a single document approach.

7.2.3 Evaluation of Bootstrapped Template Detection

To evaluate how well the bootstrapped TD algorithm works we will use once again the evaluation framework developed in chapter 5. A few small adaptations need to be made to the evaluation framework, though, in order to deal with the slightly changed environment the TD algorithm expects.

As the TD algorithm will collect documents during the extraction process, the evaluation framework must provide this data as well. Certainly, the TD algorithms could crawl directly the WWW to download the referenced documents, but, in this case, it is difficult to guarantee that the documents will be exactly the same in each evaluation run. Slightly changed additional contents, e.g. due to an additional content which lists the latest news, missing or temporarily unavailable documents and changes of the templates, e.g. due to a web site redesign, can cause different circumstances for each evaluation run. Only if the evaluation framework has full control over all documents the TD algorithm can access, the results are comparable and independent of the time of the evaluation run. For this purpose, the evaluation packages are extended to contain not only the documents for which the main content is to be extracted, but also all the web pages referenced by these documents. The supplementary documents are stored in the evaluation package together with their full URL.

As the TD algorithm is implemented as a proxy server and entirely transparent for each document request, the question remains, how to gain full control over all the data it is

7.2 Automatic Training Set Creation

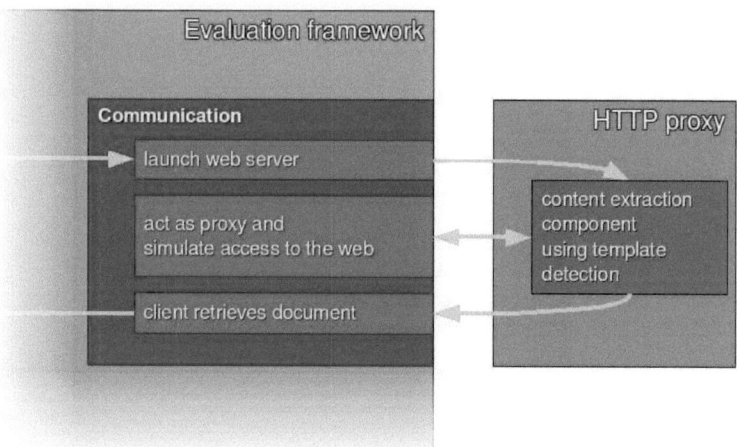

Figure 7.11: The evaluation framework simulates the web access for the CE proxy.

reading from the Internet. The answer is to employ another proxy. Pretending the CE proxy to be in a situation where it cannot access the WWW directly, but has to use a relaying HTTP proxy itself, will channel all the network traffic through a single point. At this point we insert the evaluation framework again. It acts as a proxy and accepts all forwarded requests from the CE proxy. But, instead of relaying them to the "real" web, it uses the documents stored in the evaluation package. Figure 7.11 shows the small modification in the overall process of an evaluation run as it was depicted in figure 5.5. In this way, in each evaluation run the TD algorithm sees always the same documents. If it requests a document which is not contained in the evaluation package, the evaluation framework proxy answers with an HTTP 404 error code, signalling the document was not found.

As base line for comparison we will employ again the "plain" pseudo-extraction method which corresponds to not using CE at all. For comparison with the single document methods we incorporate the results of the good performing DSC and ACCB approaches.

Given, that the evaluation packages used for the single document algorithms are lacking the supplementary files, we need to create new training sets. We will use documents from three German and two Italian online news web sites with a gold standard for the text of their main content. The test data in these packages comprises 746 documents with an outlined main content and 10,994 documents referenced by hyperlinks. The documents used in these tests were different from the ones used for fixing the distance threshold for the single linkage clustering to avoid interferences between the two experiments. Except for the documents from Spiegel online, the evaluation data was also taken from different web sites.

183

7 Template Clustering and Detection

Table 7.6: Average F1 results of the bootstrapped TD algorithm, DSC and ACCB

	espresso	heise	repubblica	spiegel	telepolis
accb-r40	0.759	0.912	0.970	0.884	0.930
cp-cluster	0.748	0.758	0.836	0.640	0.903
cps-cluster	0.748	0.741	0.823	0.640	0.899
ctss-cluster	0.748	0.743	0.819	0.640	0.904
dsc	0.722	0.886	0.934	0.918	0.865
plain	0.542	0.548	0.701	0.549	0.861

We cluster, for each of the documents, the set of linked pages to determine training sets for the entropy based TD algorithm we described in 7.2.2. The clustering is based on distances obtained from the three suitable distance measures CP, CPS and CTSS. The document frequency threshold used for discarding a text fragment corresponds to considering a text redundant if it appears in more than a third of the documents in the training set. Having extracted the presumed main content by eliminating redundant texts, we compare the remaining contents with our gold standard. The same procedure – without the detour of building training sets – is used for the DSC, ACCB and the plain approach and, in their case, corresponds to the original evaluation concept.

Table 7.6 summarises the results of the experiments, showing the average word sequence F1 score obtained for the CE process on the web documents of the five different news web sites. The complete results under all performance measures can be found in appendix B.2. The first point to notice is that the performance of the entropy based TD is always above the alternative of not using CE at all. This demonstrates the applicability of the approach. It suggests as well, that the generated training sets are suitable for the TD task. Otherwise the results would be comparable to the performance of the plain method as no redundant template information would be found and accordingly no texts would be removed.

Further, all the three underlying distance measures lead to the same quality in the results. For some test documents there are slight differences in performance, but the variations are not significant enough to derive a superiority of one of the approaches. This confirms again the comparable performance of the distance measures in clustering template based documents. It further allows to favour the simple path based CP distance measure, as it is slightly faster in comparison to the other two measures.

Compared with DSC and ACCB the results are not as conclusive. For the documents taken from the online versions of L'espresso and Telepolis the entropy based approach delivers better results than DSC, for the other three web sites the results are worse. In comparison to the F1 scores of ACCB the TD approach is always inferior. Looking more closely at the performance in the recall and precision measures underlying F1 can help to explain this observation. The entropy based algorithm always scores a very high, often even a perfect recall value, i.e. the extractor almost certainly finds the main content. The precision instead is not as good, which means that some other contents are not filtered out even though they ought to be. Thus, the precision improvements compared with the plain series are usually not of the same magnitude as those of DSC and ACCB. DSC and ACCB however never score a perfect recall. In the light of the F1 measure, this tradeoff of sacrificing recall for improving precision favours the single document algorithms.

An explanation for the poorer precision performance of the entropy based CE method can be found in the way the extractor is working. If a text fragment is created by a WCMS in the context of a particular document – e.g. a list of related links – it might not appear in the same form on any other linked page found in the training set. Accordingly, these texts will not be discovered as redundant and will not be removed from the document. The problem, however, is common to all entropy based TD methods and can appear even for perfect training sets.

Looking at the results, the entropy based algorithm might be a suitable solution for applications which require a high recall and which can easily handle additional data. A typical scenario for such an application is streamlining web pages for displaying them on small screen devices or pre-processing them for screen readers. Mutilating the main content by extracting too little of it is obviously counterproductive in these cases, while the user can easily ignore some wrongly extracted additional content. Also some of the scenarios described in the last chapter as motivation for the LSI and LP algorithms fall in this category.

Another drawback of the TD algorithms is the time they need. While most traditional CE algorithms process an HTML document within fractions of a second, any algorithm needing a training set takes longer as we can see in figure 7.12. Downloading the linked documents, calculating the distance matrix and applying the TD algorithm is very time consuming and renders this approach so far unsuitable for an effective on-the-fly extraction of the main content.

7.2.4 Conclusions about Bootstrapping Template Detection

With the incorporation of the automatic training set creation into a TD algorithm, we managed to bring together the two major benefits from the worlds of TD and CE. Combining the possibility of working "out of the box" and without the need of explicitly providing a training set with the theoretic underpinning of TD algorithms allows to create a new class of CE algorithms. Already a variation of the simple algorithm of Ma et al. provides quite good results. Employing more sophisticated web document segmentation methods and more detailed algorithms for detecting redundant information might improve the precision score obtained by the bootstrapping approach.

For time critical applications that need to perform CE on-the-fly, the approach is not yet suitable, though. Crawling the linked documents and clustering the thereby created document collection is a very time consuming task. There are, however, several ways to speed up the process. Parallelising the crawling process and the calculation of the

7 Template Clustering and Detection

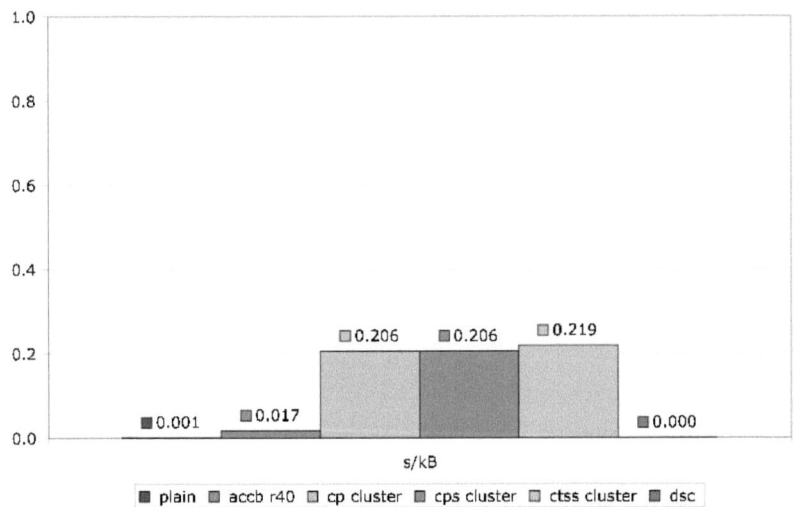

Figure 7.12: Time performance of ACCB, DSC and the clustering TD algorithms.

distance matrix is a first measure to take. Another possibility could be to limit the size of the generated training set, as the time complexity for computing the distance matrix, underlying the clustering, is of quadratic order. A further improvement could be to reduce the necessity to download all referenced documents by selecting only those links which seem promising. This would mean to guide the crawling process to retrieve documents based on the same template.

A different and quite applied issue is to build in a fallback solution, in case no suitable training documents for TD are found during the cluster analysis. A quick, easy and straight forward solution would be to use a single document CE algorithm if the training set contains very few documents or only the initial one. Depending on the scenario we could simply use ACCB or DSC for this purpose.

8 Conclusions and Future Work

In this thesis we have dealt with several topics in the context of CE. In this chapter we summarise shortly the contributions and formulate the conclusions which can be drawn from the results. Afterwards we will take a look at possible directions in which to drive future work. An interesting aspect in this context will be the role of CE for the Web-as-corpus initiative and the relation of CE to HTML 5, for which the W3C has released the first working draft of the specifications in January 2008.

8.1 Results and Conclusions

The main results and contributions of this thesis fall in four categories: the survey of CE algorithms and related techniques, the objective evaluation of CE methods, the development of new single document CE algorithms and the automatic creation of training sets for TD. We will now look at the results in these four areas separately.

Survey of CE Algorithms: As the topic of CE so far has rarely been addressed on its own, an overview of the algorithms in this field was still lacking. Hence, the *survey of currently available CE and TD algorithms* is certainly the first contribution made by this thesis. While discussing related work in chapter 3, we have seen a wide range of algorithms from both fields.

Also the *collection of different evaluation models* for CE methods is a result of this survey. The different purposes, aims and application contexts of the extraction systems and algorithms revealed a wide range of different approaches for evaluating the performance of a CE system. From involving human users over specialised and application specific tests to general purpose evaluation measures, we have seen a wide range of concepts to capture the performance of a system or even to compare different solutions.

All of these *existing evaluation measures proved to have drawbacks*, though. The lack of subjectivity, the impossibility to automate the evaluation procedure and, thus, the incapability to evaluate a method on a large set of data, as well as problems of divergence between evaluation result and actual performance were the main critics for existing evaluation procedures.

Evaluation of CE methods: Given the lack of objective and adequate evaluation measures for CE, we have developed a way to map the evaluation of CE algorithms into the

8 Conclusions and Future Work

domain of IR. This allowed us to use accepted and field-tested IR evaluation measures for the purpose of detecting the performance of a CE system. The result is a collection of *objective and reliable measures to capture the extraction performance, the stability and the time performance of CE algorithms.*

We *implemented our evaluation approach* in a framework which is highly platform independent and extensible for new evaluation measures. This framework allowed the evaluation of all the CE methods and systems we came across. Its first application was to *evaluate and rank the existing CE algorithms*. Comparing the results of this evaluation with the subjective impression we had of the extraction performance of the algorithms, we can say that the new measures reflect very well the perceived performance of the systems.

The comparison of the existing algorithms revealed that *DSC is the best performing CE algorithm* – even though it was never intended for this purpose. BTE is a good CE solution as well, but it takes too long to deliver the results. The heuristics of Crunch, instead, might be slightly outdated and seem not to work properly on some modern documents. LQF has an intrinsic problem in discovering additional contents which are not characterised by hyperlinks. However, these algorithms more or less succeed in finding the main content. Some are more precise, others have a high recall, but all of them can be said to be a better option than not using CE at all. FeatureExtractor and K-FeatureExtractor, instead, do not comply with this demand. They fall far behind in their extraction performance and are not a serious option for CE applications. The reason that they delivered good results in the comparison with the InfoDiscoverer algorithm was due to block based IR measures employed for evaluation. We provided some practical examples to demonstrate the general problem of this in the CE context actually quite frequently used evaluation approach.

Other insights we gained during the evaluation were *typical scenarios where most CE algorithms have problems* and tend to deliver poor results. Short main contents, in particular in combination with long additional contents are one problem. An adequate solution to detect those contents is still missing. The second scenario for which we detected a drop in performance consisted of fragmented main contents with a high rate of in-text hyperlinks. Wiki based web documents are a good example of it.

New Single Document CE Algorithms: Our next contribution, after the evaluation framework, was the *introduction of new single document algorithms*. With *LSI and LP* we used ideas from other fields, like wrapper induction and TD, to find the smallest DOM sub-tree which still contains all of the main content in a document. Evaluation showed that the approaches are not suitable in general. For both algorithms we found documents on which their heuristics make unsustainable assumptions about the main content and the CE fails entirely. An open question is, how the discovery of these problems affects the original environment of the algorithms.

The *content code blurring approach*, instead, turned out to be a very good CE algorithm. It is based on the idea of finding homogeneously formatted regions in a web document, as a uniform format is quite characteristic for the main content. In its ACCB form it even outperforms DSC in the major part of the cases. ACCB comes along with some adaptations which have been specifically designed to handle cases of fragmented main content with a high rate of in-text links. During evaluation it turned out, that this adaptation does not cause drawbacks on other documents and might even improve the extraction performance in general. Hence, given our results we can say that *ACCB is the best performing general purpose CE algorithm at the moment*.

Automatic Creation of Training Sets for TD: The problems of LSI and LP demonstrated impressively how the heuristics of single document algorithms can fail. As TD algorithms are not as susceptible to this problem, our next step was to develop a way to *transform multi document TD solutions into single document CE algorithms*. The most important prerequisite for bridging the gap between CE and TD was the possibility to build training sets automatically. This also requires a way to detect different template structures in a set of documents. *Clustering the web documents in sets according to their underlying templates* promised to meet this requirement. The few approaches to this task, which were reported in related research work, had either not been successful or had not really been analysed for their success.

We have analysed several distance measures and cluster analysis methods for web documents to see whether template clustering was feasible. Comparing distance measures based on tree edit distances, DOM tree paths, tag vectors and tag sequences, we discovered that in combination with a hierarchical single linkage clustering it is actually the simpler distance measures which perform best. Given our data, they resulted even in a perfect clustering of the templates. Hence, we managed to obtain *clustering results of previously unseen quality* and thereby proved that template clustering is feasible.

This insight was used to *implement an automatic training set construction* for a simple TD algorithm. First we used a limited web crawler to find candidate documents for the training set, starting from the initial document for which the main content is to be detected. Then we clustered the retrieved documents according to their underlying templates and chose the cluster featuring the initial document as training set for an entropy based TD algorithm.

The results of this process are promising. The algorithm works well and scores particularly high recall results. Though not achieving the same quality of ACCB under the F1 measure, it shows that automating TD is possible. Furthermore, as our way of building the training set is entirely independent from the employed TD algorithm, we can use it to turn virtually every multi document TD algorithm into a single document CE approach.

8 Conclusions and Future Work

8.2 Future Work

The incorporation of the automatic training set creation into more sophisticated TD algorithms and the evaluation of their performance is one of the tasks for future work. Using algorithms like InfoDiscoverer, SST or the approach based on Page Partitioning, it would be interesting to see the performance of a high quality bootstrapped TD.

Improving the time performance is another issue in this context. Technical improvements, like speeding up the bootstrapping process by parallelising the crawler and the construction of the distance matrix, will already improve the situation. A further speedup can be achieved by optimising the clustering algorithm in this very context. Given the good separation of the clusters it might even be possible to omit calculating the full distance matrix. Restricting the size of the training set and stopping the crawling process when enough suitable documents have been found is another option. This is particularly promising in combination with guiding the crawler to first follow those URLs, which might more likely lead to documents that are based on the same template.

In the context of single document CE algorithms there remain a few unsolved problems as well. Discovery of short main contents – especially in the vicinity of longer additional contents – remains a challenge. Tackling CE from a more semantic point of view would be a pretty new approach to single document CE. Instead of using syntactic characteristics to discover and outline the main content, a basic "understanding" of the contents of a document could provide very good hints of what belongs to the main content and what not. Hence, including natural language processing is another direction in which CE could be driven.

Also the ACCB algorithm can benefit from some fine tuning. The construction of the content code vector and the settings of its initial values for the blurring process seem to be a good starting point for further refinements. Using blurring filters different from the one for Gaussian blurring and exploring better the parameter space might improve the performance still a bit as well.

A general problem, common to both CE and TD solutions, are the developments in the Web 2.0 context. In particular, the advent and adolescence of the AJAX technologies allows to modify documents after they have been loaded and displayed in the browser. This is a problem, as the apperance of such a document is dynamic and cannot be deduced from the HTML source code alone. The dynamic aspects are contributed by JavaScript code and XML contents which are downloaded from a web server in the background while the page is being displayed and which are then incorporated into the document. This behaviour is not compatible with the classical CE and TD approaches.

Another problem with modern web pages might be the option of personalisation. If a web document has a unique look and layout for each user, it is difficult to make general assumptions about a template structure, and the CE algorithms might behave very differently for different users, even for the same main content.

A last interesting topic to mention here is to evaluate the influence of CE filters on WM tasks such as content classification or IE. An open question is, if in the end a successful

CE serves or hinders these tasks. Both results are possible and it would be interesting to know what happens under which circumstances.

8.3 Content Extraction and Web-as-Corpus

Web-as-corpus is the name of a special interest group (SIGWAC) of the Association for Computer Linguistics (ACL). The aim of the group is to develop methodologies to exploit the vast amount of text on the WWW as a source for linguistic data, i.e. as corpus for text analysis.

One of the major issues when using web documents as data for linguistic analysis is the noisiness of the texts. Therefore, SIGWAC introduced in 2007 the CLEANEVAL competition for the 3rd WAC workshop. The task of CLEANEVAL was basically to perform CE on arbitrary web documents, and thereby prepare them for inclusion in a web corpus. The participants to the competition had to filter the main content out of a given set of web documents in English and Chinese language. In addition to extracting the main content the task also demanded to deduce a very rough structure of the text, outlining headlines, paragraphs and lists.

Several research groups participated to the contest and the created extracts were compared with a gold standard using a Levenshtein distance. The performance was measured as a percentage of similarity between gold standard and extract – the precise algorithm is not described explicitly. However, leaving aside the structure detection, the evaluation methodology seems quite similar to the one introduced in chapter 5.

None of the algorithms analysed in this thesis participated in the CLEANEVAL competition, though. It would be interesting to extend the winning algorithms of our evaluation, like ACCB, DSC or a sophisticated TD algorithm, to cope with structure detection and run them on the CLEANEVAL data. Chances are good, that they might deliver competitive results.

In any case, the web-as-corpus project is an interesting application for CE. And the results of the research work following this track might provide interesting contributions for the CE and TD methods. Surprisingly, so far the two communities do not seem to be aware of each other.

8.4 Content Extraction and HTML 5

The topic of CE itself might soon become more interesting in a different environment, too. The first working draft of the HTML 5 specifications [W3C08] has been published on the 22nd of January 2008. Among the newly introduced features are concepts to differentiate between the kinds of content and to outline specific sections in a document. The kinds of content are supposed to declare whether a content is e.g. meta data, interactive or prose. The specific sections in a document extend existing concepts like the quotations or headlines by articles, navigation, headers, footers and the so-called aside sections. The

8 Conclusions and Future Work

semantic definition of the article section corresponds quite well to the main content, while the aside sections reflect additional, but still related contents. Navigation, header and footer, instead, would typically be examples of additional contents.

If the proposed concept will become part of the eventual W3C recommendation for the HTML 5 specifications, CE might change its role. On one hand it might be used as a converter from old document formats to the new HTML 5, on the other hand it could be specialised to incorporate the new tags in the extraction process.

Converting documents from old formats to new ones will probably be interesting even on the long run. One reason are legacy documents which simply will not be converted and in case of necessity will have to be transformed on-the-fly by external filters. Another reason are new documents which simply do not adhere to the specifications. One of the lessons learned in the short history of the web is that format specifications are handled in a very lax way by the community. Web document authors and even authoring software do not or at least not always comply with the de-facto standards of the W3C.

A change towards specialisation of CE would mean, instead, that CE algorithms use the additional information to operate in a more reliable but also more specific way. They could focus on categorising the contents better than what the standard permits. Classifying contents as main content, closely related content or additional content can be done more fine-grained, e.g. as suggested by Di Iorio's Pentaformat [Di 07].

This application of CE may also be used for the purpose of search engine fraud detection. After all, just because the author outlines certain contents as the main content does not necessarily mean that they actually are. Clearly an interest of introducing the new section tags is to aid search engines in creating a better index of web documents[1]. CE algorithms can verify the tagging of a document to detect manipulations and misleading markup.

So, even with the advent of HTML 5, CE will most likely not become obsolete; it might actually become even more useful. In any case, the development and the direction the new specifications have taken underline the importance of knowing the main content in a web document and thereby the importance of CE.

---

[1]This is probably also one of the reasons why one of the editors of the working draft, namely Ian Hickson, is an employee of Google.

A Test Data

The tables presented here describe how the evaluation packages for single document and multi document CE algorithms have been composed. Of particular interest might be how the main content is determined for the automatically generated evaluation documents.

A.1 Evaluation Packages for Single Document Algorithms

The packages for evaluation of single document algorithms contain for each document mainly the original HTML source code and the extracted text for the main content. They are used in chapter 5 and 6.

bbc	
Web site	BBC online
URL	http://news.bbc.co.uk
Type	General news
Language	English
No. of documents	1000
Main content	Determination via specialised automatic extractor. The headline is identified via the embedding table element with a class attribute of sh, the article body is wrapped into the two comments <!-- S BO --> and <!-- E BO -->.

chip	
Web site	Chip online
URL	http://www.chip.de
Type	Product reviews and technology news
Language	German
No. of documents	361
Main content	Determination via specialised automatic extractor. The content slots are recognised via particular comments. The title is wrapped into the comments <!-- mn-title --> and <!-- /mn-title -->, the main article in the comments <!-- mn-text --> and <!-- /mn-text -->.

A Test Data

economist	
Web site	Economist.com
URL	http://www.economist.com
Type	Economical, political and business news
Language	English
No. of documents	250
Main content	Determination via specialised automatic extractor. The headline is identified via a comment `<!-- top-title -->`. The article text follows the first comment `<!-- col -->` in a p element. Nested additional contents in the article are recognised via the class attribute `info`.

espresso	
Web site	L'espresso
URL	http://espresso.repubblica.it
Type	General news and reportages
Language	Italian
No. of documents	139
Main content	Determination via specialised automatic extractor. Several nested elements indicate the location of the title, the teaser and the main text. The title is embedded in an `h1` headline element, the teaser in the first `b` element following the title and the article text is contained in a `div` element with class attribute `didascalia`. Nested additional contents are recognised via the class attributes `data` or `paging`.

golem	
Web site	Golem
URL	http://www.golem.de
Type	IT related news
Language	German
No. of documents	1000
Main content	Determination via specialised automatic extractor. The title and a subtitle are contained in an `h3` and an `h4` element respectively. They are further indicated by the class attributes `artikelhead` for the title and `artikelsubhead` for the subtitle. The article text, instead, is embedded between the comments `<!-- content -->` and `<!-- /content -->`.

A.1 Evaluation Packages for Single Document Algorithms

heise	
Web site	Heise online
URL	http://www.heise.de
Type	Technology news
Language	German
No. of documents	1000
Main content	Determination via specialised automatic extractor. All of the main content is marked up via non-HTML tags `HEISETEXT`. The nested additional contents are identified via another non-standard element `cadv` or a `span` element with class attribute `ISI_IGNORE`.

manual	
Web site	Manual selection of pages
URL	different sources
Type	News, e-commerce, manuals, references
Language	English, German, Italian
No. of documents	65
Main content	Manually created package. Using a Firefox Extension (see p. 115), a human user outlined the main content in a web document in the browser window. The documents were taken from several different web sites, like online news, e-commerce, manuals, etc. From each web site several documents were taken to reduce the risk of including outlier documents.

A Test Data

repubblica	
Web site	La Repubblica.it
URL	http://www.repubblica.it
Type	General news
Language	Italian
No. of documents	1000
Main content	Determination via specialised automatic extractor. The main content consists of several parts, all of which are indicated by particular comments. The comments marking the beginning of a main content fragment are `<!-- inizio OCCHIELLO -->`, `<!-- inizio TITOLO -->`, `<!-- inizio SOMMARIO -->` and `<!-- inizio TESTO -->`, the end of the fragments is indicated by `<!-- fine OCCHIELLO -->`, `<!-- fine TITOLO -->`, `<!-- fine SOMMARIO -->` and `<!-- fine TESTO -->` respectively. Embedded commercials can be recognised via the comments `<!-- inserto -->` and `<!-- /inserto -->`.

slashdot	
Web site	Slashdot
URL	http://slashdot.org
Type	IT news and rumours
Language	English
No. of documents	364
Main content	Determination via specialised automatic extractor. The title of slashdot documents is obtained from the HTML `title` element by stripping off the prefix "SLASHDOT |". The short main content of a news is found in a `div` element with class attribute `intro`.

A.1 Evaluation Packages for Single Document Algorithms

spiegel	
Web site	Spiegel online
URL	http://www.spiegel.de
Type	General news
Language	German
No. of documents	1000
Main content	Determination via specialised automatic extractor. The title of a document is obtained from the HTML `title` element. The teaser text is indicated by a `p` element with class attribute `spIntrotext`. The article text is embedded in a `div` element with id `spArticleBody`. As the article might contain nested `div` elements with main content, the number of opening and closing `div` tags is counted to determine when the main content `div` is closed.

telepolis	
Web site	Telepolis
URL	http://www.telepolis.de
Type	General news
Language	German
No. of documents	1000
Main content	Determination via specialised automatic extractor. All of the main content is marked up via non-HTML tags `HEISETEXT`. However, this section contains additional contents. The main content inside it is found via `h1`, `h2` or `h3` headline elements or `p` elements with class attributes `fliess` or `zitat`.

wiki	
Web site	Wikipedia
URL	http://de.wikipedia.org
Type	Encyclopaedia
Language	German
No. of documents	1000
Main content	Determination via specialised automatic extractor. The article title is indicated by an `h1` element with class attribute `firstHeading`, the article itself is embedded in the comments `<!-- start content -->` and `<!-- end content -->`.

A Test Data

yahoo	
Web site	Yahoo! News
URL	http://news.yahoo.com
Type	General news
Language	English
No. of documents	1000
Main content	Determination via specialised automatic extractor. The headline is identified via an `h1` element. The main content is a `div` element with id `storybody`. As nested `div` elements indicate additional contents, the number of opening and closing `div` tags is counted and only the contents on the highest level are extracted.

zdf	
Web site	ZDF heute.de
URL	http://www.heute.de
Type	General news
Language	German
No. of documents	422
Main content	Determination via specialised automatic extractor. The main content consists of a teaser and the main text. The teaser is found in a `div` element with class attribute `article-box-content`, the main text in a `div` element with class attribute `artikel-inhalt-text`.

A.2 Evaluation Packages for Multi Document Algorithms

The evaluation packages used for multi document CE algorithms in chapter 7 additionally contain all those documents which are referenced via hyperlinks. The extraction rules for the main content are exactly the same as for the single document packages. Hence, the tables merely list the number of documents with an outlined main content and the number of hyperlinked documents in the packages.

espresso	
Web site	L'espresso
URL	http://espresso.repubblica.it
No. of documents	18
Referenced documents	237

heise	
Web site	Heise online
URL	http://www.heise.de
No. of documents	197
Referenced documents	3206

repubblica	
Web site	La Repubblica.it
URL	http://www.repubblica.it
No. of documents	112
Referenced documents	642

spiegel	
Web site	Spiegel online
URL	http://www.spiegel.de
No. of documents	371
Referenced documents	5827

telepolis	
Web site	Telepolis
URL	http://www.telepolis.de
No. of documents	47
Referenced documents	1082

A Test Data

B Evaluation Results

The following pages summarise the results of all the evaluation runs made in the context of this thesis. The results are presented in tabular form as the most compact mean. The evaluation results for single document CE algorithms are listed in B.1, the results for TD based multi document approaches in B.2.

The table list F1 measure, recall, precision and the estimate for the standard deviation of F1 for the following underlying document models (see 5.2.2): character sequence (CS), word sequence (WS), bag of words (BoW) and set of words (SoW). The processing time is normalised to seconds per kilobyte. All experiments were conducted on the same system with a 2.6 GHz Pentium 4 processor and 512 MB RAM, which was used to run the CE applications.

There are few cases in which the plain method does not achieve a recall value of 1.0 which seems to contradict the theoretic background. This effect is caused by problems in resolving the encoding of the HTML source code. Some special characters had not been resolved correctly when determining the main content for the gold standard. As this problem affects all CE methods equally the relative performance is not affected.

B.1 Single Document Algorithms

The following results are compiled from the evaluation runs conducted for the comparison of existing and new single document CE methods in chapter 5 and 6. The evaluated methods comprise Body Text Extraction (bte) (see 3.2.2), content code blurring in the character based version (ccb-r40), the adapted character based version (accb-r40) and the token based version (tccb-25) (see 6.4), Crunch (crunch) (see 3.2.1), Document Slope Curves (dsc) (see 3.2.3), Link Quota Filters (see 3.2.4) with a link quota threshold of 0.25 (lqf-25), 0.5 (lqf-50) and 0.75 (lqf-75), largest size increase (lsi) (see 6.2), largest pagelet (lp-7) (see 6.3), FeatureExtractor (fe) and K-FeatureExtractor (kfe) (see 3.2.5). The plain method corresponds to not using any CE filter at all and serves as baseline (see 5.4.2).

The evaluation packages comprise the documents taken from the web sites of BBC, Chip, The Economist, l'espresso, Golem, Heise online, La Repubblica, Slashdot, Spiegel online, Telepolis, Wikipedia, Yahoo! news and ZDF heute online. The manual package consists of different web documents taken from a wide range of web sites. Details about size, composition and creation of the single packages are given in appendix A.

B Evaluation Results

Table B.1: Evaluation results single document algorithms: average F1 (CS)

	bbc	chip	economist	espresso	golem	heise	manual	repubblica	slashdot	spiegel	telepolis	wiki	yahoo	zdf
accb-r40	0.939	0.722	0.896	0.881	0.958	0.920	0.484	0.970	0.190	0.871	0.913	0.678	0.739	0.928
bte	0.668	0.272	0.749	0.835	0.547	0.670	0.452	0.846	0.117	0.749	0.930	0.858	0.601	0.884
ccb-r40	0.938	0.745	0.918	0.882	0.939	0.851	0.487	0.966	0.189	0.870	0.916	0.400	0.749	0.928
crunch	0.754	0.390	0.823	0.816	0.887	0.830	0.430	0.892	0.136	0.734	0.915	0.754	0.742	0.784
dsc	0.929	0.738	0.891	0.872	0.959	0.883	0.485	0.926	0.282	0.908	0.869	0.652	0.785	0.855
fe	0.149	0.161	0.044	0.080	0.277	0.304	0.271	0.172	0.276	0.043	0.152	0.280	0.211	0.089
kfe	0.682	0.318	0.706	0.080	0.371	0.581	0.436	0.188	0.225	0.713	0.828	0.640	0.692	0.527
lqf-25	0.833	0.521	0.722	0.669	0.932	0.806	0.429	0.832	0.144	0.811	0.914	0.733	0.703	0.580
lqf-50	0.826	0.520	0.709	0.667	0.822	0.801	0.423	0.819	0.133	0.802	0.912	0.800	0.667	0.579
lqf-75	0.799	0.496	0.683	0.666	0.763	0.781	0.413	0.819	0.123	0.779	0.913	0.824	0.644	0.572
lsi	0.889	0.216	0.868	0.850	0.574	0.719	0.414	0.876	0.128	0.732	0.945	0.830	0.788	0.611
lp-7	0.956	0.714	0.885	0.865	0.532	0.717	0.420	0.931	0.364	0.901	0.934	0.583	0.229	0.728
plain	0.588	0.184	0.599	0.628	0.521	0.580	0.375	0.698	0.108	0.553	0.868	0.814	0.578	0.507
tccb-25	0.931	0.844	0.906	0.881	0.947	0.823	0.469	0.920	0.280	0.915	0.906	0.653	0.765	0.748

Table B.2: Evaluation results single document algorithms: average recall (CS)

	bbc	chip	economist	espresso	golem	heise	manual	repubblica	slashdot	spiegel	telepolis	wiki	yahoo	zdf
accb-r40	0.937	0.925	0.958	0.898	0.928	0.934	0.872	0.965	0.940	0.906	0.919	0.559	0.850	0.919
bte	1.000	0.999	0.991	0.968	1.000	0.998	0.905	0.999	0.999	0.973	0.997	0.809	0.999	1.000
ccb-r40	0.936	0.895	0.948	0.898	0.890	0.815	0.863	0.956	0.900	0.895	0.918	0.291	0.849	0.919
crunch	0.994	0.993	0.999	0.959	0.981	0.947	0.937	0.996	0.970	0.982	0.998	0.752	0.999	1.000
dsc	0.902	0.923	0.915	0.868	0.938	0.865	0.792	0.941	0.917	0.925	0.838	0.552	0.894	0.808
fe	0.083	0.100	0.027	0.069	0.166	0.196	0.246	0.146	0.216	0.023	0.088	0.197	0.165	0.049
kfe	0.655	0.791	0.823	0.069	0.399	0.755	0.721	0.164	0.649	0.793	0.819	0.596	0.816	0.559
lqf-25	0.994	1.000	0.998	0.965	1.000	0.977	0.946	1.000	0.998	0.985	0.997	0.689	0.999	1.000
lqf-50	0.995	1.000	0.999	0.968	1.000	0.983	0.950	1.000	1.000	0.987	1.000	0.861	0.999	1.000
lqf-75	0.995	1.000	0.999	0.968	1.000	0.987	0.960	1.000	1.000	0.989	1.000	0.917	0.999	1.000
lsi	0.985	0.770	0.997	0.936	0.988	0.867	0.911	0.991	0.945	0.945	0.999	0.985	0.989	0.925
lp-7	0.987	0.966	0.958	0.960	0.542	0.789	0.681	0.979	0.695	0.849	0.988	0.500	0.147	0.831
plain	1.000	1.000	1.000	0.969	1.000	1.000	1.000	1.000	1.000	1.000	1.000	1.000	1.000	1.000
tccb-25	0.926	0.838	0.950	0.887	0.911	0.894	0.835	0.897	0.932	0.898	0.906	0.548	0.879	0.669

B.1 Single Document Algorithms

Table B.3: Evaluation results single document algorithms: average precision (CS)

	bbc	chip	economist	espresso	golem	heise	manual	repubblica	slashdot	spiegel	telepolis	wiki	yahoo	zdf
accb-r40	0.943	0.602	0.853	0.918	0.991	0.913	0.391	0.984	0.118	0.856	0.934	1.000	0.672	0.950
bte	0.514	0.160	0.619	0.766	0.382	0.524	0.354	0.758	0.064	0.627	0.897	0.942	0.441	0.804
ccb-r40	0.943	0.646	0.917	0.919	0.998	0.912	0.397	0.985	0.126	0.863	0.942	1.000	0.688	0.950
crunch	0.618	0.247	0.718	0.739	0.811	0.751	0.312	0.819	0.077	0.603	0.869	0.774	0.602	0.654
dsc	0.964	0.625	0.894	0.931	0.989	0.923	0.423	0.931	0.191	0.917	0.936	0.874	0.720	0.943
fe	1.000	0.472	0.630	0.447	0.970	0.938	0.636	0.628	0.489	0.616	0.988	0.777	0.460	0.654
kfe	0.938	0.279	0.734	0.447	0.401	0.721	0.454	0.624	0.213	0.744	0.933	0.793	0.633	0.729
lqf-25	0.726	0.358	0.584	0.528	0.873	0.703	0.311	0.733	0.081	0.702	0.866	0.826	0.556	0.420
lqf-50	0.714	0.358	0.568	0.524	0.703	0.693	0.305	0.716	0.074	0.689	0.862	0.768	0.514	0.419
lqf-75	0.676	0.336	0.536	0.523	0.623	0.663	0.294	0.716	0.068	0.657	0.862	0.763	0.488	0.412
lsi	0.840	0.127	0.821	0.823	0.431	0.661	0.331	0.849	0.072	0.673	0.921	0.751	0.667	0.493
lp-7	0.928	0.576	0.846	0.828	0.540	0.693	0.454	0.900	0.271	0.976	0.919	0.965	0.734	0.667
plain	0.429	0.103	0.442	0.477	0.357	0.423	0.258	0.563	0.059	0.399	0.787	0.704	0.418	0.350
tccb-25	0.940	0.934	0.895	0.929	0.990	0.799	0.407	0.973	0.220	0.963	0.942	1.000	0.700	0.960

Table B.4: Evaluation results single document algorithms: stability (CS)

	bbc	chip	economist	espresso	golem	heise	manual	repubblica	slashdot	spiegel	telepolis	wiki	yahoo	zdf
accb-r40	0.033	0.106	0.120	0.196	0.025	0.066	0.252	0.088	0.155	0.120	0.141	0.253	0.148	0.077
bte	0.120	0.076	0.149	0.182	0.093	0.154	0.248	0.152	0.083	0.137	0.148	0.170	0.132	0.091
ccb-r40	0.035	0.105	0.149	0.196	0.046	0.109	0.251	0.090	0.153	0.122	0.141	0.286	0.145	0.077
crunch	0.104	0.090	0.138	0.175	0.043	0.084	0.237	0.105	0.097	0.134	0.146	0.119	0.112	0.098
dsc	0.050	0.117	0.150	0.195	0.066	0.112	0.234	0.119	0.206	0.148	0.140	0.193	0.147	0.145
fe	0.088	0.032	0.039	0.092	0.117	0.181	0.186	0.252	0.083	0.027	0.106	0.198	0.064	0.043
kfe	0.370	0.141	0.332	0.092	0.069	0.343	0.262	0.231	0.115	0.309	0.258	0.283	0.220	0.406
lqf-25	0.081	0.098	0.155	0.154	0.024	0.114	0.241	0.144	0.096	0.109	0.145	0.191	0.128	0.131
lqf-50	0.083	0.098	0.154	0.153	0.059	0.113	0.239	0.147	0.090	0.114	0.145	0.134	0.131	0.131
lqf-75	0.087	0.097	0.154	0.153	0.072	0.115	0.236	0.147	0.088	0.119	0.145	0.121	0.131	0.131
lsi	0.166	0.052	0.229	0.205	0.148	0.271	0.247	0.238	0.087	0.250	0.149	0.172	0.117	0.206
lp-7	0.063	0.107	0.204	0.197	0.246	0.287	0.210	0.154	0.178	0.146	0.165	0.291	0.070	0.283
plain	0.132	0.059	0.152	0.145	0.090	0.146	0.228	0.183	0.069	0.159	0.143	0.127	0.132	0.132
tccb-25	0.056	0.240	0.148	0.197	0.051	0.159	0.260	0.152	0.261	0.167	0.162	0.305	0.162	0.241

B Evaluation Results

Table B.5: Evaluation results single document algorithms: average F1 (WS)

	bbc	chip	economist	espresso	golem	heise	manual	repubblica	slashdot	spiegel	telepolis	wiki	yahoo	zdf
accb-r40	0.924	0.703	0.890	0.875	0.959	0.916	0.419	0.968	0.177	0.861	0.908	0.682	0.732	0.929
bte	0.676	0.262	0.736	0.835	0.532	0.674	0.409	0.842	0.113	0.749	0.927	0.853	0.602	0.875
ccb-r40	0.923	0.716	0.914	0.876	0.939	0.841	0.420	0.964	0.160	0.858	0.913	0.403	0.742	0.929
crunch	0.756	0.342	0.815	0.810	0.837	0.810	0.382	0.887	0.123	0.706	0.910	0.725	0.738	0.772
dsc	0.937	0.708	0.881	0.862	0.958	0.877	0.403	0.925	0.252	0.902	0.859	0.594	0.780	0.847
fe	0.147	0.015	0.002	0.035	0.273	0.264	0.141	0.099	0.067	0.002	0.143	0.236	0.109	0.015
kfe	0.677	0.276	0.697	0.035	0.200	0.580	0.357	0.097	0.077	0.689	0.823	0.593	0.673	0.491
lqf-25	0.834	0.502	0.732	0.667	0.926	0.791	0.387	0.826	0.135	0.790	0.906	0.690	0.708	0.579
lqf-50	0.826	0.502	0.720	0.666	0.806	0.787	0.381	0.816	0.127	0.775	0.906	0.752	0.670	0.578
lqf-75	0.798	0.473	0.694	0.665	0.735	0.767	0.374	0.816	0.118	0.749	0.906	0.785	0.644	0.571
lsi	0.886	0.070	0.842	0.838	0.554	0.645	0.376	0.877	0.076	0.722	0.942	0.764	0.781	0.574
lp-7	0.954	0.698	0.835	0.863	0.319	0.603	0.322	0.918	0.177	0.893	0.931	0.574	0.060	0.623
plain	0.595	0.173	0.613	0.624	0.502	0.575	0.371	0.704	0.106	0.549	0.858	0.823	0.582	0.514
tccb-25	0.914	0.842	0.903	0.871	0.947	0.821	0.404	0.918	0.269	0.910	0.902	0.660	0.758	0.745

Table B.6: Evaluation results single document algorithms: average recall (WS)

	bbc	chip	economist	espresso	golem	heise	manual	repubblica	slashdot	spiegel	telepolis	wiki	yahoo	zdf
accb-r40	0.927	0.913	0.952	0.894	0.929	0.930	0.717	0.962	0.905	0.902	0.911	0.566	0.838	0.921
bte	0.999	0.999	0.956	0.946	1.000	0.998	0.805	0.997	0.996	0.983	0.995	0.808	0.999	1.000
ccb-r40	0.925	0.875	0.948	0.894	0.890	0.806	0.706	0.954	0.748	0.889	0.911	0.295	0.838	0.921
crunch	0.993	0.988	0.982	0.963	0.981	0.944	0.815	0.996	0.911	0.978	0.998	0.731	0.996	0.999
dsc	0.900	0.902	0.909	0.860	0.936	0.859	0.601	0.938	0.750	0.924	0.822	0.510	0.887	0.803
fe	0.082	0.009	0.001	0.022	0.163	0.172	0.115	0.100	0.056	0.001	0.081	0.173	0.084	0.008
kfe	0.655	0.758	0.803	0.022	0.222	0.749	0.593	0.106	0.271	0.781	0.809	0.569	0.796	0.537
lqf-25	0.993	1.000	0.981	0.969	1.000	0.971	0.838	1.000	0.986	0.980	0.996	0.658	0.998	1.000
lqf-50	0.995	1.000	0.982	0.972	1.000	0.979	0.843	1.000	1.000	0.982	1.000	0.818	0.998	1.000
lqf-75	0.995	1.000	0.982	0.972	1.000	0.984	0.869	1.000	1.000	0.985	1.000	0.880	0.999	1.000
lsi	0.975	0.272	0.968	0.901	0.988	0.755	0.816	0.991	0.521	0.934	0.996	0.907	0.985	0.858
lp-7	0.982	0.952	0.895	0.937	0.303	0.640	0.522	0.963	0.315	0.843	0.985	0.494	0.038	0.686
plain	1.000	1.000	0.984	0.973	1.000	1.000	1.000	1.000	1.000	1.000	1.000	1.000	1.000	1.000
tccb-25	0.914	0.833	0.949	0.878	0.913	0.882	0.681	0.892	0.908	0.897	0.898	0.557	0.866	0.669

B.1 Single Document Algorithms

Table B.7: Evaluation results single document algorithms: average precision (WS)

	bbc	chip	economist	espresso	golem	heise	manual	repubblica	slashdot	spiegel	telepolis	wiki	yahoo	zdf
accb-r40	0.924	0.581	0.846	0.913	0.991	0.909	0.345	0.983	0.110	0.842	0.928	1.000	0.667	0.949
bte	0.523	0.153	0.612	0.764	0.368	0.528	0.322	0.753	0.062	0.623	0.893	0.923	0.443	0.789
ccb-r40	0.924	0.614	0.911	0.915	0.998	0.900	0.347	0.984	0.108	0.847	0.939	1.000	0.682	0.949
crunch	0.622	0.210	0.713	0.727	0.733	0.720	0.279	0.812	0.069	0.571	0.861	0.735	0.598	0.638
dsc	0.984	0.591	0.890	0.922	0.990	0.917	0.361	0.930	0.174	0.907	0.926	0.779	0.716	0.931
fe	1.000	0.039	0.023	0.138	0.911	0.701	0.310	0.168	0.104	0.018	0.907	0.559	0.274	0.096
kfe	0.927	0.177	0.636	0.138	0.223	0.721	0.351	0.160	0.057	0.633	0.928	0.665	0.599	0.471
lqf-25	0.727	0.341	0.601	0.524	0.863	0.683	0.281	0.725	0.076	0.676	0.854	0.759	0.562	0.419
lqf-50	0.715	0.341	0.586	0.520	0.680	0.674	0.275	0.711	0.070	0.656	0.851	0.718	0.518	0.418
lqf-75	0.675	0.315	0.553	0.520	0.587	0.644	0.266	0.711	0.065	0.621	0.851	0.726	0.488	0.411
lsi	0.841	0.041	0.790	0.808	0.411	0.605	0.305	0.849	0.043	0.664	0.919	0.692	0.659	0.466
lp-7	0.929	0.561	0.794	0.821	0.342	0.589	0.333	0.890	0.139	0.963	0.914	0.934	0.201	0.579
plain	0.436	0.096	0.459	0.471	0.340	0.417	0.254	0.571	0.057	0.396	0.772	0.717	0.421	0.356
tccb-25	0.918	0.934	0.889	0.920	0.988	0.801	0.359	0.971	0.212	0.954	0.938	1.000	0.694	0.951

Table B.8: Evaluation results single document algorithms: stability (WS)

	bbc	chip	economist	espresso	golem	heise	manual	repubblica	slashdot	spiegel	telepolis	wiki	yahoo	zdf
accb-r40	0.035	0.107	0.147	0.206	0.025	0.072	0.274	0.089	0.153	0.135	0.154	0.257	0.161	0.078
bte	0.119	0.074	0.153	0.189	0.095	0.147	0.253	0.155	0.083	0.137	0.151	0.205	0.133	0.091
ccb-r40	0.037	0.116	0.155	0.206	0.047	0.121	0.277	0.091	0.154	0.143	0.154	0.291	0.159	0.078
crunch	0.102	0.084	0.146	0.172	0.056	0.091	0.245	0.107	0.093	0.146	0.147	0.137	0.113	0.100
dsc	0.052	0.136	0.164	0.204	0.068	0.119	0.265	0.124	0.222	0.164	0.166	0.234	0.154	0.152
fe	0.087	0.012	0.005	0.100	0.117	0.209	0.193	0.257	0.040	0.013	0.104	0.197	0.049	0.024
kfe	0.369	0.172	0.342	0.100	0.055	0.341	0.281	0.241	0.055	0.321	0.265	0.302	0.245	0.425
lqf-25	0.081	0.096	0.159	0.152	0.028	0.114	0.246	0.146	0.094	0.123	0.147	0.227	0.129	0.131
lqf-50	0.083	0.096	0.158	0.151	0.066	0.112	0.244	0.149	0.087	0.132	0.147	0.165	0.132	0.131
lqf-75	0.086	0.095	0.157	0.151	0.078	0.113	0.238	0.149	0.085	0.135	0.147	0.145	0.132	0.132
lsi	0.183	0.083	0.221	0.204	0.150	0.378	0.252	0.236	0.092	0.268	0.152	0.165	0.119	0.268
lp-7	0.090	0.114	0.262	0.200	0.387	0.422	0.234	0.200	0.230	0.195	0.170	0.293	0.039	0.413
plain	0.132	0.056	0.156	0.143	0.090	0.142	0.227	0.184	0.070	0.163	0.144	0.127	0.133	0.132
tccb-25	0.067	0.240	0.154	0.207	0.052	0.170	0.281	0.156	0.263	0.177	0.175	0.307	0.175	0.244

B Evaluation Results

Table B.9: Evaluation results single document algorithms: average F1 (BoW)

	bbc	chip	economist	espresso	golem	heise	manual	repubblica	slashdot	spiegel	telepolis	wiki	yahoo	zdf
accb-r40	0.924	0.709	0.895	0.878	0.959	0.918	0.436	0.969	0.186	0.868	0.912	0.682	0.747	0.931
bte	0.676	0.262	0.737	0.836	0.532	0.675	0.424	0.843	0.113	0.753	0.927	0.858	0.603	0.875
ccb-r40	0.923	0.720	0.918	0.879	0.939	0.847	0.437	0.965	0.184	0.865	0.917	0.403	0.755	0.931
crunch	0.758	0.344	0.815	0.812	0.840	0.816	0.394	0.887	0.130	0.708	0.910	0.742	0.739	0.772
dsc	0.937	0.713	0.891	0.866	0.958	0.882	0.449	0.927	0.273	0.904	0.868	0.602	0.785	0.854
fe	0.147	0.017	0.002	0.043	0.273	0.270	0.165	0.101	0.106	0.002	0.146	0.252	0.116	0.017
kfe	0.684	0.281	0.702	0.043	0.290	0.583	0.384	0.100	0.136	0.697	0.829	0.604	0.687	0.496
lqf-25	0.835	0.502	0.732	0.672	0.926	0.794	0.399	0.826	0.136	0.792	0.907	0.716	0.708	0.579
lqf-50	0.827	0.502	0.721	0.669	0.806	0.789	0.393	0.816	0.127	0.777	0.906	0.772	0.670	0.578
lqf-75	0.800	0.473	0.694	0.669	0.735	0.768	0.383	0.816	0.118	0.751	0.906	0.803	0.645	0.571
lsi	0.888	0.104	0.842	0.843	0.554	0.663	0.389	0.877	0.104	0.727	0.942	0.768	0.786	0.584
lp-7	0.955	0.709	0.836	0.864	0.361	0.630	0.367	0.921	0.262	0.894	0.931	0.574	0.089	0.647
plain	0.595	0.173	0.613	0.627	0.502	0.575	0.371	0.704	0.106	0.549	0.858	0.823	0.582	0.514
tccb-25	0.914	0.847	0.907	0.874	0.947	0.828	0.423	0.921	0.276	0.912	0.907	0.660	0.767	0.751

Table B.10: Evaluation results single document algorithms: average recall (BoW)

	bbc	chip	economist	espresso	golem	heise	manual	repubblica	slashdot	spiegel	telepolis	wiki	yahoo	zdf
accb-r40	0.927	0.921	0.958	0.897	0.929	0.932	0.750	0.964	0.957	0.909	0.919	0.566	0.857	0.924
bte	0.999	0.999	0.959	0.947	1.000	0.999	0.831	0.997	0.997	0.990	0.996	0.812	1.000	1.000
ccb-r40	0.925	0.881	0.953	0.897	0.890	0.812	0.741	0.955	0.891	0.896	0.919	0.295	0.853	0.923
crunch	0.995	0.993	0.982	0.964	0.984	0.951	0.844	0.996	0.972	0.982	0.998	0.750	0.997	1.000
dsc	0.900	0.909	0.919	0.864	0.936	0.863	0.682	0.942	0.859	0.926	0.837	0.516	0.895	0.811
fe	0.082	0.011	0.001	0.026	0.163	0.175	0.137	0.102	0.091	0.001	0.083	0.185	0.090	0.010
kfe	0.662	0.773	0.809	0.026	0.320	0.753	0.628	0.109	0.461	0.790	0.821	0.579	0.814	0.543
lqf-25	0.994	1.000	0.982	0.975	1.000	0.974	0.870	1.000	0.992	0.982	0.997	0.683	0.998	1.000
lqf-50	0.996	1.000	0.983	0.977	1.000	0.981	0.874	1.000	1.000	0.985	1.000	0.840	0.999	1.000
lqf-75	0.997	1.000	0.983	0.977	1.000	0.985	0.893	1.000	1.000	0.988	1.000	0.902	0.999	1.000
lsi	0.978	0.393	0.968	0.907	0.988	0.780	0.848	0.991	0.759	0.945	0.996	0.911	0.992	0.874
lp-7	0.983	0.967	0.895	0.938	0.349	0.673	0.574	0.966	0.490	0.844	0.985	0.495	0.057	0.719
plain	1.000	1.000	0.984	0.977	1.000	1.000	1.000	1.000	1.000	1.000	1.000	1.000	1.000	1.000
tccb-25	0.914	0.839	0.955	0.881	0.913	0.890	0.720	0.897	0.947	0.899	0.907	0.557	0.878	0.676

B.1 Single Document Algorithms

Table B.11: Evaluation results single document algorithms: average precision (BoW)

	bbc	chip	economist	espresso	golem	heise	manual	repubblica	slashdot	spiegel	telepolis	wiki	yahoo	zdf
accb-r40	0.924	0.585	0.851	0.916	0.992	0.911	0.358	0.983	0.115	0.848	0.932	1.000	0.680	0.952
bte	0.523	0.153	0.613	0.766	0.368	0.528	0.335	0.753	0.062	0.626	0.894	0.929	0.443	0.789
ccb-r40	0.924	0.617	0.914	0.918	0.998	0.907	0.361	0.984	0.122	0.854	0.942	1.000	0.693	0.952
crunch	0.623	0.212	0.713	0.729	0.736	0.727	0.287	0.812	0.073	0.573	0.861	0.752	0.598	0.639
dsc	0.984	0.595	0.899	0.926	0.990	0.922	0.400	0.932	0.186	0.909	0.934	0.791	0.721	0.939
fe	1.000	0.045	0.025	0.188	0.911	0.717	0.363	0.179	0.158	0.019	0.920	0.605	0.284	0.112
kfe	0.935	0.180	0.640	0.188	0.312	0.724	0.383	0.173	0.100	0.640	0.933	0.677	0.611	0.477
lqf-25	0.729	0.341	0.602	0.527	0.863	0.686	0.290	0.725	0.076	0.678	0.855	0.789	0.563	0.419
lqf-50	0.716	0.341	0.586	0.523	0.680	0.676	0.283	0.711	0.070	0.657	0.851	0.736	0.518	0.418
lqf-75	0.676	0.315	0.553	0.522	0.587	0.646	0.272	0.711	0.065	0.623	0.851	0.741	0.489	0.411
lsi	0.842	0.061	0.790	0.813	0.411	0.619	0.314	0.849	0.058	0.667	0.919	0.696	0.664	0.474
lp-7	0.930	0.569	0.795	0.823	0.382	0.614	0.399	0.892	0.198	0.964	0.915	0.935	0.293	0.598
plain	0.436	0.096	0.459	0.473	0.340	0.417	0.254	0.571	0.057	0.396	0.772	0.717	0.421	0.356
tccb-25	0.918	0.938	0.893	0.923	0.988	0.807	0.374	0.974	0.216	0.956	0.942	1.000	0.702	0.957

Table B.12: Evaluation results single document algorithms: stability (BoW)

	bbc	chip	economist	espresso	golem	heise	manual	repubblica	slashdot	spiegel	telepolis	wiki	yahoo	zdf
accb-r40	0.035	0.103	0.144	0.206	0.025	0.070	0.273	0.088	0.157	0.134	0.144	0.257	0.154	0.075
bte	0.119	0.075	0.152	0.189	0.095	0.147	0.257	0.155	0.083	0.135	0.151	0.201	0.133	0.091
ccb-r40	0.037	0.113	0.152	0.207	0.047	0.117	0.275	0.089	0.161	0.141	0.145	0.291	0.153	0.075
crunch	0.103	0.085	0.146	0.172	0.055	0.087	0.245	0.107	0.096	0.146	0.147	0.128	0.113	0.100
dsc	0.052	0.133	0.160	0.204	0.068	0.114	0.269	0.120	0.219	0.161	0.146	0.229	0.149	0.144
fe	0.087	0.015	0.005	0.100	0.117	0.204	0.196	0.257	0.069	0.014	0.104	0.200	0.050	0.025
kfe	0.372	0.175	0.343	0.100	0.067	0.343	0.281	0.241	0.093	0.323	0.259	0.303	0.244	0.428
lqf-25	0.081	0.097	0.159	0.152	0.028	0.112	0.245	0.146	0.093	0.123	0.147	0.216	0.128	0.131
lqf-50	0.084	0.097	0.158	0.152	0.066	0.111	0.243	0.149	0.087	0.132	0.147	0.154	0.132	0.131
lqf-75	0.087	0.095	0.158	0.151	0.078	0.113	0.238	0.149	0.085	0.135	0.147	0.135	0.132	0.132
lsi	0.176	0.073	0.221	0.204	0.150	0.352	0.250	0.236	0.089	0.263	0.151	0.166	0.117	0.255
lp-7	0.083	0.110	0.261	0.200	0.360	0.389	0.226	0.190	0.208	0.190	0.169	0.292	0.047	0.381
plain	0.132	0.056	0.156	0.143	0.090	0.142	0.227	0.184	0.070	0.163	0.144	0.127	0.133	0.132
tccb-25	0.067	0.238	0.151	0.207	0.052	0.163	0.280	0.153	0.264	0.176	0.164	0.307	0.170	0.242

B Evaluation Results

Table B.13: Evaluation results single document algorithms: average F1 (SoW)

	bbc	chip	economist	espresso	golem	heise	manual	repubblica	slashdot	spiegel	telepolis	wiki	yahoo	zdf
accb-r40	0.921	0.701	0.903	0.874	0.979	0.929	0.498	0.981	0.272	0.865	0.923	0.726	0.809	0.956
bte	0.682	0.309	0.750	0.831	0.541	0.656	0.493	0.848	0.196	0.747	0.932	0.872	0.661	0.905
ccb-r40	0.921	0.716	0.926	0.875	0.966	0.869	0.498	0.978	0.264	0.863	0.929	0.456	0.825	0.956
crunch	0.773	0.612	0.843	0.818	0.892	0.819	0.479	0.913	0.222	0.803	0.929	0.734	0.784	0.830
dsc	0.957	0.708	0.901	0.866	0.970	0.900	0.491	0.945	0.341	0.904	0.888	0.638	0.864	0.885
fe	0.222	0.021	0.004	0.058	0.365	0.325	0.185	0.112	0.109	0.003	0.205	0.309	0.184	0.026
kfe	0.696	0.329	0.706	0.058	0.279	0.572	0.423	0.113	0.151	0.689	0.846	0.623	0.745	0.503
lqf-25	0.832	0.550	0.705	0.637	0.930	0.798	0.471	0.826	0.223	0.803	0.914	0.736	0.777	0.587
lqf-50	0.825	0.550	0.697	0.636	0.816	0.794	0.466	0.813	0.212	0.788	0.912	0.767	0.736	0.586
lqf-75	0.807	0.525	0.673	0.635	0.758	0.766	0.460	0.813	0.202	0.764	0.912	0.796	0.710	0.580
lsi	0.885	0.126	0.851	0.841	0.582	0.654	0.458	0.879	0.159	0.734	0.951	0.770	0.783	0.593
lp-7	0.946	0.749	0.842	0.864	0.360	0.624	0.407	0.918	0.263	0.916	0.938	0.619	0.111	0.653
plain	0.605	0.246	0.626	0.599	0.529	0.576	0.460	0.704	0.185	0.557	0.861	0.813	0.652	0.549
tccb-25	0.913	0.869	0.919	0.873	0.969	0.832	0.481	0.948	0.357	0.914	0.922	0.694	0.837	0.794

Table B.14: Evaluation results single document algorithms: average recall (SoW)

	bbc	chip	economist	espresso	golem	heise	manual	repubblica	slashdot	spiegel	telepolis	wiki	yahoo	zdf
accb-r40	0.957	0.952	0.950	0.894	0.969	0.957	0.757	0.982	0.950	0.916	0.929	0.619	0.878	0.958
bte	1.000	0.999	0.941	0.944	1.000	0.999	0.833	0.998	0.997	0.987	0.997	0.836	0.999	1.000
ccb-r40	0.955	0.916	0.947	0.894	0.938	0.851	0.747	0.976	0.873	0.905	0.929	0.346	0.876	0.957
crunch	0.993	0.993	0.973	0.956	0.988	0.954	0.838	0.997	0.965	0.981	0.998	0.745	0.997	0.999
dsc	0.937	0.935	0.917	0.865	0.956	0.895	0.683	0.967	0.837	0.928	0.862	0.573	0.924	0.849
fe	0.129	0.014	0.002	0.036	0.232	0.221	0.154	0.113	0.096	0.002	0.122	0.233	0.126	0.015
kfe	0.702	0.778	0.803	0.036	0.339	0.760	0.632	0.121	0.408	0.798	0.840	0.624	0.838	0.558
lqf-25	0.994	1.000	0.974	0.970	1.000	0.978	0.866	1.000	0.991	0.982	0.997	0.722	0.998	1.000
lqf-50	0.995	1.000	0.974	0.974	1.000	0.984	0.871	1.000	1.000	0.985	1.000	0.863	0.999	1.000
lqf-75	0.996	1.000	0.975	0.974	1.000	0.987	0.890	1.000	1.000	0.988	1.000	0.917	0.999	1.000
lsi	0.978	0.380	0.950	0.907	0.992	0.783	0.839	0.991	0.701	0.956	0.997	0.894	0.996	0.873
lp-7	0.983	0.976	0.879	0.930	0.367	0.678	0.572	0.966	0.429	0.882	0.987	0.535	0.073	0.705
plain	1.000	1.000	0.976	0.973	1.000	1.000	1.000	1.000	1.000	1.000	1.000	1.000	1.000	1.000
tccb-25	0.944	0.871	0.948	0.879	0.956	0.913	0.722	0.943	0.944	0.906	0.922	0.602	0.903	0.733

B.1 Single Document Algorithms

Table B.15: Evaluation results single document algorithms: average precision (SoW)

	bbc	chip	economist	espresso	golem	heise	manual	repubblica	slashdot	spiegel	telepolis	wiki	yahoo	zdf
accb-r40	0.892	0.561	0.868	0.912	0.989	0.909	0.418	0.987	0.171	0.835	0.936	1.000	0.758	0.961
bte	0.527	0.185	0.636	0.759	0.375	0.506	0.399	0.759	0.112	0.618	0.895	0.926	0.504	0.835
ccb-r40	0.892	0.593	0.930	0.914	0.998	0.902	0.421	0.988	0.175	0.841	0.948	1.000	0.785	0.961
crunch	0.642	0.448	0.756	0.742	0.816	0.727	0.369	0.851	0.130	0.692	0.887	0.740	0.656	0.717
dsc	0.983	0.576	0.915	0.925	0.989	0.921	0.440	0.939	0.236	0.905	0.936	0.772	0.823	0.949
fe	1.000	0.053	0.028	0.199	0.911	0.713	0.361	0.193	0.148	0.021	0.918	0.631	0.433	0.127
kfe	0.916	0.217	0.646	0.199	0.277	0.706	0.410	0.183	0.108	0.621	0.937	0.665	0.681	0.480
lqf-25	0.722	0.384	0.565	0.487	0.870	0.689	0.356	0.722	0.129	0.691	0.861	0.777	0.646	0.426
lqf-50	0.711	0.384	0.555	0.484	0.693	0.681	0.350	0.703	0.122	0.670	0.856	0.708	0.593	0.425
lqf-75	0.686	0.360	0.526	0.484	0.615	0.640	0.342	0.703	0.116	0.637	0.855	0.718	0.561	0.418
lsi	0.833	0.077	0.813	0.809	0.436	0.606	0.379	0.849	0.093	0.667	0.927	0.706	0.655	0.483
lp-7	0.913	0.615	0.815	0.830	0.364	0.599	0.429	0.885	0.204	0.964	0.919	0.934	0.282	0.616
plain	0.444	0.142	0.472	0.443	0.364	0.417	0.329	0.567	0.104	0.401	0.771	0.702	0.494	0.388
tccb-25	0.886	0.944	0.916	0.924	0.986	0.794	0.432	0.976	0.271	0.953	0.948	1.000	0.791	0.961

Table B.16: Evaluation results single document algorithms: stability (SoW)

	bbc	chip	economist	espresso	golem	heise	manual	repubblica	slashdot	spiegel	telepolis	wiki	yahoo	zdf
accb-r40	0.035	0.095	0.137	0.206	0.023	0.063	0.264	0.079	0.154	0.123	0.128	0.253	0.127	0.061
bte	0.107	0.071	0.138	0.185	0.085	0.147	0.250	0.146	0.096	0.133	0.129	0.195	0.116	0.075
ccb-r40	0.037	0.106	0.144	0.206	0.035	0.104	0.267	0.080	0.158	0.130	0.128	0.308	0.124	0.061
crunch	0.088	0.085	0.128	0.163	0.041	0.080	0.249	0.090	0.106	0.113	0.126	0.130	0.096	0.080
dsc	0.048	0.126	0.154	0.205	0.056	0.101	0.257	0.111	0.216	0.157	0.139	0.227	0.118	0.132
fe	0.102	0.018	0.007	0.114	0.144	0.231	0.199	0.261	0.063	0.017	0.130	0.205	0.072	0.034
kfe	0.378	0.195	0.339	0.114	0.063	0.339	0.277	0.244	0.085	0.314	0.255	0.302	0.245	0.431
lqf-25	0.073	0.084	0.141	0.144	0.026	0.113	0.244	0.132	0.101	0.112	0.125	0.204	0.100	0.120
lqf-50	0.074	0.084	0.141	0.143	0.056	0.112	0.243	0.135	0.097	0.121	0.124	0.149	0.107	0.119
lqf-75	0.074	0.084	0.141	0.143	0.066	0.113	0.237	0.135	0.096	0.123	0.124	0.132	0.110	0.120
lsi	0.167	0.097	0.206	0.211	0.153	0.360	0.252	0.228	0.104	0.267	0.128	0.148	0.106	0.266
lp-7	0.085	0.098	0.257	0.198	0.381	0.395	0.226	0.188	0.211	0.189	0.145	0.267	0.056	0.407
plain	0.117	0.062	0.140	0.136	0.084	0.136	0.229	0.169	0.082	0.152	0.122	0.121	0.116	0.121
tccb-25	0.065	0.239	0.144	0.208	0.040	0.163	0.278	0.152	0.249	0.175	0.149	0.314	0.146	0.243

B Evaluation Results

Table B.17: Evaluation results single document algorithms: average time in s/kB

	bbc	chip	economist	espresso	golem	heise	manual	repubblica	slashdot	spiegel	telepolis	wiki	yahoo	zdf
accb-r40	0.000	0.008	0.015	0.016	0.009	0.012	0.020	0.014	0.013	0.015	0.052	0.028	0.013	0.000
bte	0.049	0.404	0.411	0.412	0.162	0.381	0.413	0.043	1.901	1.000	0.183	0.329	0.180	0.134
ccb-r40	0.007	0.008	0.015	0.016	0.009	0.011	0.018	0.011	0.013	0.016	0.052	0.024	0.013	0.000
crunch	0.027	0.012	0.014	0.033	0.033	0.032	0.047	0.048	0.019	0.018	0.077	0.073	0.024	0.028
dsc	0.001	0.001	0.002	0.002	0.001	0.001	0.001	0.000	0.001	0.001	0.003	0.002	0.001	0.000
fe	0.000	0.001	0.001	0.001	0.001	0.001	0.001	0.001	0.001	0.001	0.001	0.001	0.001	0.000
kfe	0.000	0.001	0.007	0.001	0.002	0.005	0.015	0.001	0.002	0.005	0.035	0.013	0.006	0.003
lqf-25	0.000	0.003	0.016	0.013	0.004	0.010	0.017	0.003	0.009	0.009	0.051	0.012	0.010	0.000
lqf-50	0.004	0.003	0.016	0.010	0.004	0.011	0.017	0.000	0.009	0.009	0.051	0.013	0.011	0.001
lqf-75	0.001	0.003	0.017	0.011	0.004	0.011	0.017	0.000	0.009	0.009	0.050	0.014	0.011	0.000
lsi	0.000	0.001	0.002	0.002	0.001	0.001	0.002	0.000	0.001	0.002	0.003	0.007	0.002	0.000
lp-7	0.000	0.001	0.002	0.002	0.001	0.001	0.001	0.001	0.001	0.002	0.003	0.001	0.001	0.000
plain	0.000	0.000	0.001	0.001	0.000	0.000	0.000	0.000	0.000	0.000	0.000	0.000	0.000	0.000
tccb-25	0.000	0.000	0.002	0.002	0.001	0.001	0.001	0.001	0.001	0.001	0.004	0.003	0.001	0.000

B.2 Multi Document Algorithms

The results in this section are compiled from the evaluation runs conducted for the comparison of multi document methods based on bootstrapping TD in chapter 7. The evaluated methods comprise an entropy based TD algorithm using a the common paths (cp-cluster), the common path shingle (cps-cluster) and the common tag sequence shingle (ctss-cluster) distance measures (see 7.1.1) for template clustering. As reference served the adapted content code blurring (accb-r40) (see 6.4), the Document Slope Curve algorithm (dsc) (see 3.2.3) and the plain method (see 5.4.2).

The evaluation packages comprise the documents taken from the web sites of l'espresso, Heise online, La Repubblica, Spiegel online and Telepolis, as well as all the web documents that were referenced via hyperlinks. Details about size, composition and creation of the packages are given in appendix A.

Table B.18: Evaluation results multi document algorithms: average F1 (CS)

	espresso	heise	repubblica	spiegel	telepolis
accb-r40	0.767	0.920	0.970	0.887	0.934
cp-cluster	0.750	0.764	0.838	0.640	0.908
cps-cluster	0.750	0.747	0.823	0.640	0.904
ctss-cluster	0.750	0.748	0.820	0.640	0.910
dsc	0.751	0.895	0.941	0.920	0.872
plain	0.545	0.554	0.689	0.539	0.871

Table B.19: Evaluation results multi document algorithms: average recall (CS)

	espresso	heise	repubblica	spiegel	telepolis
accb-r40	0.890	0.916	0.964	0.926	0.922
cp-cluster	0.963	0.987	0.996	0.998	1.000
cps-cluster	0.963	0.988	0.997	0.998	1.000
ctss-cluster	0.963	0.988	0.997	0.998	1.000
dsc	0.878	0.879	0.945	0.943	0.819
plain	0.971	0.996	0.998	0.999	1.000

B Evaluation Results

Table B.20: Evaluation results multi document algorithms: average precision (CS)

	espresso	heise	repubblica	spiegel	telepolis
accb-r40	0.786	0.933	0.981	0.856	0.955
cp-cluster	0.668	0.643	0.745	0.485	0.840
cps-cluster	0.668	0.621	0.722	0.485	0.833
ctss-cluster	0.668	0.623	0.719	0.485	0.842
dsc	0.750	0.936	0.947	0.905	0.953
plain	0.406	0.398	0.549	0.382	0.780

Table B.21: Evaluation results multi document algorithms: stability (CS)

	espresso	heise	repubblica	spiegel	telepolis
accb-r40	0.293	0.067	0.047	0.073	0.076
cp-cluster	0.248	0.133	0.140	0.135	0.077
cps-cluster	0.248	0.142	0.139	0.135	0.077
ctss-cluster	0.248	0.142	0.142	0.135	0.078
dsc	0.280	0.110	0.080	0.089	0.103
plain	0.228	0.144	0.166	0.142	0.080

Table B.22: Evaluation results multi document algorithms: average F1 (WS)

	espresso	heise	repubblica	spiegel	telepolis
accb-r40	0.759	0.912	0.970	0.884	0.930
cp-cluster	0.748	0.758	0.836	0.640	0.903
cps-cluster	0.748	0.741	0.823	0.640	0.899
ctss-cluster	0.748	0.743	0.819	0.640	0.904
dsc	0.722	0.886	0.934	0.918	0.865
plain	0.542	0.548	0.701	0.549	0.861

B.2 Multi Document Algorithms

Table B.23: Evaluation results multi document algorithms: average recall (WS)

	espresso	heise	repubblica	spiegel	telepolis
accb-r40	0.875	0.907	0.962	0.925	0.920
cp-cluster	0.964	0.981	0.996	0.997	0.998
cps-cluster	0.964	0.983	0.997	0.997	0.998
ctss-cluster	0.964	0.983	0.997	0.997	0.998
dsc	0.793	0.868	0.937	0.944	0.813
plain	0.975	0.997	0.998	0.999	1.000

Table B.24: Evaluation results multi document algorithms: average precision (WS)

	espresso	heise	repubblica	spiegel	telepolis
accb-r40	0.780	0.926	0.981	0.850	0.950
cp-cluster	0.663	0.637	0.744	0.485	0.833
cps-cluster	0.663	0.616	0.723	0.485	0.826
ctss-cluster	0.663	0.617	0.719	0.486	0.835
dsc	0.722	0.928	0.940	0.900	0.942
plain	0.403	0.391	0.564	0.392	0.765

Table B.25: Evaluation results multi document algorithms: stability (WS)

	espresso	heise	repubblica	spiegel	telepolis
accb-r40	0.301	0.071	0.047	0.079	0.083
cp-cluster	0.247	0.132	0.143	0.137	0.080
cps-cluster	0.247	0.140	0.141	0.137	0.080
ctss-cluster	0.247	0.140	0.145	0.137	0.081
dsc	0.294	0.118	0.106	0.102	0.118
plain	0.228	0.142	0.166	0.144	0.084

B Evaluation Results

Table B.26: Evaluation results multi document algorithms: average F1 (BoW)

	espresso	heise	repubblica	spiegel	telepolis
accb-r40	0.765	0.914	0.971	0.889	0.933
cp-cluster	0.749	0.759	0.838	0.640	0.903
cps-cluster	0.749	0.742	0.824	0.640	0.899
ctss-cluster	0.749	0.743	0.821	0.640	0.904
dsc	0.738	0.887	0.936	0.919	0.872
plain	0.544	0.548	0.702	0.549	0.861

Table B.27: Evaluation results multi document algorithms: average recall (BoW)

	espresso	heise	repubblica	spiegel	telepolis
accb-r40	0.888	0.909	0.964	0.930	0.924
cp-cluster	0.966	0.982	0.998	0.998	0.998
cps-cluster	0.966	0.984	0.998	0.998	0.998
ctss-cluster	0.966	0.983	0.998	0.998	0.998
dsc	0.818	0.870	0.939	0.946	0.821
plain	0.978	0.997	0.999	0.999	1.000

Table B.28: Evaluation results multi document algorithms: average precision (BoW)

	espresso	heise	repubblica	spiegel	telepolis
accb-r40	0.785	0.928	0.982	0.855	0.953
cp-cluster	0.665	0.637	0.746	0.485	0.833
cps-cluster	0.665	0.616	0.724	0.485	0.826
ctss-cluster	0.665	0.618	0.720	0.486	0.835
dsc	0.739	0.930	0.942	0.902	0.949
plain	0.404	0.391	0.564	0.392	0.765

B.2 Multi Document Algorithms

Table B.29: Evaluation results multi document algorithms: stability (BoW)

	espresso	heise	repubblica	spiegel	telepolis
accb-r40	0.300	0.069	0.044	0.077	0.077
cp-cluster	0.247	0.132	0.144	0.137	0.080
cps-cluster	0.247	0.140	0.142	0.137	0.080
ctss-cluster	0.247	0.140	0.146	0.137	0.081
dsc	0.295	0.116	0.101	0.099	0.105
plain	0.228	0.142	0.166	0.144	0.084

Table B.30: Evaluation results multi document algorithms: average F1 (SoW)

	espresso	heise	repubblica	spiegel	telepolis
accb-r40	0.778	0.923	0.983	0.886	0.943
cp-cluster	0.764	0.754	0.849	0.634	0.899
cps-cluster	0.765	0.738	0.835	0.634	0.895
ctss-cluster	0.765	0.739	0.832	0.634	0.900
dsc	0.744	0.900	0.951	0.918	0.893
plain	0.534	0.561	0.697	0.549	0.860

Table B.31: Evaluation results multi document algorithms: average recall (SoW)

	espresso	heise	repubblica	spiegel	telepolis
accb-r40	0.884	0.931	0.982	0.934	0.934
cp-cluster	0.958	0.978	0.997	0.997	0.999
cps-cluster	0.958	0.981	0.997	0.997	0.999
ctss-cluster	0.958	0.980	0.997	0.997	0.999
dsc	0.812	0.893	0.964	0.945	0.850
plain	0.975	0.997	0.998	0.999	1.000

B Evaluation Results

Table B.32: Evaluation results multi document algorithms: average precision (SoW)

	espresso	heise	repubblica	spiegel	telepolis
accb-r40	0.802	0.922	0.986	0.847	0.958
cp-cluster	0.683	0.631	0.762	0.478	0.822
cps-cluster	0.683	0.610	0.741	0.478	0.816
ctss-cluster	0.683	0.612	0.736	0.478	0.825
dsc	0.744	0.925	0.945	0.900	0.951
plain	0.392	0.402	0.556	0.390	0.760

Table B.33: Evaluation results multi document algorithms: stability (SoW)

	espresso	heise	repubblica	spiegel	telepolis
accb-r40	0.287	0.062	0.032	0.078	0.061
cp-cluster	0.223	0.127	0.142	0.130	0.062
cps-cluster	0.223	0.136	0.140	0.130	0.062
ctss-cluster	0.223	0.135	0.142	0.130	0.063
dsc	0.283	0.099	0.098	0.099	0.093
plain	0.213	0.131	0.156	0.133	0.066

Table B.34: Evaluation results multi document algorithms: average time in s/kB

	espresso	heise	repubblica	spiegel	telepolis
accb-r40	0.017	0.017	0.013	0.013	0.062
cp-cluster	0.131	0.206	0.119	0.282	0.169
cps-cluster	0.103	0.206	0.131	0.197	0.180
ctss-cluster	0.119	0.219	0.099	0.209	0.199
dsc	0.001	0.000	0.000	0.001	0.002
plain	0.001	0.001	0.000	0.000	0.000

C Glossary

Adapted content code blurring (ACCB): Adapted version of the character based content code blurring. Ignores hyperlink elements to cope with the problematic cases of documents in which the main content contains a lot of interspersed hyperlinks. (see p. 147)

Attribute: Attributes are the characteristics of instances in information retrieval and data mining. The instances are in fact described by the values their attributes have. Attributes are equivalent to features. (see p. 29)

Body text extraction (BTE): Content extraction algorithm based on a tokenisation of web documents into word and tag tokens. The main content is characterised as a continuous subsequence of these tokens which contains most words while excluding most tags. (see p. 49)

Common paths (CP): A path in a DOM tree is a sequence of nodes from the root node to a leaf node. Comparing the sets of paths which appear in two documents allows to compute a distance for document structures. (see p. 163)

Common path shingles (CPS): Applying shingling to the paths in a DOM tree results in path shingles. Comparing the sets of path shingles which appear in two documents allows to compute a distance for document structures. (see p. 165)

Common tag sequence shingles (CTSS): Tag sequence shingles are shingles of a fixed length build from the sequence of tags as they appear in a web document. Comparing the sets of tag sequence shingles of two documents allows to compute a distance for document structures. (see p. 166)

Content code blurring (CCB): Character based content extraction algorithm which involves a technique similar to Gaussian blurring filters. The blurring filter is applied to the content code vector. CCB is aiming on finding those regions in an HTML document which contain a homogeneously formatted text. (see p. 147)

Content code ratio: A value which resembles the amount of content and code in a certain source code region. The content code ratio is used by content code blurring and the derived variations to decide which parts of a web document to extract. (see p. 143)

Content code vector: The content code vector is a vector representation of the sequence of atomic content and code elements in an HTML document. The content code ratio

C Glossary

is deduced from the content code vector in an iterative process. An entry in the vector resembles a single character for CCB and ACCB and a tag or a word token for TCCB. (see p. 143)

Content extraction (CE): The process of locating the main content in a web document. The algorithms are usually based on heuristics to find the main content in a single document or apply template detection techniques on a collection of multiple documents. (see p. 16)

Crawler: A program which uses the hyperlink structure of the WWW to find and analyse web pages. Crawlers are an essential part of web search engines and harvest the documents for further analysis. Via its hyperlinks, each crawled document provides new URLs for the Crawler to visit. (see p. 9)

Crunch: Crunch is a DOM based CE framework. It combines several heuristics for filtering web documents. It was designed to improve accessibility for screen readers or small screen devices like mobile phones or PDAs. (see p. 49)

Comma separated values (CSV): A simple and text based format for storing tabular data. The values of each cell in a table are separated by a previously specified character. This character usually is a comma, a semicolon, a blank or a tabulator character. Due to its simplicity, the CSV format is commonly used for exchanging data between different applications. (see p. 109)

Dendrogram: A tree structure to represent the results of a hierarchical cluster analysis. The tree expresses which clusters are merged at which point of the cluster hierarchy. (see p. 168)

Document slope curve (DSC): A function to represent the distribution of words and tags in a web document. Each word and each tag are considered to be a token. The document slope curve is defined on the tokens sequence and assigns the i-th token the number of tag tokens encountered so far in the document. The DSC content extraction algorithm is based on finding plateaus in this curve. (see p. 51)

DOM: The document object model is a programming language independent reference model of data structures and functions for accessing and modifying the data in SGML/XML based documents. The hierarchic structure of the documents based on those markup languages is represented by a tree structure. (see p. 23)

Dunn index: The Dunn index is a measure of how good the items in a cluster configuration are divided with respect to a certain distance matrix. The Dunn index is the quotient of the minimal distance between items from different clusters divided by the maximum distance between items from the same cluster. It does not necessarily take into account a ground truth. (see p. 172)

Entropy: In classical information theory the entropy is a measure for the information contained in a transmitted message. It is based on the probability for certain contents to appear in a message or – better – the uncertainty about the contents of the message. It is used frequently in template detection algorithms to determine frequent parts of a document. (see p. 37)

F1: A quality measure for evaluating information retrieval tasks. F1 combines precision and recall in a single measure. F1 is defined to be $F1 = \frac{2 \cdot r \cdot p}{r+p}$. (see p. 35)

False negative: Characterisation of an instance which would have been relevant to a given query but was not retrieved. (see p. 33)

False positive: Characterisation of an instance which is not relevant to a given query but was retrieved. (see p. 33)

Feature: Features or attributes are the characteristics of instances in information retrieval and data mining. The instances are in fact described by the values that their features have. (see p. 29)

FeatureExtractor: A single document content extraction algorithm, which segments a document in blocks and assigns certain features to each block. As features serve the words of the contained texts and particular HTML elements, like images or JavaScript. The extraction process finds the block which corresponds best to a certain desired feature. While for classical content extraction the desired feature is text, the algorithm can also handle other kinds of contents by using, for instance, images as desired feature. (see p. 57)

Gold standard: The gold standard is the best known classification or clustering for instances which can be used for training or evaluation. The gold standard does not necessarily correspond to the real classification or clustering, neither to the best. In cases where the truth is simply not known, other ways to determine this best result are commonly used, e.g. to employ experts' opinions. (see p. 32)

Ground truth: When testing classification or clustering algorithms it is necessary to provide test data for which the correct classification or clustering is known. This true classification or clustering is referred to as the ground truth. (see p. 32)

Hierarchical clustering: Hierarchical clustering starts with each instance forming a cluster on its own. These clusters are iteratively merged according to some scheme until only one large cluster remains. The order in which the clusters have been merged can be represented in a dendrogram. (see p. 168)

Instance: An object or data item which is part of larger collection. Information retrieval tasks correspond to finding those instances in the set which are relevant to a given query. Also the objects in a training set for machine learning algorithms are referred to as instances. (see p. 29)

C Glossary

K-FeatureExtractor: A single document content extraction algorithm, which extends FeatureExtractor with a refinement which involves clustering those document blocks that correspond best to the desired content. (see p. 57)

k-means: An iterative cluster analysis algorithm which needs a parameter k of how many clusters to form. The instances are initially assigned to one of the k clusters randomly. In each iteration step, the algorithm computes a centroid for each cluster. A centroid is a value representing the centre of a cluster, e.g. an average value or an object which lies centrally to all other instance in the cluster. Afterwards all instances are reassign to the cluster, for which they have minimum distance to its centroid. (see p. 167)

Largest size increase (LSI): The largest size increase occurs at the node in the DOM tree which contributes strongest to the visible content in a web document. The detection of this node was used in the XWRAP elite system to find data rich regions for wrapper induction. The same algorithm can also be used for content extraction. (see p. 137)

Levenshtein distance: The Levenshtein distance for strings computes a distance based on the changes which are necessary to convert one string into another one. These changes like inserting, deleting and replacing single characters have a certain cost and the distance corresponds to the minimum cost for the transformation. (see p. 163)

Link quota filter (LQF): A heuristic content extraction algorithm which is quite wide spread. The basic concept is to locate regions or blocks in a web document which contain a high ratio of hyperlinks. These regions very likely represent navigation menus or link lists and, hence, are considered additional contents which are removed. (see p. 53)

Longest common subsequence (LCS): The longest common subsequence of two strings is a sequence of characters which can be found in both strings, possibly interrupted by other interspersed characters, and there is no longer sequence with this property. (see p. 103)

Longest common tag subsequence (LCTS): The longest common tag subsequence is defined similarly to the longest common subsequence for strings. The difference is that it operates on a sequence of tags. It can be used to define a distance measure for document structures. (see p. 165)

Naïve Bayes (NB) classifier: A classification algorithm based on the Bayes theorem for conditional probability. It considers the features of the instance to be independent random variables. Estimating from a training set the conditional probabilities for the values, i.e. the realisations of the features given a certain category, it deduces the category for a new instance by looking at the values the features have. (see p. 39)

Pagelet: The term pagelet was introduced by Bar-Yossef and Rajagopalan. It describes a self-contained region with a single topic or function, e.g. a link list, a search function element or the main content. (see p. 62)

Plain (extraction method): The plain method in the evaluation of content extraction algorithms corresponds to not using any extraction system. This means a document is compared in its original form to the gold standard for the main content. The method represents the alternative of not employing content extraction techniques and, hence, serves as a baseline in the comparison. (see p. 121)

Precision: A quality measure for evaluating information retrieval tasks. The precision is the ratio of relevant items in a result set. It can be combined with the recall measure into the F1 measure. (see p. 34)

Proxy: A proxy server relays requests in a client server architecture. It takes the role of a server, as it accepts requests from the client. In the same time it is a client itself as it acts like a client when forwarding the request to a server. Proxy servers are used for connecting separated networks in a single point or to control or modify the transmitted data. (see p. 108)

Rand index: The Rand index measures how far a computed cluster configuration agrees with a known ground truth. An agreement corresponds to a division of different items in different clusters or in grouping similar items together in the same cluster. A disagreement corresponds to grouping different items together or separating similar items. The Rand index is the ratio of agreements to the sum of agreements and disagreements. (see p. 174)

Recall: A quality measure for evaluating information retrieval tasks. The recall is the ratio of relevant retrieved items to all relevant items. It can be combined with the precision measure into the F1 measure. (see p. 34)

Single linkage: A hierarchical clustering algorithm which iteratively always merges those two clusters for which the distance between two contained items is minimal over all inter-cluster distances. (see p. 169)

Shingle: Shingles are the fragments of a longer sequence which all have the same length. Shingling can be used to approximate the similarity of two sequences quite efficient. (see p. 63)

Tag vector (TV): A tag vector is vector which counts how often each tag appears in a document. This vector representation can be used to compute a distance for document structures. (see p. 165)

Template: An empty framework document which provides solely a layout. It is filled with different contents to create a final document. Templates are a standard technology of web content management systems. (see p. 9)

C Glossary

Template detection: The attempt to deduce a common template structure from a collection of web documents. It corresponds to a reverse engineering of templates and can serve content extraction algorithms. (see p. 18)

Token based content code blurring (TCCB): Token based version of the content code blurring algorithm. Ignores hyperlink elements and bases the construction of the content-code vector on tag and word tokens. (see p. 147)

Tree edit distance (TED): A tree edit distance computes a distance between tree structures by determining the minimum cost for transforming one tree into the other one. The RTDM algorithm can be used to compute a tree edit distance efficiently and particularly for DOM trees. (see p. 163)

True negative (TN): Characterisation of an instance which was not relevant to a given query and has not been retrieved. (see p. 33)

True positive (TP): Characterisation of an instance which was relevant to a given query and has been retrieved. (see p. 33)

Web content management system (WCMS): Web content management systems support the maintenance of a web site in a systematic way. These information system separate at least layout, content and the structure of a web site and organise the access via different roles, e.g. of authors, editors, technical staff, designers, etc. Web content management systems appear in very different forms are by now quite wide spread. They are also considered to be responsible for most of the redundant and additional contents on the web. (see p. 8)

Web mining: Describes data mining with a focus on the world wide web and related fields. Web mining is typically subdivided into web data mining, web linkage mining or web usage mining. Web data mining are all task which try to find information in the documents on the web, web linkage mining is operating mainly on the hyperlink structure and web usage mining analyses the behaviour of web user, e.g. by looking at the access log files of a server. (see p. 36)

Wrapper: A wrapper is a program which is intended to harvest structured data from web documents which are all based on the same template. Typical application scenarios for wrappers are to retrieve information about products from an online shop or to extract contact data from phone lists. (see p. 43)

D Abbreviations

ACCB	adapted content code blurring
BPM	bi-gram proximity matrix
BTE	body text extraction
CCB	content code blurring
CE	content extraction
CMS	content management system
CP	common path
CPS	common path shingles
CSV	comma separated values
CTSS	common tag sequence shingles
DM	data mining
DMOZ	Open Directory Project
DOM	document object model
DSC	document slope curve
ECMS	enterprise content management system
ERA	extensible rendering architecture
F1	F1-measure
F-D (matrix)	feature document matrix
FN	false negative
FP	false positive
HF	highest fanout
IBDF	inverse block-document frequency
IE	information extraction
IR	information retrieval
kB	kilobyte
LCS	longest common subsequence
LCTS	longest common tag subsequence
LP	largest pagelet
LQF	link quota filter
LSI	largest size increase
LTC	largest tag count
MDS	multi dimensional scaling
MI	mutual information
NB	Naïve Bayes
NLP	natural language processing

D Abbreviations

p	precision
PDA	personal digital assistant
r	recall
RSS	really simple syndication
RTDM	restricted top down tree mapping algorithm
SAX	simple API for XML
SVM	support vector machines
TCCB	token based content code blurring
TD	template detection
TF-IDF	term frequency – inverse document frequency
TM	text mining
TN	true negative
TP	true positive
TPM	tri-gram proximity matrix
TV	tag vector
UFRE	union-free regular expression
W3C	World Wide Web Consortium
WCMS	web content management system
WM	web mining
WWW	World Wide Web

List of Tables

2.1 The confusion matrix assigns the result of a binary classification of a single item into one of four categories. 34
5.1 The confusion matrix for block based evaluation of a CE algorithm which has made one mistake. 100
5.2 Overview of the automatically generated test packages. 116
5.3 Word sequence F1 scores for all packages and CE algorithms. 125
6.1 Evaluation results of new single document algorithms: average F1 (WS). . 150
6.2 Recall for LSI, LP and Crunch in direct comparison 155
7.1 Web documents used for evaluating template clustering approaches. 171
7.2 Dunn index I_{Dunn} for all distance measures. 174
7.3 Evaluation of k-median clustering based on the different distance measures for $k = 5$ (Average of 100 repetitions) 177
7.4 Evaluation of single linkage clustering for five clusters 177
7.5 Evaluation of single linkage with a distance threshold chosen according to the gaps in the distance histograms. 179
7.6 Average F1 results of the bootstrapped TD algorithm, DSC and ACCB . . 184
B.1 Evaluation results single document algorithms: average F1 (CS) 202
B.2 Evaluation results single document algorithms: average recall (CS) 202
B.3 Evaluation results single document algorithms: average precision (CS) . . . 203
B.4 Evaluation results single document algorithms: stability (CS) 203
B.5 Evaluation results single document algorithms: average F1 (WS) 204
B.6 Evaluation results single document algorithms: average recall (WS) 204
B.7 Evaluation results single document algorithms: average precision (WS) . . 205
B.8 Evaluation results single document algorithms: stability (WS) 205
B.9 Evaluation results single document algorithms: average F1 (BoW) 206
B.10 Evaluation results single document algorithms: average recall (BoW) . . . 206
B.11 Evaluation results single document algorithms: average precision (BoW) . 207
B.12 Evaluation results single document algorithms: stability (BoW) 207
B.13 Evaluation results single document algorithms: average F1 (SoW) 208
B.14 Evaluation results single document algorithms: average recall (SoW) 208
B.15 Evaluation results single document algorithms: average precision (SoW) . . 209
B.16 Evaluation results single document algorithms: stability (SoW) 209

List of Tables

B.17 Evaluation results single document algorithms: average time in s/kB . . . 210
B.18 Evaluation results multi document algorithms: average F1 (CS) 211
B.19 Evaluation results multi document algorithms: average recall (CS) 211
B.20 Evaluation results multi document algorithms: average precision (CS) . . . 212
B.21 Evaluation results multi document algorithms: stability (CS) 212
B.22 Evaluation results multi document algorithms: average F1 (WS) 212
B.23 Evaluation results multi document algorithms: average recall (WS) 213
B.24 Evaluation results multi document algorithms: average precision (WS) . . 213
B.25 Evaluation results multi document algorithms: stability (WS) 213
B.26 Evaluation results multi document algorithms: average F1 (BoW) 214
B.27 Evaluation results multi document algorithms: average recall (BoW) 214
B.28 Evaluation results multi document algorithms: average precision (BoW) . . 214
B.29 Evaluation results multi document algorithms: stability (BoW) 215
B.30 Evaluation results multi document algorithms: average F1 (SoW) 215
B.31 Evaluation results multi document algorithms: average recall (SoW) 215
B.32 Evaluation results multi document algorithms: average precision (SoW) . . 216
B.33 Evaluation results multi document algorithms: stability (SoW) 216
B.34 Evaluation results multi document algorithms: average time in s/kB 216

List of Figures

1.1 An example of a WCMS generated web document as it is presented by a standard browser. 13
1.2 The lower part of the WCMS generated web document. 14
1.3 Four screenshots from CSS Zen Garden: the same HTML document has a different appearance due to different CSS definitions. 18

2.1 The DOM inspector of the Mozilla Firefox browser allows displaying the DOM tree of an HTML document. 24
2.2 A more vivid and artistic representation of the DOM tree of a web document. 25
2.3 Screenshot of a template based web document in which the content slots are highlighted. 27

3.1 The cumulative tag token distribution in a web document represented as a function. The arrows mark the plateau which corresponds to the main content. 51
3.2 Example of an extraction rule formulated in the XML syntax of elISA. . . 60
3.3 Bar-Yossef and Rajagopalan's template criterion: documents d_1, d_2 and d_3 form a connected component for pagelet p_1, hence, qualifying p_1 as template. 64
3.4 The DOM tree of a simple document and the according PST. The rectangular structures in the PST correspond to style nodes, the oval structures to element nodes. 69

4.1 Slashdot news article with user discussion. 91
4.2 Additional information embedded in a BBC news article. 92

5.1 Overview of the components of the evaluation framework. 110
5.2 Details of the component for managing the evaluation packages. 111
5.3 Details of the communication component. 111
5.4 Details of the evaluation component. 112
5.5 Process of an evaluation run. 113
5.6 The Firefox browser with the activated extension for outlining the main content. 115
5.7 Original form of the Yahoo news article prior to any CE. 118
5.8 The Yahoo news article filtered with Crunch. 119
5.9 The Yahoo news article filtered with BTE. 120
5.10 The Yahoo news article filtered with DSC. 121

List of Figures

5.11 The Yahoo news article filtered with K-FeatureExtractor. 122
5.12 The Yahoo news article filtered with LQF and a threshold of 0.25. 123
5.13 F1 performance of the CE algorithms on the heise package. 124
5.14 Precision performance of the CE algorithms on the heise package. 128
5.15 Recall performance of the CE algorithms on the heise package. 128
5.16 F1 performance of the CE algorithms on the slashdot package. 129
5.17 F1 performance of the CE algorithms on the wiki package. 130
5.18 Precision performance of the CE algorithms on the wiki package. 131
5.19 Recall performance of the CE algorithms on the wiki package. 131
5.20 Stability of the CE algorithms on the heise package. 132
5.21 Time performance of the CE algorithms on the heise package. 133

6.1 A fragment of an HTML document and its source code. 142
6.2 A Gauss filter blurs an image by spreading the colour information of a pixel to its neighbour pixels according to a Gauss distribution. 145
6.3 Blurring a character vector interpreted as greyscale image. 146
6.4 A document from the chip web site in its original form. 151
6.5 LSI often extracts the content rich side bar of chip documents. 152
6.6 DOM tree of a chip document with the two sub-trees of the main content region and the content rich side bar. 153
6.7 A document from the yahoo web site in its original form. 154
6.8 Due to the DOM structure LP extracts only one paragraph of the main content of a yahoo document. 155
6.9 Average F1 performance of CCB, ACCB and TCCB on the heise package in comparison with DSC. 156
6.10 Time performance of LP, LSI, CCB, ACCB and TCCB on the heise package in comparison with DSC, LQF and Crunch. 157
6.11 Stability of CCB, ACCB and TCCB on the heise package in comparison with DSC. 158

7.1 The k-means algorithm is using centroids to form clusters. 167
7.2 A cluster configuration which has too complicated shapes for k-means clustering. 168
7.3 Example of a dendrogram. 169
7.4 Single linkage clustering can handle also tricky shaped clusters. 169
7.5 A cluster configuration which might be difficult for single linkage clustering. 170
7.6 Time needed to compute the distance matrix with the different distance measures, depending on the number of documents. 172
7.7 Visual interpretation of the distance matrices for 500 template based documents from five web sites. 173
7.8 Using MDS to map the documents into a two dimensional space while maintaining the distances. 175
7.9 Distribution of distances for all distance measures (logarithmic scale) . . . 178

List of Figures

7.10 The process of building a clean TD training set for a single seed document. 181
7.11 The evaluation framework simulates the web access for the CE proxy. . . . 183
7.12 Time performance of ACCB, DSC and the clustering TD algorithms. . . . 186

List of Figures

List of Algorithms

3.1	Finn's BTE algorithm.	52
3.2	DSC algorithm.	54
3.3	Linkquota function.	55
3.4	A simple LQF algorithm	56
3.5	Decomposing a document into blocks according to Debnath et al.	58
3.6	Building block tree structures in InfoDiscoverer	66
3.7	RTDM	73
6.1	LSI: finding the node with the largest size increase	138
6.2	Page partitioning of Bar-Yossef and Rajagopalan	140
6.3	CCB	148
7.1	RTDM (linear space)	164

LIST OF ALGORITHMS

Bibliography

[ABS00]   Serge Abiteboul, Peter Buneman, and Dan Suciu, editors. *Data on the Web*. Morgan Kaufmann Publishers, 2000.

[AEAB05] Raihan Al-Ekram, Archana Adma, and Olga Baysal. diffX: an algorithm to detect changes in multi-version XML documents. In *CASCON '05: Proceedings of the 2005 conference of the Centre for Advanced Studies on Collaborative research*, pages 1–11. IBM Press, 2005.

[AIS93]   Rakesh Agrawal, Tomasz Imieliński, and Arun Swami. Mining association rules between sets of items in large databases. In *SIGMOD '93: Proceedings of the 1993 ACM SIGMOD international conference on Management of data*, pages 207–216, New York, NY, USA, 1993. ACM Press.

[AK97]   Naveen Ashish and Craig A. Knoblock. Semi-Automatic Wrapper Generation for Internet Information Sources. In *COOPIS '97: Proceedings of the Second IFCIS International Conference on Cooperative Information Systems*, pages 160–169, Washington, DC, USA, 1997. IEEE Computer Society.

[Arc08]   Internet Archive. The internet archive. http://www.archive.org, 2008.

[AS94]   Rakesh Agrawal and Ramakrishnan Srikant. Fast Algorithms for Mining Association Rules in Large Databases. In *VLDB '94: Proceedings of the 20th International Conference on Very Large Data Bases*, pages 487–499, San Francisco, CA, USA, 1994. Morgan Kaufmann Publishers Inc.

[BDGM95] Sergey Brin, James Davis, and Héctor García-Molina. Copy detection mechanisms for digital documents. In *SIGMOD '95: Proceedings of the 1995 ACM SIGMOD international conference on Management of data*, pages 398–409, New York, NY, USA, 1995. ACM.

[BFG01]   Robert Baumgartner, Sergio Flesca, and Georg Gottlob. The Elog Web Extraction Language. In *LPAR '01: Proceedings of the 8th International Conference on Logic for Programming, Artificial Intelligence, and Reasoning*, volume 2250 of *Lecture Notes in Computer Science*, pages 548–560. Springer, December 2001.

[BGMP01] Orkut Buyukkokten, Hector Garcia-Molina, and Andreas Paepcke. Seeing the whole in parts: text summarization for web browsing on handheld devices. In

Bibliography

                WWW '01: Proceedings of the 10th international conference on World Wide Web, pages 652–662, New York, NY, USA, 2001. ACM Press.

[BGMZ97]   Andrei Z. Broder, Steven C. Glassman, Mark S. Manasse, and Geoffrey Zweig. Syntactic Clustering of the Web. *Computer Networks*, 29(8-13):1157–1166, 1997.

[BH03]   Michael Berthold and David J. Hand, editors. *Intelligent Data Analysis*. Springer, Berlin, 2nd edition, 2003.

[BLHL01]   Tim Berners-Lee, James Hendler, and Ora Lassila. The Semantic Web. *Scientific American*, 284(5):34–43, May 2001.

[BP98]   Sergey Brin and Lawrence Page. The anatomy of a large-scale hypertextual Web search engine. *Comput. Netw. ISDN Syst.*, 30(1-7):107–117, 1998.

[Bro02]   David Brownell. *SAX2*. O'Reilly, 1st edition, 2002.

[BST07]   Darcy Benoit, Devin Slauenwhite, and André Trudel. On the path to a World Wide Web census: A large scale survey. In *ITA '07: Proceedings of the 2nd International Conference on Internet Technologies and Applications*, pages 354–363, September 2007.

[But04]   David Buttler. A short survey of document structure similarity algorithms. In *IC '04: Proceedings of the International Conference on Internet Computing*, pages 3–9. CSREA Press, 2004.

[BWR+05]   Michael Bolin, Matthew Webber, Philip Rha, Tom Wilson, and Robert C. Miller. Automation and customization of rendered web pages. In *UIST '05: Proceedings of the 18th annual ACM symposium on User interface software and technology*, pages 163–172, New York, NY, USA, 2005. ACM Press.

[BYR02]   Ziv Bar-Yossef and Sridhar Rajagopalan. Template detection via data mining and its applications. In *WWW '02: Proceedings of the 11th International Conference on World Wide Web*, pages 580–591, New York, NY, USA, 2002. ACM Press.

[BZTZ00]   Heino Büchner, Oliver Zschau, Dennis Traub, and Rik Zahradka. *Web Content Management – Websites professionell betreiben*. Galileo Press, Bonn, 1st edition, 2000.

[CBMW98]   Isabel F. Cruz, Slava Borisov, Michael A. Marks, and Timothy R. Webbs. Measuring structural similarity among web documents: preliminary results. In *EP '98: Proceedings of the 7th international Conference on Electronic Publishing, Artistic Imaging, and Digital Typography,*, pages 513 – 524, 1998.

Bibliography

[CDK+99]   Soumen Chakrabarti, Byron E. Dom, S. Ravi Kumar, Prabhakar Raghavan, Sridhar Rajagopalan, Andrew Tomkins, David Gibson, and Jon Kleinberg. Mining the Web's Link Structure. *Computer*, 32(8):60–67, 1999.

[CFGM02]   Abdur Chowdhury, Ophir Frieder, David Grossman, and Mary Catherine McCabe. Collection statistics for fast duplicate document detection. *ACM Trans. Inf. Syst.*, 20(2):171–191, 2002.

[Cha03]   Soumen Chakrabarti. *Mining the Web*. Morgan Kaufmann Publishers, San Francisco, 2003.

[CKP07]   Deepayan Chakrabarti, Ravi Kumar, and Kunal Punera. Page-level template detection via isotonic smoothing. In *WWW '07: Proceedings of the 16th International Conference on World Wide Web*, pages 61–70, New York, NY, USA, 2007. ACM Press.

[CL96]   Jim Cowie and Wendy Lehnert. Information extraction. *Commun. ACM*, 39(1):80–91, 1996.

[CM98]   Valter Crescenzi and Giansalvatore Mecca. Grammars have exceptions. *Inf. Syst.*, 23(9):539–565, 1998.

[CMM03]   Valter Crescenzi, Paolo Merialdo, and Paolo Missier. Fine-grain web site structure discovery. In *WIDM '03: Proceedings of the 5th ACM international workshop on Web information and data management*, pages 15–22, New York, NY, USA, 2003. ACM Press.

[CMZ03]   Yu Chen, Wei-Ying Ma, and Hong-Jiang Zhang. Detecting web page structure for adaptive viewing on small form factor devices. In *WWW '03: Proceedings of the 12th international conference on World Wide Web*, pages 225–233, New York, NY, USA, 2003. ACM Press.

[CSP08]   Dan Connolly, Mike Smith, and Steven Pemberton. W3C HTML Working Group Home Page. http://www.w3.org/html, 2008.

[CW84]   John G. Cleary and Ian H. Witten. Data compression using adaptive coding and partial string matching. *IEEE Transactions on Communications*, COM-32(4):396–402, April 1984.

[DDL+90]   Scott C. Deerwester, Susan T. Dumais, Thomas K. Landauer, George W. Furnas, and Richard A. Harshman. Indexing by Latent Semantic Analysis. *Journal of the American Society of Information Science*, 41(6):391–407, 1990.

[DH99]   Jeffrey Dean and Monika R. Henzinger. Finding related pages in the world wide web. In *WWW '99: Proceeding of the eighth international conference on World Wide Web*, pages 1467–1479, New York, NY, USA, 1999. Elsevier North-Holland, Inc.

Bibliography

[Di 07]   Angelo Di Iorio. *Pattern-Based Segmentation of Digital Documents: Model and Implementation*. PhD thesis, University of Bologna, 2007.

[DMG05a]   Sandip Debnath, Prasenjit Mitra, and C. Lee Giles. Automatic extraction of informative blocks from webpages. In *SAC '05: Proceedings of the 2005 ACM Symposium on Applied Computing*, pages 1722–1726, New York, NY, USA, 2005. ACM Press.

[DMG05b]   Sandip Debnath, Prasenjit Mitra, and C. Lee Giles. Identifying content blocks from web documents. In *Foundations of Intelligent Systems*, Lecture Notes in Computer Science, pages 285–293, 2005.

[DMO+04]   Bonnie Dorr, Christof Monz, Douglas Oard, Stacy President, and David Zajic. Extrinsic Evaluation of Automatic Metrics for Summarization. Technical Report LAMP-TR-115,CAR-TR-999,CS-TR-4610,UMIACS-TR-2004-48, University of Maryland, College Park and BBN Technologies, July 2004.

[Ehr07]   Marc Ehrig. *Ontology Alignment – Bridging the Semantic Gap*. Springer, 2007.

[Fer03]   Reginald Ferber. *Information Retrieval – Suchmodelle und Data-Mining-Verfahren für Textsammlungen und das Web*. dpunkt.verlag GmbH, Heidelberg, 2003.

[FGM+99]   R. Fielding, J. Gettys, J. Mogul, H. Frystyk, L. Masinter, P. Leach, and T. Berners-Lee. Hypertext transfer protocol – HTTP/1.1. RFC 2616, June 1999.

[Fin05]   Aidan Finn. BTE: Body text extraction. http://www.aidanf.net/software/bte-body-text-extraction, 2005. (22. May 2007).

[FKS01]   Aidan Finn, Nicholas Kushmerick, and Barry Smyth. Fact or fiction: Content classification for digital libraries. In *DELOS Workshop: Personalisation and Recommender Systems in Digital Libraries*, 2001.

[FMM+05]   Sergio Flesca, Giuseppe Manco, Elio Masciari, Luigi Pontieri, and Andrea Pugliese. Exploiting structural similarity for effective web information extraction. In Frank Neven, Thomas Schwentick, and Dan Suciu, editors, *Foundations of Semistructured Data*, number 05061 in Dagstuhl Seminar Proceedings. Internationales Begegnungs- und Forschungszentrum fuer Informatik (IBFI), Schloss Dagstuhl, Germany, 2005.

[FR08]   Ben Fry and Casey Reas. Processing. http://www.processing.org, 2008.

Bibliography

[Fre98]   Dayne Freitag. Information extraction from HTML: Application of a general machine learning approach. In *AAAI '98/IAAI '98: Proceedings of the fifteenth National/tenth Conference on Artificial Intelligence/Innovative Applications of Artificial Intelligence*, pages 517–523, Menlo Park, CA, USA, 1998. American Association for Artificial Intelligence.

[GBKS06] Suhit Gupta, Hila Becker, Gail Kaiser, and Salvatore Stolfo. Verifying genre-based clustering approach to content extraction. In *WWW '06: Proceedings of the 15th International Conference on World Wide Web*, pages 875–876, New York, NY, USA, 2006. ACM Press.

[GGM05]   Zoltán Gyöngyi and Hector Garcia-Molina. Web spam taxonomy. In Brian D.Davison, editor, *AIRWEB '05: Proceedings of the First International Workshop on Adversarial Information Retrieval on the Web, held in conjunction with WWW '05*, pages 39–47, New York, NY, USA, 2005. ACM Press.

[GKB+04] Georg Gottlob, Christoph Koch, Robert Baumgartner, Marcus Herzog, and Sergio Flesca. The Lixto data extraction project - back and forth between theory and practice. In *PODS '04: Proceedings of the Twenty-third ACM SIGACT-SIGMOD-SIGART Symposium on Principles of Database Systems*, pages 1–12. ACM, June 2004.

[GKG+05] Suhit Gupta, Gail E. Kaiser, Peter Grimm, Michael F. Chiang, and Justin Starren. Automating Content Extraction of HTML Documents. *World Wide Web*, 8(2):179–224, 2005.

[GKNG03] Suhit Gupta, Gail Kaiser, David Neistadt, and Peter Grimm. DOM-based content extraction of HTML documents. In *WWW '03: Proceedings of the 12th International Conference on World Wide Web*, pages 207–214, New York, NY, USA, 2003. ACM Press.

[GKS05]   Suhit Gupta, Gail Kaiser, and Salvatore Stolfo. Extracting context to improve accuracy for HTML content extraction. In *WWW '05: Special Interest Tracks and Posters of the 14th International conference on World Wide Web*, pages 1114–1115, New York, NY, USA, 2005. ACM Press.

[Glö03]   Michael Glöggler. *Suchmaschinen im Internet*. Springer-Verlag, Berlin, 2003.

[Got07]   Thomas Gottron. Evaluating content extraction on HTML documents. In *ITA '07: Proceedings of the 2nd International Conference on Internet Technologies and Applications*, pages 123–132, September 2007.

[Got08a] Thomas Gottron. Bridging the gap: From multi document template detection to single document content extraction. In *EuroIMSA '08: Proceedings of the*

Bibliography

IASTED Conference on Internet and Multimedia Systems and Applications 2008, pages 66–71. ACTA Press, Calgary, March 2008.

[Got08b]   Thomas Gottron. Clustering template based web documents. In *ECIR '08: Proceedings of the 30th European Conference on Information Retrieval*, pages 40–51. Springer, March 2008.

[Got08c]   Thomas Gottron. Content code blurring: A new approach to content extraction. In *DEXA '08: 19th International Workshop on Database and Expert Systems Applications*, pages 29 – 33. IEEE Computer Society, September 2008.

[GPT05]   David Gibson, Kunal Punera, and Andrew Tomkins. The volume and evolution of web page templates. In *WWW '05: Special Interest Tracks and Posters of the 14th International Conference on World Wide Web*, pages 830–839, New York, NY, USA, 2005. ACM Press.

[GRVB98]   Jean-Robert Gruser, Louiqa Raschid, María Esther Vidal, and Laura Bright. Wrapper generation for web accessible data sources. In *CoopIS '98: Proceedings of the 3rd Conference on Cooperative Information Systems*, pages 14–23, Los Alamitos, CA, USA, August 1998. IEEE Computer Society.

[GS93]   J.R. Galliers and Karen Spärck Jones. Evaluating natural language processing systems. Technical Report UCAM-CL-TR-291, University of Cambridge, Computer Laboratory, February 1993.

[GTG+08]   Fabrizio Giustina, Andy Tripp, Russell Gold, Gary L. Peskin, and Sami Lempinen. JTidy – HTML Parser and Pretty-Printer in Java, 2008. (26. May 2008).

[Gup06]   Suhit Gupta. *Context-Based Content Extraction of HTML Documents*. PhD thesis, Columbia University, 2006.

[HBP01]   Wei Han, David Buttler, and Calton Pu. Wrapping Web Data into XML. *SIGMOD Rec.*, 30(3):33–38, 2001.

[HFAN98]   Gerald Huck, Peter Fankhauser, Karl Aberer, and Erich Neuhold. Jedi: Extracting and synthesizing information from the web. In *CoopIS '98: Proceedings of the 3rd Conference on Cooperative Information Systems*, pages 32–41, Los Alamitos, CA, USA, August 1998. IEEE Computer Society.

[Hir75]   D. S. Hirschberg. A linear space algorithm for computing maximal common subsequences. *Commun. ACM*, 18(6):341–343, 1975.

[HK05]   Andrew Hogue and David Karger. Thresher: Automating the unwrapping of semantic content from the World Wide Web. In *WWW '05: Proceedings of the 14th International Conference on World Wide Web*, pages 86–95, New York, NY, USA, 2005. ACM Press.

[HMGM97]   Joachim Hammer, Jason McHugh, and Hector Garcia-Molina. Semistructured data: The Tsimmis experience. In *ADBIS '97: Proceedings of the First East-European Symposium on Advances in Databases and Information Systems*, pages 1–8. Nevsky Dialect, September 1997.

[HMS02]   Monika R. Henzinger, Rajeev Motwani, and Craig Silverstein. Challenges in web search engines. *SIGIR Forum*, 36(2):11–22, 2002.

[HQW06]   Gerhard Heyer, Uwe Quasthoff, and Thomas Wittig. *Text Mining: Wissensrohstoff Text*. W3L, Bochum, 2006.

[HS77]   James W. Hunt and Thomas G. Szymanski. A fast algorithm for computing longest common subsequences. *Commun. ACM*, 20(5):350–353, 1977.

[HS94]   Frank Halasz and Mayer Schwartz. The Dexter hypertext reference model. *Commun. ACM*, 37(2):30–39, 1994.

[HS07]   Andreas Hotho and Gerd Stumme. Mining the World Wide Web – Methods, Applications, and Perspectives. *Künstliche Intelligenz*, 3:5–8, 2007.

[HWW08]   Philippe Le Hégaret, Ray Whitmer, and Lauren Wood. W3C DOM Working Group Home Page. http://www.w3.org/DOM, 2008.

[JAKN03]   Sachindra Joshi, Neeraj Agrawal, Raghu Krishnapuram, and Sumit Negi. A bag of paths model for measuring structural similarity in web documents. In *KDD '03: Proceedings of the ninth ACM SIGKDD International Conference on Knowledge Discovery and Data Mining*, pages 577–582, New York, NY, USA, 2003. ACM Press.

[KCLH02]   Hung-Yu Kao, Ming-Syan Chen, Shian-Hua Lin, and Jan-Ming Ho. Entropy-based link analysis for mining web informative structures. In *CIKM '02: Proceedings of the eleventh international conference on Information and knowledge management*, pages 574–581, New York, NY, USA, 2002. ACM Press.

[KGB05]   Gail Kaiser, Suhit Gupta, and Hila Becker. Crunch – a web proxy for HTML content extraction. http://www.psl.cs.columbia.edu/crunch/, 2005. (22. May 2007).

[KHC05]   Hung-Yu Kao, Jan-Ming Ho, and Ming-Syan Chen. WISDOM: Web Intra-page Informative Structure Mining Based on Document Object Model. *IEEE Transactions on Knowledge and Data Engineering*, 17(5):614–627, 2005.

Bibliography

[KK07] Per M. Koch and Susanne Koch. The size of the World Wide Web. http://www.pandia.com/sew/383-web-size.html, 2007. (25. February 2007).

[KL05] J. Kangasharju and T. Lindholm. A sequence-based type-aware interface for XML processing. In M. H. Hamza, editor, *EuroIMSA '05: Ninth IASTED International Conference on Internet and Multimedia Systems and Applications*, pages 83–88. ACTA Press, February 2005.

[Kle98] Jon M. Kleinberg. Authoritative sources in a hyperlinked environment. In *SODA '98: Proceedings of the ninth Annual ACM-SIAM Symposium on Discrete algorithms*, pages 668–677, Philadelphia, PA, USA, 1998. Society for Industrial and Applied Mathematics.

[Kle99] Jon M. Kleinberg. Authoritative Sources in a Hyperlinked Environment. *J. ACM*, 46(5):604–632, 1999.

[KLHC04] Hung-Yu Kao, Shian-Hua Lin, Jan-Ming Ho, and Ming-Syan Chen. Mining Web Informative Structures and Contents Based on Entropy Analysis. *IEEE Transactions on Knowledge and Data Engineering*, 16(1):41–55, 2004.

[KRRT06] Ravi Kumar, Prabhakar Raghavan, Sridhar Rajagopalan, and Andrew Tomkins. Core algorithms in the CLEVER system. *ACM Trans. Inter. Tech.*, 6(2):131–152, 2006.

[Kru64] J. B. Kruskal. Nonmetric Multidimensional Scaling: A Numerical Method. *Psychometrika*, 29(2):115–129, 1964.

[Kru06] Steve Krug. *Don't make me think – Web Usability*. mitp, Heidelberg, 2nd edition, 2006.

[Kus99] Nicholas Kushmerick. Learning to remove Internet advertisements. In *AGENTS '99: Proceedings of the third annual conference on Autonomous Agents*, pages 175–181, New York, NY, USA, 1999. ACM Press.

[Kus00] Nicholas Kushmerick. Wrapper verification. *World Wide Web*, 3(2):79–94, 2000.

[KWD97] Nicholas Kushmerick, Daniel S. Weld, and Robert B. Doorenbos. Wrapper induction for information extraction. In *IJCAI 1997: Intl. Joint Conference on Artificial Intelligence*, pages 729–737, 1997.

[Lev65] Vladimir I. Levenshtein. Binary codes capable of correcting deletions, insertions, and reversals. *Doklady Akademii Nauk SSSR*, 163(4):845–848, 1965.

[LFDB05] Gitte Lindgaard, Gary Fernandes, Cathy Dudek, and J. Browñ. Attention web designers: You have 50 milliseconds to make a good first impression! *Behaviour & Information Technology*, 25(2):115–126, 2005.

[LG94]   David D. Lewis and William A. Gale. A sequential algorithm for training text classifiers. In *SIGIR '94: Proceedings of the 17th annual international ACM SIGIR conference on Research and development in information retrieval*, pages 3–12, New York, NY, USA, 1994. Springer-Verlag New York, Inc.

[LH02]   Shian-Hua Lin and Jan-Ming Ho. Discovering informative content blocks from web documents. In *KDD '02: Proceedings of the eighth ACM SIGKDD International Conference on Knowledge Discovery and Data Mining*, pages 588–593, New York, NY, USA, 2002. ACM Press.

[Liu07]   Bing Liu. *Web Data Mining – Exploring Hyperlinks, Contents, and Usage Data*. Springer, 2007.

[LKT06]   Tancred Lindholm, Jaakko Kangasharju, and Sasu Tarkoma. Fast and simple XML tree differencing by sequence alignment. In *DocEng '06: Proceedings of the 2006 ACM Symposium on Document Engineering*, pages 75–84, New York, NY, USA, 2006. ACM Press.

[LM06]   Amy N. Langville and Carl D. Meyer. *Google's PageRank and Beyond: The Science of Search Engine Rankings*. Princeton University Press, Princeton, 2006.

[Lot02]   Tony Loton. *Web Content Mining with Java: Techniques for exploiting the World Wide Web*. Wiley, Chichester, England, 2002.

[LRNdST02] Alberto H. F. Laender, Berthier A. Ribeiro-Neto, Altigran S. da Silva, and Juliana S. Teixeira. A brief survey of web data extraction tools. *SIGMOD Rec.*, 31(2):84–93, 2002.

[Mac00]   Joshua P. MacDonald. File system support for delta compression, 2000. Master thesis, University of California at Berkeley.

[Mar99]   Daniel Marcu. The automatic construction of large-scale corpora for summarization research. In *SIGIR '99: Proceedings of the 22nd annual international ACM SIGIR conference on Research and development in information retrieval*, pages 137–144, New York, NY, USA, 1999. ACM Press.

[MB08]   Rob Malda and Jeff Bates. Slashdot: News for nerds, stuff that matters. http://www.slashdot.org/, 2008.

[MBC+03]   Kathleen McKeown, Regina Barzilay, John Chen, David Elson, David Evans, Judith Klavans, Ani Nenkova, Barry Schiffman, and Sergey Sigelman. Columbia's newsblaster: New features and future directions. In *Proceedings of NAACL-HLT'03, Demonstrations*, May 2003.

Bibliography

[MBE+01]   Kathleen R. McKeown, Regina Barzilay, David Evans, Vasileios Hatzivassiloglou, Barry Schiffman, and Simone Teufel. Columbia multi-document summarization: Approach and evaluation. In *Proceedings of the Workshop on Text Summarization, ACM SIGIR Conference 2001*. DARPA/NIST, Document Understanding Conference, September 2001.

[Meg08]   David Megginson. SAX project home page. http://www.saxproject.org/, 2008.

[MGCC03]   Ling Ma, Nazli Goharian, Abdur Chowdhury, and Misun Chung. Extracting unstructured data from template generated web documents. In *CIKM '03: Proceedings of the twelfth international conference on Information and knowledge management*, pages 512–515, New York, NY, USA, 2003. ACM Press.

[MOC05]   Constantine Mantratzis, Mehmet Orgun, and Steve Cassidy. Separating XHTML content from navigation clutter using DOM-structure block analysis. In *HYPERTEXT '05: Proceedings of the sixteenth ACM conference on Hypertext and hypermedia*, pages 145–147, New York, NY, USA, 2005. ACM Press.

[MW03]   Angel R. Martinez and Edward J. Wegman. Encoding of text to preserve "meaning". In *ACAS 2003: Proceedings of the Eighth U.S. Army Conference on Applied Statistics*, pages 27–39, 2003.

[MyS07]   MySQL AB. *MySQL 5.1 Reference Manual*, August 2007.

[oST08]   National Institute of Standards and Technology. Text retrieval conference (TREC) home page. http://trec.nist.gov/, 2008.

[PBC+02]   David Pinto, Michael Branstein, Ryan Coleman, W. Bruce Croft, Matthew King, Wei Li, and Xing Wei. QuASM: a system for question answering using semi-structured data. In *JCDL '02: Proceedings of the 2nd ACM/IEEE-CS joint conference on Digital libraries*, pages 46–55, New York, NY, USA, 2002. ACM Press.

[Pea01]   Karl Pearson. On lines and planes of closest fit to systems of points in space. *Philosophical Magazine*, 2(6):559–572, 1901.

[Pem08]   Steven Pemberton. W3C XHTML2 working group home page. http://www.w3.org/markup, 2008.

[PN05]   François Paradis and Jian-Yun Nie. Filtering contents with bigrams and named entities to improve text classification. In *AIRS 2005: Proceedings of the Second Asia Information Retrieval Symposium*, pages 135–146, 2005.

Bibliography

[Por80] Martin F. Porter. An algorithm for suffix stripping. *Program*, 14(3):130–137, July 1980.

[PS05] Gautam Pant and Padmini Srinivasan. Learning to Crawl: Comparing Classification Schemes. *ACM Trans. Inf. Syst.*, 23(4):430–462, 2005.

[Rag03] Dave Raggett. Clean up your web pages with HTML TIDY, November 2003. (16. Octobre 2007).

[RAH01] A. F. R. Rahman, H. Alam, and R. Hartono. Content extraction from HTML documents. In *WDA 2001: Proceedings of the First International Workshop on Web Document Analysis*, pages 7–10, 2001.

[Ran71] William M. Rand. Objective Criteria for the Evaluation of Clustering Methods. *Journal of the American Statistical Association*, 66(336):846–850, December 1971.

[Ran07] Default english stopwords, googles stopwords list. http://www.ranks.nl/tools/stopwords.html, 2007. (9. August 2007).

[RGdL04] D. C. Reis, P. B. Golgher, A. S. da Silva, and A. F. Laender. Automatic web news extraction using tree edit distance. In *WWW '04: Proceedings of the 13th International Conference on World Wide Web*, pages 502–511, New York, NY, USA, 2004. ACM Press.

[RHJ99] Dave Raggett, Arnaud Le Hors, and Ian Jacobs. HTML 4.01 Specification. W3C Recommendation, December 1999.

[Sal08] Marcel Salathé. Websites as Graphs. http://www.aharef.info/static/htmlgraph/, 2008.

[SBLK05] Adam Schenker, Horst Bunke, Mark Last, and Abraham Kandel. *Graph-Theoretic Techniques for Web Content Mining*. World Scientific, 2005.

[SCY+04] Dou Shen, Zheng Chen, Qiang Yang, Hua-Jun Zeng, Benyu Zhang, Yuchang Lu, and Wei-Ying Ma. Web-page classification through summarization. In *SIGIR '04: Proceedings of the 27th annual international ACM SIGIR conference on Research and development in information retrieval*, pages 242–249, New York, NY, USA, 2004. ACM Press.

[SGM00] Alexander Strehl, Joydeep Ghosh, and Raymond Mooney. Impact of similarity measures on web-page clustering. In *AAAI 2000: Proceedings of the 17th National Conference on Artificial Intelligence: Workshop of Artificial Intelligence for Web Search*, pages 58–64. AAAI, July 2000.

[Sha48] Claude .E. Shannon. A mathematical theory of communication. *Bell System Technical Journal*, 27:379–423 and 623–656, July and October 1948.

Bibliography

[She07]   Dave Shea. CSS Zen Garden. http://www.csszengarden.com/, 2007. (13. August 2007).

[Sin04]   Munindar P. Singh, editor. *Practical Handbook of Internet Computing*. Chapman Hall & CRC Press, Baton Rouge, 2004.

[Ski98]   Steven S. Skiena, editor. *The Algorithm Design Manual*. Springer Verlag, New York, 1998.

[SM83]   Gerard Salton and Michael J. McGill. *Introduction to Modern Information Retrieval*. McGraw-Hill Book Company, New York, 1983.

[SM97]   João Carlos Setubal and João Meidanis. *Introduction to Computational Molecular Biology*. PWS Publishing Company, Boston, 1997.

[Smi02]   Lindsay I. Smith. A tutorial on principal components analysis. Technical report, February 2002.

[SMW03]   Benno Stein, Sven Meyer zu Eißen, and Frank Wißbrock. On Cluster Validity and the Information Need of Users. In M. H. Hanza, editor, *IAI '03: Proceedings of the 3rd IASTED International Conference on Artificial Intelligence and Applications*, pages 216–221. ACTA Press, Calgary, September 2003.

[SNZG06]   Lei Shi, Cheng Niu, Ming Zhou, and Jianfeng Gao. A DOM tree alignment model for mining parallel data from the web. In *ACL '06: Proceedings of the 21st International Conference on Computational Linguistics and the 44th annual meeting of the ACL*, pages 489–496, Morristown, NJ, USA, 2006. Association for Computational Linguistics.

[Sod97]   Stephen Soderland. Learning to extract text-based information from the World Wide Web. In *KDD '97: Proceedings of Third International Conference on Knowledge Discovery and Data Mining*, pages 251–254. AAAI, 1997.

[Spe99]   Paul Spencer, editor. *Professional XMLDesign and Implementation*. Wrox Press, Birmingham, 1999.

[Tea07]   TeaShark. TeaShark mobile phone browser. http://www.teashark.com/, 2007. (5. December 2007).

[Tri99]   Andrew Tridgell. *Efficient Algorithms for Sorting and Synchronization*. PhD thesis, Australian National University, February 1999.

[TSK06]   Pang-Ning Tan, Michael Steinbach, and Vipin Kumar. *Introduction to Data Mining*. Pearson, 2006.

[Val01]   Gabriel Valiente. An efficient bottom-up distance between trees. In *SPIRE 2001: Proceedings of the 8th international symposium on String Processing and Information Retrieval*, pages 212–219, November 2001.

[VdC04]   Fabio Vitali, Angelo di Iorio, and Elisa Ventura Campori. Rule-based structural analysis of web pages. In *DAS 2004: Proceedings of the 6th International Workshop on Document Analysis Systems*, volume 3163 of *Lecture Notes in Computer Science*, pages 425–437. Springer, July 2004.

[VdP+06]   Karane Vieira, Altigran S. da Silva, Nick Pinto, Edleno S. de Moura, João M. B. Cavalcanti, and Juliana Freire. A fast and robust method for web page template detection and removal. In *CIKM '06: Proceedings of the 15th ACM international conference on Information and knowledge management*, pages 258–267, New York, NY, USA, 2006. ACM Press.

[VR79]   C. J. Van Rijsbergen. *Information Retrieval*. Butterworths, 2nd edition, 1979.

[W3C98]   Document Object Model (DOM) Level 1 Specification. W3C Recommendation, October 1998.

[W3C99a]   XML path language (XPath) version 1.1. W3C Recommendation, November 1999.

[W3C99b]   XSL Transformation (XSLT) version 1.1. W3C Recommendation, November 1999.

[W3C00]   Document Object Model (DOM) Level 2 Core Specification. W3C Recommendation, November 2000.

[W3C04]   Document Object Model (DOM) Level 3 Core Specification. W3C Recommendation, April 2004.

[W3C06a]   Mobile Web Best Practice 1.0 Proposed Recommendation. W3C Proposed Recommendation, November 2006.

[W3C06b]   XHTML 2.0. W3C Working Draft, July 2006.

[W3C07]   XHTML 1.1 - module-based XHTML - second edition. W3C Recommendation, February 2007.

[W3C08]   HTML 5 Working Draft. W3C Working Draft, January 2008.

[WBMT99]   Ian H. Witten, Zane Bray, Malika Mahoui, and W. J. Teahan. Text mining: A new frontier for lossless compression. In *Data Compression Conference*, pages 198–207, 1999.

Bibliography

[WF00]   Ian H. Witten and Eibe Frank. *Data Mining*. Morgan Kaufmann Publishers, 1st edition, 2000.

[Wil88] Peter Willett. Recent trends in hierarchic document clustering: a critical review. *Inf. Process. Manage.*, 24(5):577–597, 1988.

[Wit04] Ian H. Witten. Text mining. In Munindar P. Singh, editor, *Practical Handbook of Internet Computing*. Chapman Hall & CRC Press, Baton Rouge, 2004.

[WJ05]   Tarquin Mark Wilton-Jones. Extensible rendering architecture. White paper, Opera Software ASA, September 2005.

[WMB94] Ian H. Witten, Alistair Moffat, and Timothy C. Bell. *Managing Gigabytes : Compressing and Indexing Documents and Images*. van Nostrand, New York, 1st edition, 1994.

[WZ02]   Weinan Wang and Osmar R. Zaïane. Clustering web sessions by sequence alignment. In *DEXA '02: Proceedings of the 13th International Workshop on Database and Expert Systems Applications*, pages 394–398, Washington, DC, USA, 2002. IEEE Computer Society.

[WZC95] Jason T. L. Wang, Kaizhong Zhang, and Gung-Wei Chirn. Algorithms for approximate graph matching. *Information Sciences*, 82(1–2):45–74, January 1995.

[Yan91] Wuu Yang. Identifying syntactic differences between two programs. *Software-Practice and Experience*, 21(7):739–755, 1991.

[YLL03] Lan Yi, Bing Liu, and Xiaoli Li. Eliminating noisy information in web pages for data mining. In *KDD '03: Proceedings of the ninth ACM SIGKDD International Conference on Knowledge Discovery and Data Mining*, pages 296–305, New York, NY, USA, 2003. ACM Press.

[YLZ+05] Jun Yan, Ning Liu, Benyu Zhang, Shuicheng Yan, Zheng Chen, Qiansheng Cheng, Weiguo Fan, and Wei-Ying Ma. OCFS: optimal orthogonal centroid feature selection for text categorization. In *SIGIR '05: Proceedings of the 28th annual international ACM SIGIR conference on Research and development in information retrieval*, pages 122–129, New York, NY, USA, 2005. ACM Press.

[YP97]   Yiming Yang and Jan O. Pedersen. A comparative study on feature selection in text categorization. In *ICML '97: Proceedings of the Fourteenth International Conference on Machine Learning*, pages 412–420, San Francisco, CA, USA, 1997. Morgan Kaufmann Publishers Inc.

[YRK03] Guizhen Yang, I. V. Ramakrishnan, and Michael Kifer. On the complexity of schema inference from web pages in the presence of nullable data attributes. In *CIKM '03: Proceedings of the twelfth International Conference on Information and Knowledge Management*, pages 224–231, New York, NY, USA, 2003. ACM Press.

[ZA02] Osmar R. Zaïane and Maria-Luiza Antonie. Classifying text documents by associating terms with text categories. In *ADC '02: Proceedings of the 13th Australasian database conference*, pages 215–222, Darlinghurst, Australia, Australia, 2002. Australian Computer Society, Inc.

[ZE98] Oren Zamir and Oren Etzioni. Web document clustering: a feasibility demonstration. In *SIGIR '98: Proceedings of the 21st annual international ACM SIGIR conference on Research and development in information retrieval*, pages 46–54, New York, NY, USA, 1998. ACM Press.

[ZL05] Yanhong Zhai and Bing Liu. Web data extraction based on partial tree alignment. In *WWW '05: Proceedings of the 14th international conference on World Wide Web*, pages 76–85, New York, NY, USA, 2005. ACM Press.

[Zsc08] Oliver Zschau. Contentmanager.de - Das Content Management Portal. http://www.contentmanager.de/, 2008.

Bibliography

Index

ACCB, 141, 147, 177, 183
ACL, 185, 191
adapted CCB, *see* ACCB, *see* ACCB
additional content, 1, 7, 9, 16
    deleting, 89, 95
    hiding, 89, 95
    replacing, 89, 95
advertisements, 9, 15
AJAX, 87, 93
algorithm
    Hirschberg, 79, 85, 106, 112
    HITS, 3, 9
    Hunt and Szymanski, 79, 86
    Kruskal, 161, 167
    LCS, 79, 85, 106, 112
    longest common subsequence, 79, 85
    Page Partitioning, 133, 139
    PageRank, 3, 9
    Porter stemming, 33, 39
    Valiente, 77, 84
API components, 103, 109
application specific test, 73, 80, 92, 98
artificial neural networks, 33, 39
artistic DOM representation, 18, 25
Association for Computer Linguistics, 185, 191
atomic content element
    CCB, 137, 143
    smallest content unit, 96, 102
attribute, 23, 29
authority, 58, 64
automatic extraction, 38, 44
automatically generated test packages, 110, 116

bag of words, 30, 36, 98, 104
baseline, 115, 122
bi-gram, 31, 37
bi-gram proximity matrix, 31, 37
binary classification, 27, 33
binary content, 83, 89
blogging system, 3, 9
Body Text Extraction, 43, *see* BTE, 49, *see* BTE
bootstrapping TD, 173, 179
BPM, 31, 37
Brin, Sergey, 3, 9
BTE, 43, 44, 49, 50, 112, 118, 137, 143
Buttler, David, 159, 165

cascading style sheets, 11, 17
case folding, 32, 38
CCB, 141, 147
CE
    definition, 10, 16
    formal definition, 87, 92
    function, 87, 93
    global techniques, 11, 17, 36, 42
    heuristics, 11, 17
    level of granularity, 96, 102
    local techniques, 11, 17, 36, 42
    on-the-fly, 42, 48, 179, 185
    practical realisation, 88, 94
CE algorithms
    ACCB, 141, 147
    BTE, 43, 49
    CCB, 141, 147
    Crunch, 43, 49
    DSC, 44, 50

Index

elISA, 53, 59
FeatureExtractor, 51, 57
K-FeatureExtractor, 51, 57
LQF, 47, 53
TCCB, 141, 147
character sequence, 96, 102
characteristic performance curve (CE), 117, 123
χ^2 test, 31, 37
CLEANEVAL, 185, 191
Clever search system, 58, 64
closely related meta data, 84, 90
cluster analysis
    k-means, 161, 167
    k-median, 161, 168
    hierarchical, 162, 168
    multidimensional scaling, 161, 166
    single linkage, 163, 169
CMS, see WCMS, see WCMS
code, 135, 141
commercials, 9, 15
common path shingles, 159, 165
common paths, 157, 163
common tag sequence shingles, 160, 166
communication component, 104, 110
composite importance, 63, 70
concept, 23, 29
concept description, 23, 29
confusion matrix, 27, 34, 94, 99
constrained device test, 74, 80
content, 135, 141
    additional, 1, 7
    advertisements, 9, 15
    animated GIF, 9, 15
    atomic element, 96, 102
    atomic item, 96, 102
    commercials, 9, 15
    copyright notice, 9, 15
    core content, 10, 16
    detagged, 108, 114
    factual articles, 43, 49
    Flash, 9, 15

functional elements, 9, 15
highly formatted, 135, 141
homogeneously formatted, 135, 141
ignoring content, 5, 11
kinds of, 6, 12
link list, 9, 15
main content, 1, 7, 9, 15, 16
navigation, 9, 15
noise, 10, 16
opinionated articles, 43, 49
optional information, 84, 90
PDF, 84, 89
primary content, 10, 16
principal content, 10, 16
redundant, 4, 10
smallest unit, 96, 102
syndication, 5, 11
template elements, 9, 15
template generated, 10, 16
user discussion, 84, 90
content block, 59, 65
content code blurring, 135, 140
content code ratio, 138, 143
content code vector, 137, 143
content extraction, see CE, see CE
content management system, see WCMS, see WCMS
content, primary, 9, 15
ContentExtractor, 61, 67, 175, 181
core content, 10, 16, 83, 89
core content detection, 10, 16
CP, 157, 163
CPS, 159, 165
crawler, 3, 9, 174, 180
Crunch, 43, 49, 111, 117, 144, 150
CSS, 11, 17
CSS Zen Garden, 11, 17
CSV, 103, 109
CTSS, 160, 166
Cumulative tag distribution, 44, 50

data management component, 103, 109

Index

data mining, 23, 29
Dave Raggett, 16, 22
David Buttler, 159, 165
deleting additional contents, 89, 95
dendrogram, 162, 168
detagged content, 70, 77, 88, 94, 108, 114
detail page, 37, 43
diffX, 77, 83
digital library, 43, 49
directory, 2, 8
dissimilarity function, 25, 31
distance function, 24, 30
distance matrices, 165, 171
distance measure
    CP, 157, 163
    CPS, 159, 165
    CTSS, 160, 166
    LCTS, 160, 165
    RTDM, 157, 163
    tree edit distance, 157, 163
    TV, 159, 165
DMOZ, 2, 8
document
    as graph, 18, 25
    duplicate detection, 57, 63, 68, 74
    HTML, 1, 7
    kinds of content, 1, 6, 7, 12
    models for evaluation, 96, 102
    near duplicate, 155, 161
    representation (CCB), 137, 143
    restructuring, 89, 95
    scanning, 5, 11
    template, 4, 9
document frequency, 68, 74, 176, 182
Document Object Model, 17, 23
document slope curve, *see* DSC, *see* DSC
document type definition, 77, 83
DOM, 17, 23, 43, 49
DOM inspector, 18, 24
DSC, 44, 50, 113, 119, 137, 143, 144, 150, 177, 183
DTD, 77, 83

Dunn index, 166, 172
duplicate document detection, 57, 63, 68, 74

e-learning, 130, 136
E-measure, 29, 35
ECMS, 3, 9
element nodes, 62, 69
elISA, 53, 59, 130, 136
entropy, 175, 181
ERA, 54, 60
Euclidean distances, 161, 166
evaluation component, 106, 112
evaluation framework
    single document algorithms, 101, 107, 143, 149
    TD, 176, 182
evaluation of wrappers, 39, 44
evaluation package, 102, 108
evaluation run, 103, 107, 109, 113, 177, 183
example, 23, 29
extended content, 84, 90
Extensible Rendering Architecture, 54, 60
Extensible Stylesheet Language, 16, 22
extracted content, 96, 102
extraction of informative blocks, 10, 16

F-D matrix, 59, 66, 69, 75
F-measure, 29, 35
F1-measure, 29, 35
false negative, 27, 33
false positive, 27, 33
f_{CE}, 87, 93
fe, 117, 123
feature entropy, 59, 66
feature-document matrix, 59, 66
FeatureExtractor, 51, 57, 61, 67, 114, 120
filtering additional contents, 6, 12
Firefox extension, 103, 109, 115
Flash, 9, 15
FN, 27, 33
formal definition (CE), 87, 92

251

Index

FP, 27, 33
frequent item set, 58, 65
functional elements, 9, 15

Gaussian blurring filter, 139, 144
genre classifier, 43, 49
global noise, 5, 10
global techniques (CE), 11, 17, 36, 42
gold standard, 26, 32, 95, 101
Google, 3, 9
ground truth, 26, 32
guided crawler, 180, 186

heuristics for content extraction, 43, 49
HF, 38, 44, 131, 137
hiding additional contents, 89, 95
hierarchical clustering, 162, 168
hierarchical top-down tree matching, 157, 163
highest fanout, 38, 44, 131, 137
highly formatted content, 135, 141
Hirschberg, 79, 85, 106, 112
HITS, 3, 5, 9, 11, 33, 39, 58, 64, 68, 74
homogeneously formatted content, 135, 141
HTML
    comments, 135, 141
    document, 1, 7
    entities, 108, 114, 137, 143
    format, 16, 21
    parser, 17, 23, 110, 116
    version 5, 185, 191
hub, 58, 64
human user evaluation, 72, 78, 91, 97
Hunt, 79, 86
Hypertext IR Principles, 56, 62

I-Match, 68, 74
IBDF, 62, 68
illegal copies of web site, 5, 11
importance, 63, 69
index, 30, 36
indirect evaluation, 74, 81, 92, 98
InfoDiscoverer, 59, 65, 175, 181

information coverage tree, 69, 76
information integration, 130, 136
information overload, 40, 46
information retrieval, 22, 28
informative structure
    page, 69, 75
    web site, 68, 74
instance, 23, 29
instance based methods, 33, 39
inter-site redundancy, 4, 10
intra-site redundancy, 4, 10
intrapage informative structure, 69, 76
inverse block-document frequency, 62, 68
inverted index, 30, 36
IR, 22, 28
IR-based evaluation measures, 75, 82, 93, 99
IsaWiki, 53, 59, 130, 136

JavaScript, 11, 17, 18, 24
Jon Kleinberg, 3, 9
JTidy, 17, 22, 111, 117, 133, 138

k nearest neighbour, 33, 39
K-FeatureExtractor, 51, 57, 61, 67, 114, 120
k-means clustering, 33, 39, 65, 71
k-means clustering, 161, 167
k-median clustering, 161, 168
k-mer, 31, 37
kfe, 117, 123
kinds of content, 6, 12
Kleinberg, Jon, 3, 9
Kruskal, 161, 167

LAMIS, 68, 69, 74, 75
landmark, 38, 44
largest pagelet, 133, 139
largest size increase, 38, 44, 131, 137
largest tag count, 38, 44, 131, 137
Larry Page, 3, 9
LCS, 79, 85, 97, 103, 106, 112
LCTS, 160, 165

252

$lcts(D_1, D_2)$, 160, 166
level of granularity, 96, 102
Levenshtein distance, 157, 163
Lexical Affinity Principle, 56, 62
lift charts, 30, 36
link analysis, 69, 75
link list, 9, 15, 47, 53
Link Quota Filter, 47, see LQF, 53, see LQF
link-ratio, 43, 49
link/text removal ratio, 47, 55
list page, 37, 43
local noise, 5, 10
local techniques (CE), 11, 17, 36, 42
longest common subsequence, 79, 85, see LCS, see LCS
longest common tag subsequence, 160, 165
LP, 133, 139
LQF, 47, 53
LSI, 38, 44, 131, 137
LTC, 38, 44, 131, 137

machine learning, 23, 29
main content, 9, 16, 96, 102
    definition, 1, 7, 9, 15, 83, 89
    extraction, 88, 94
    marking, 88, 94
managed web site, 3, 9
manual package, 109, 115
manually created wrappers, 37, 43
market basket analysis, 58, 65
marking the main content, 88, 94
markup language, 16, 21
maximality, 25, 31
MDS, 161, 166
meaningful node, 64, 70
metric, 24, 30
metric MDS, 161, 167
MI, 170, 176
mirror pages, 5, 11
Mobile Web Initiative, 55, 61
multi document algorithms, 11, 17

multidimensional scaling, 161, 166
mutual information, 170, 176

n-gram, 31, 37
Naïve Bayes classifier, 33, 39, 65, 71, 93, 98
named entities, 39, 45
named tokens, 39, 45
natural language processing, 33, 39, 40, 46, 78, 84
navigation, 9, 15
NB, 33, 39, 65, 71, 93, 98
NE, 39, 45
ne-pattern, 67, 72
near duplicate documents, 155, 161
nearest neighbour, 33, 39
NEG, 37, 42
Newsblaster, 75, 81
Newsblaster test, 75, 81
NLP, 33, 39, 40, 46, 78, 84
node extraction pattern, 67, 72
noisy contents, 10, 16
noisy node, 64, 70
nominal attributes, 23, 29
non-metric distance, 25, 31
non-metric MDS, 161, 167
non-negativity, 24, 25, 30, 31
NP-completeness (TD), 37, 43
numeric attributes, 23, 29

on-the-fly extraction, 42, 48, 179, 185
Open Directory Project, 2, 8
Opera Mini, 54, 60

$p(D)$, 157, 163
package, 102, 108
Page Partitioning, 55, 62, 133, 139, 143, 149
Page Style Tree, 63, 69
Page, Larry, 3, 9
pagelet, 56, 62, 133, 139, 175, 181
pagelet candidate, 143, 149
PageRank, 3, 5, 9, 11, 33, 39

Index

Pandia, 2, 8
parallelisation, 106, 112
path language, 16, 22
PCA, 161, 167
PDF content, 84, 89
Pentaformat, 54, 60, 186, 192
personal information management, 130, 136
plain method (CE), 115, 121
Porter stemming algorithm, 33, 39, 59, 66
POS, 37, 42
practical content extraction, 88, 94
precision, 28, 34
precision recall charts, 29, 36
primary content, 9, 10, 15, 16, 83, 89
primary content location phase, 132, 137
principal component analysis, 161, 167
principal content, 10, 16, 83, 89
printer friendly layout, 174, 180
Processing, 18, 25
proximity matrix, 31, 37
proxy, 133, 139, 176, 183
$ps(D)$, 159, 165
PST, 63, 69
publishing concept, 3, 9
purity, 170, 176

Quaero, 6, 12
QuASM, 44, 50

Rand index, 168, 174
ranking, 5, 11
really simple syndication, 7, 12
recall, 28, 34
receiver operating characteristics, 30, 36
redundant content, 4, 10
regular expression, 67, 72
relevant items, 26, 32
Relevant Linkage Principle, 56, 62
rendering information, 10, 11, 16, 17
replacing additional contents, 89, 95
restricted top-down mapping, 65, 71
result set, 26, 32
retrieved items, 26, 32

ROC curves, 30, 36
RSS, 7, 12
RTDM, 65, 71, 157, 163
rule deduction, 33, 39

SAT-problem, 37, 43
SAX, 17, 23
scanning, 5, 10, 11, 16
screen reader, 5, 11, 179, 185
screen reader test, 74, 80, 92, 98
search engine, 2, 5, 8, 11
   CE support, 10, 16
   crawler, 3, 9
   Google, 3, 9
   HITS, 3, 9
   PageRank, 3, 9
   ranking, 3, 9
Semantic Web, 10, 16
semi-structured data, 131, 137
separation of content and layout(WCMS), 3, 9
separation of primary content blocks, 10, 16
Sergey Brin, 3, 9
set of words, 98, 104
SGML, 16, 22
Shannon, 31, 37, 60, 66
shingles, 57, 63, 159, 165
SIGWAC, 185, 191
similarity function, 24, 30
similarity measure, 25, 31
simple API for XML, 17, 23
single document algorithms, 11, 17
single linkage clustering, 163, 169
Site Style Trees, 62, 68
size of the WWW, 2, 7
Slashdot, 84, 90
slot, 19, 26
small screen devices, 179, 185
source code, 10, 16, 22
specialised content extractors, 95, 101, 110, 116

Index

SST, 62, 68, 70, 76
stability criterion, 99, 105
standard deviation, 100, 106
statistical methods, 33, 39
stemming, 32, 38
stop word, 32, 38
string representation of web documents, 15, 21
structurally significant element, 50, 56
structured data, 37, 43, 131, 137
style node, 62, 69
superfluous white space, 108, 114, 132, 138
support vector machines, 33, 39
symmetry, 24, 25, 30, 31
systematic web site, 3, 9
Szymanski, 79, 86

table of content pages, 68, 75
tag, 16, 22
tag token, 44, 50
tag vector, 159, 165
TCCB, 141, 147
TD
    complexity, 12, 19
    definition, 12, 18
TD algorithms
    ContentExtractor, 61, 67
    document frequency based filter, 67, 74
    InfoDiscoverer, 59, 65
    Page Partitioning, 55, 62
    RTDM, 65, 71
    SiteStyleTrees, 62, 68
TeaShark, 55, 61
template, 19, 26
    analysis, 130, 136
    definition, 4, 9
    elements, 9, 15
    recognition, 55, 61
    reverse engineering, 12, 18
    structures, 11, 17

template detection, *see* TD, *see* TD
template generated contents, 10, 16
template table detection ratio, 68, 74
template-hash, 70, 76
term frequency-inverse document frequency, 31, 37
text encoding, 16, 22
text mining, 30, 36
text understanding, 40, 46
TF-IDF, 31, 37, 59, 66
Tidy, 16, 22
time performance, 100, 106
TM, 30, 36
TN, 27, 33
TOC page, 68, 75, 174, 180
token based CCB, *see* TCCB, *see* TCCB
topic drift, 68, 75
Topical Unity Principle, 56, 62
TP, 27, 33
TPM, 31, 37
transformation component (XSL), 16, 22
tree matching, 157, 163
tree traversal, 134, 140
tri-gram, 31, 37
tri-gram proximity matrix, 31, 37
triangle inequality, 24, 30
true negative, 27, 33
true positive, 27, 33
$ts(D)$, 160, 166
TV, 159, 165

UFRE, 37, 42
union-free regular expression, 37, 42
user discussion, 84, 90

$v(D)$, 159, 165
vaguely structured data, 41, 47
Valiente, 77, 84
visually impaired user, 5, 11

W3C, 16, 21, 34, 40, 55, 61
WCMS, 2, 8, 19, 26, 174, 180
    basic features, 3, 9

Index

    features, 3, 9
    hierarchy information, 4, 10
    managed web site, 3, 9
    redundant content, 4, 10
    template, 4, 9
    types of, 3, 9
Web 2.0, 2, 8, 84, 88, 90, 93
web content management system, *see* WCMS,
    see WCMS
web crawler, 3, 9
web directory, 2, 8
    classification of documents, 2, 8
    DMOZ, 2, 8
    editors, 2, 8
    Open Directory Project, 2, 8
web informative structure mining, 69, 76
web search engine, 2, 8
web site
    content, 3, 9
    illegal copy, 5, 11
    layout, 3, 9
    mirror, 5, 11
    structure, 3, 9
web-as-corpus, 185, 191
winner block (FeatureExtractor), 51, 58
winner set (K-FeatureExtractor, 52, 59
WISDOM, 69, 75
WM, 30, 36
word sequence, 97, 103
word token, 44, 50
workflow management, 3, 9
World Wide Web, 1, 7
World Wide Web Consortium, 16, 21
wrapper, 37, 43, 131, 137
    evaluation, 39, 44
    induction, 38, 43
    verification, 38, 44
wrapper induction, 11, 17
WWW, 1, 7
    growth rate, 4, 10
    redundant content, 4, 10
    size of, 2, 7

Xerces, 17, 23
XHTML, 16, 21
XML, 16, 21, 22, 38, 44
XPath, 16, 22, 53, 59
XSL, 16, 22
XSLT, 16, 22, 53, 59
XWRAP elite, 38, 44, 131, 137

Yahoo, 2, 8

Zen Garden (CSS), 11, 17
zip-format, 103, 109

Die VDM Verlagsservicegesellschaft sucht für wissenschaftliche Verlage abgeschlossene und herausragende

Dissertationen, Habilitationen, Diplomarbeiten, Master Theses, Magisterarbeiten usw.

für die kostenlose Publikation als Fachbuch.

Sie verfügen über eine Arbeit, die hohen inhaltlichen und formalen Ansprüchen genügt, und haben Interesse an einer honorarvergüteten Publikation?

Dann senden Sie bitte erste Informationen über sich und Ihre Arbeit per Email an *info@vdm-vsg.de*.

Sie erhalten kurzfristig unser Feedback!

VDM Verlagsservicegesellschaft mbH
Dudweiler Landstr. 99
D - 66123 Saarbrücken

Telefon +49 681 3720 174
Fax +49 681 3720 1749

www.vdm-vsg.de

Die VDM Verlagsservicegesellschaft mbH vertritt

Printed by Books on Demand GmbH, Norderstedt / Germany